# GROUNDING COSMOPOLITANISM

# GROUNDING COSMOPOLITANISM

*From Kant to the Idea of a Cosmopolitan Constitution*

GARRETT WALLACE BROWN

EDINBURGH
University Press

First published in 2009 by
Edinburgh University Press Ltd
22 George Square, Edinburgh EH8 9LF
www.euppublishing.com

This paperback edition 2013

Typeset in 11/13.5 pt Goudy by
Servis Filmsetting Ltd, Stockport, Cheshire, and
printed and bound in the United States of America

A CIP record for this book is available from the British Library

ISBN  978 0 7486 3881 9 (hardback)
ISBN  978 0 7486 7730 6 (paperback)

# Contents

A Note on the Texts and Kant Referencing   ix
Acknowledgements   xi

Introduction   1
  I   An Abridged History of Cosmopolitan Thought and the
      Connections to Kant's Cosmopolitanism   4
  II   Contemporary Cosmopolitan Themes and the
      Distinctiveness of a Kantian Approach to
      Cosmopolitanism   9
  III   The Critiques of Cosmopolitanism and the Structure of
      Response   15
  IV   Methodology: Kant the Cosmopolitan and a Kantian
      form of Cosmopolitanism   20

Part One

1.   Kant's Cosmopolitanism   31
  I   Moral Foundations of Kant's Cosmopolitanism   33
  II   Cosmopolitanism, Globalization and Kant's Problematic
      Theory of History   37
  III   Cosmopolitan Jurisprudence and the Foundation for a
      Cosmopolitan Matrix   44
  IV   Cosmopolitan Jurisprudence and the Development of a
      Kantian Cosmopolitan Matrix   47
  V   Conclusion   50

2.  Kant's Cosmopolitan Law and the Idea of a Cosmopolitan
    Constitution                                                          55
    I    Cosmopolitan Law and a Condition of Cosmopolitan
         Right                                                            57
    II   Cosmopolitan Right and the Laws of Hospitality                   59
    III  Kantian Constitutionalism and the Idea of a
         Cosmopolitan Constitution                                       66
    IV   Conclusion                                                      78

Part Two

3.  State Sovereignty, Federation and Kant's Cosmopolitanism              87
    I    Kant's Move from Natural Law to Lawful
         Cosmopolitanism                                                 89
    II   The Definitive Articles of Perpetual Peace and the
         Jurisprudence of Kant's Cosmopolitanism                         94
    III  The Scope of Federation in a Cosmopolitan Order                 106
    IV   Kant's Cosmopolitanism and its Relationship to
         Contemporary International Relations Theory                     110
    V    Conclusion                                                      117

4.  Cultural Difference and Kant's Cosmopolitan Law                      123
    I    Claims from Culture: Cultural Relativism and Cultural
         Pluralism                                                       126
    II   Some Confusion Regarding Cultural Communities and
         Identity                                                        128
    III  Kant's Pragmatic Anthropology and the Cosmopolitan
         Alternative to the Reductionist Sociology of Culture            131
    IV   Cultural Relativism and the Critique of Kantian
         Universalism                                                    133
    V    Coexist versus Cohere: Kant's Cosmopolitanism and
         Cultural Pluralism                                              140
    VI   Conclusion: Kantian Cosmopolitanism and Diversity               143

5.  Distributive Justice and the Capability for Effective Autonomy       149
    I    Normative Principles of Kant's Distributive Justice             150
    II   Kant's Social Welfare and Distributive Justice                  159
    III  Effective Autonomy and Capabilities for Freedom                 167

    IV   Effective Autonomy and Cosmopolitan Concerns for
         Distributive Justice       171
    V    Conclusion       178

6.  Conclusion: Applied Theory and a Continued Cosmopolitan
    Enthusiasm       186
    I     Implications of Kant's Constitutional Cosmopolitanism:
         Globalization, Global Markets and Inequality       189
    II    The Protection of Cosmopolitan Right and the Global
         Forum       191
    III  Humanitarian Assistance and Global Justice       195
    IV  The Idea of Universal Human Rights as a Basis for
         Cosmopolitan Right       198
    V    Applied Theory: Toward a Cosmopolitan Condition       202
    VI  Conclusion       210

Bibliography       217
Index       231

# A Note on the Texts and Kant Referencing

All citations to the works of Immanuel Kant will contain the bibliographical information and page references of the English translation as well as the reference information for *Kants gesammelte Schriften*, edited by the Royal Prussian Academy of Sciences (referred to as the *Akademie* edition). As is standard practice, the Akademie reference will immediately follow the page number given for the English translation. The Akademie reference will be encased within brackets at the end of the citation and will provide the volume number and page number [volume number: page(s)]. For example, [8:310] or [8:310–13]. The following translations for Kant's works have been used:

Hans Reiss (ed.) and H. B. Nisbet (trans.), *Kant's Political Writings* (Cambridge: Cambridge University Press, 1970). This collection of essays includes Kant's: (1784) "Idea for a Universal History with a Cosmopolitan Purpose," (1784) "An Answer to the Question: 'What is Enlightenment?'," (1793) "On the Common Saying: This May be True in Theory, But it Does not Apply in Practice," (1795) "Perpetual Peace: A Philosophical Sketch," and (1798) "The Contest of Faculties." In all instances, references to these essays by Kant will be related to this collection.

Immanuel Kant (1785), *Grounding for the Metaphysics of Morals*, James W. Ellington (trans.), (Cambridge: Hackett Publishing Company, 1993). In all instances, references to this work by Kant will be related strictly to this translation.

Immanuel Kant (1787), *The Critique of Pure Reason*, J. M. D. Meiklejohn (trans.), (New York: The Colonial Press, 1900). In all instances, references to this work by Kant will be related strictly to this translation. Nevertheless, it should be noted that an appendix from this text ("Transcendental Logic II, Dialectics, I, I: Of Ideas in General") is referenced without a page number for the Meiklejohn translation. This is due to the fact that the appendix appears in this translation without a page number at the end of the volume. Therefore, when citing from this appendix, I have only given the volume and page number from the *Akademie* edition. All other references to this translation will contain both the translation page number and the Akademie edition numbers.

Immanuel Kant (1790), *Critique of Judgement*, J. Meredith (trans.), (Oxford: Oxford University Press, 1973). In all instances, references to this work by Kant will be related strictly to this translation.

Immanuel Kant (1797), *The Metaphysics of Morals*, Mary Gregor (trans.), (Cambridge: Cambridge University Press, 1996). In all instances, references to this work by Kant will be related strictly to this translation.

Immanuel Kant (1798), *Anthropology from a Pragmatic Point of View*, Victor Lyle Dowdell (trans.), (Carbondale: Southern Illinois University Press, 1978). In all instances, references to this work by Kant will be related strictly to this translation.

Lastly, it should be noted that key philosophical terms and concepts are represented in italics in their first usage (for example, *kingdom of ends*) so as to highlight that the phrasing is intentional and that the term is an idea associated with the author/debate being discussed.

# Acknowledgements

While writing this book I had the wonderful opportunity to have an extended lunch with Katrin Flikschuh and Daniele Archibugi. During what developed into a two-hour discussion, we debated the meaning and nature of Kant's cosmopolitanism and how it should be understood. By the end of the conversation we agreed on one point. That whatever Kant's cosmopolitanism is, it is not easily understood. Daniele concluded our lunch by suggesting another commonplace between everyone at the table, the shared belief that Kant was not an idiot.

Throughout the trials and tribulations of writing on Kant's cosmopolitanism it is easy to sometimes feel like an idiot. To reduce this feeling I have sought expertise and valuable advice from people along the way. A number of people deserve mention for their efforts. I owe much appreciation to John Charvet who has been willing to read substantial portions of this project and who has kindly offered constructive comments while sharing a bottle of wine. In addition, Paul Kelly, Katrin Flikschuh, Daniele Archibugi, Kim Hutchings, Sujith Kumar, Richard Beardsworth, Will Smith, Brian Barry, Raffaele Marchetti, James Gregory, Girish Daswani, Kate Macdonald, Rodney Barker and John Gray are just a few who have commented on various aspects of this work and deserve mention for their keen observations. It is also important to mention that many versions of my arguments have benefited greatly from questions raised within the Political Philosophy Seminars at the London School of Economics and at the Political Theory Research Group at the University of Sheffield. My colleagues have provided wonderful criticism and support and it is my hope that I repaid the favor with my own dedication to their work.

However, there are some individuals that deserve special recognition. Cecile Fabre, who carefully read multiple versions of this project, gave the most vital assistance. Her force of logic and ability to balance criticism with unfailing support has been invaluable. She has been an outstanding friend and mentor for which I am indebted. Much appreciation is also due to David Held. Not only has he provided sage advice and criticism throughout the writing of this book, but he has also taken a strong personal interest in my overall research agenda. His guidance and enthusiastic support has made all the difference. Lastly, I am extremely grateful to Jeremy Waldron for his comments on multiple versions of this project and for the excellent suggestions he provided. Of course, any remaining deficiencies are mine alone.

There are those that say that writing a book can be a lonely and isolated experience. Gratefully I have had the opportunity to develop friendships with outstanding people who have not only provided me with wonderful companionship, but have also been excellent intellectual sparring partners with which to test my ideas. This circle of friends has eliminated any feeling of loneliness. The incomparable Martin Skewes-Cox, Sophia Money-Coutts, Ali Bohm, Valbona Muzaka, Camille Monteux, Skippy the Dog, Graham Harrison and my friends in the United States all deserve my most profound appreciation for their continued friendship and love. Furthermore, special thanks should be given to my hyperbolic friend Gavin Edwards who reminded me throughout the process of writing this book, that "there is no such thing as Kan't."

Of course an acknowledgement section wouldn't be complete without expressing one's debt to one's parents. However, there are no words that can indicate the feeling of indebtedness I feel toward them. The best I can say is that I have always felt supported and that they have been great sources of inspiration in my life. They mean the world to me and it is because of them that I have done so well in life. Although these words do not capture the depth of my gratitude and the fondness I feel for them, I think they already know how much they mean to me and that fact allows me to say no more.

The following permissions are gratefully acknowledged. A shortened version of Chapter 3, "State Sovereignty, Federation and Kant's Cosmopolitanism" appears in the *European Journal of International Relations*, vol. 11 (Dec. 2005), Sage Publication. In addition, a shorter version of Chapter 2, "Kant's Cosmopolitan Law and the Idea of a Cosmopolitan Constitution" appears in *History of Political Thought*, vol.

27, no. 3 (2006), Imprint Publishing. Lastly, parts from "Moving from Cosmopolitan Legal Theory to Legal Practice: Models of Cosmopolitan Law," *Legal Studies*, vol. 28, no. 3 (2008), Blackwell Publishing, appear in one section of Chapter 6.

Lastly, I owe considerable thanks to Nicola Ramsey, Eddie Clark, James Dale, Lianne Vella and the keen eye of Ian Brooke, all from the editorial, marketing and production team at Edinburgh University Press. They have been extremely helpful, constructive, responsive and professional. In other words, it has been an absolute pleasure to work with them and they have given me excellent direction throughout the entire process.

G. W. Brown
University of Sheffield
October 2008

# Introduction

"We cannot live for ourselves alone. Our lives are connected by a thousand invisible threads, and along these sympathetic fibers our actions run as causes and return to us as results." – Henry Melvill

The above quote shares a common spirit with the cosmopolitanism of Immanuel Kant. The spirit is implicit in that it relates the nature of human interdependency and the consequences of our behavior towards one another. Although Melvill is not usually associated with cosmopolitan theory and is generally associated with the Church of England, he was much more than a religious scholar, spending significant time writing critical essays on natural law and global ethics.[1] The quote by Melvill reflects a cosmopolitan belief of universal human coexistence, for it mirrors Kant's cosmopolitan concern, that we are all inextricably connected, that "a violation of rights in *one* part of the world is felt *everywhere*."[2] Moreover, Melvill's quote is loaded with a Kantian cosmopolitan universal principle, that humans cannot live independently of one another and therefore should act towards others as if those actions were to dictate the substance of returned consequences. This could be extended to a form of Kant's *categorical imperative*, where individuals should "act only according to the maxim whereby you can at the same time will that it should become a universal law."[3] It would seem that Melvill is in agreement with Kant's cosmopolitanism, that we should monitor our actions as if we would want our actions to be the universal actions of everyone, which ultimately "run as causes and return to us as results." Since "we cannot live for ourselves alone," Melvill, like Kant, suggests that we need to remember that our lives are unavoidably connected and that our moral actions must reflect the fact of human interdependence and unavoidable coexistence.

1

It might seem odd to introduce a book on Kantian cosmopolitanism by making a comparison with the religious teachings of Melvill. Nevertheless, the passage is a striking continuation of a long cosmopolitan legacy and highlights some of the main premises inherent in both Kantian and current cosmopolitan thought and debate. This is because cosmopolitan theory has attracted new criticisms as well as newfound interest due to the increase in the phenomenon usually described as *globalization*. Of course, there is considerable debate about what globalization is, what it entails, what effects it has, how to define it, or if it is a new phenomenon or if it is as old as history itself. Nevertheless, regardless of how we define globalization, it is also widely accepted that the world is becoming increasingly interconnected at an exponential rate and that this process has been, and will continue to be, a real fact for human relations on earth. For my purpose, I regard globalization as a real phenomenon in our lives and I define it as broadly as possible, in that it encompasses growing connection between various peoples, nations, cultures, corporations, governments, technologies, environments, economies and movements which are ultimately bound by the spherical shape of the earth.

The increase of cosmopolitan debate in conjunction with new approaches for understanding the effects of globalization illustrates that political theorists, among others, have increasingly realized the necessity to philosophically and politically address new global considerations of human interconnectedness. Most cosmopolitan theories, if not all, are premised on the fact that the world is an interconnected and interdependent community, which is bound by the spherical shape of the earth: where our moral responsibility toward all humanity should be understood as being a universal and globalized concern. For the cosmopolitan, the interconnectedness of humanity translates to a cosmopolitan ethical concern "whose primary allegiance is to the community of human beings in the entire world."[4] For Kant and Melvill, as well as with most cosmopolitan theorists, the limited sphere of the earth creates something of a common human community and provides the philosophical and moral motivation behind cosmopolitan enthusiasm.[5]

Therefore, the use of the quote by Melvill provides a simple way to relate the assumptions and premises found within the tradition of cosmopolitan theory in general, but also found within this book in particular. The first of these premises, highlighted wonderfully by Melvill, is the suggestion which underlines most globalization theories and cosmopolitan political theory. The main premise is that the world is becoming increasingly interconnected and that this increased interconnectedness has created a need to consider political issues from a broader and more universally human standpoint. Like most cosmopolitan theories, the Kantian argument developed in this book is based on the assumption that globalization creates an increasingly interconnected global community and has therefore also created a need for new theories to adjudicate the problems associated with this growing interdependence. Although there exist several arguments for and against the positive effects of globalization and the possible formulation of any global social order, these arguments seem to support, and not discredit, the standpoint that corresponding forms of normative theorizing are needed to grapple with the new benefits and burdens associated with globalization. Intuitively speaking, as the world becomes increasingly more interdependent and socially interactive, cosmopolitan concerns for peaceful coexistence and cohabitation seem to be concerns that need to be philosophically addressed. As the international environment has evolved, so must political theory and the concerns they are designed to reconcile. As Melvill suggests, we no longer live in a world of community isolation. The international arena has evolved into an extremely interdependent, culturally transient and globalized environment.[6] If this environment of global interdependence is to peacefully evolve, it is important to find recognizable moral and legal principles that not only facilitate greater cooperation, but that also protect the valuable pluralist and autonomous concerns of various communities impacted by globalization.

The second cosmopolitan belief highlighted by Melvill stems directly from the acceptance that globalization is both a real and dialectic phenomenon. In other words, globalization is dialectic in that it has two sides, one promoting more interconnectedness, resulting in greater economic markets, democracies and peace between democratic states, while also promoting greater economic inequality, ideological ethnic conflict and a failure to secure human development. The result is that globalization makes an environment for cosmopolitanism feasible, but only if we are successful in implementing the normative principles necessary to make globalization a peaceful and positive evolutionary process. Otherwise there is a real possibility that the processes of globalization will not be progressive for all of humankind, but will only continue to facilitate increased networks of possible conflict. Since the world is, so to speak, getting smaller, and the sharing of our world with others is more inevitable, we should continue to theorize about the possibility of global interaction in relation to a minimal set of normative principles. In this regard, globalization has created the need for cooperation as well as the corresponding need for a mechanism to regulate new problems associated with this interdependence. Although there exist several arguments against the positive effects of globalization and social order, I largely accept and posit a view that globalization is in fact occurring and that this phenomenon creates a corresponding need for some form of regulating normative order.[7] Without common normative principles to guide the increased benefits and burdens of global dependency, there is a greater possibility that our human interactions will become increasingly confrontational. As Kant himself developed it in *The Metaphysics of Morals*, cosmopolitanism should be understood as a set of genuinely agreed constraints governing what people can reasonably expect in the course of living alongside one another.[8] It is from a normative conception for basic rules of *cosmopolitan law* that it is possible to establish a foundation for a minimal ethical and legal cosmopolitan order: an international order that not only satisfies cosmopolitan concerns of human worth, but that is also not guilty of being imperialistic, idealistically utopian, or grossly universal beyond the minimal normative principles that make the peaceful existence of individuals, associations, cultures and states in a pluralistic global society possible.

## I. An Abridged History of Cosmopolitan Thought and the Connections to Kant's Cosmopolitanism

The cosmopolitan idea that human beings are members of a universal fraternity and share responsibilities to each other on the basis of our common humanity is not new.[9] The beginnings of this idea can be traced as far back as 1375 BC to the Egyptian Akhnaton, who advocated a universal monotheism where all humans owed each other equal moral duties regardless of political affiliation.[10] Nevertheless, the term cosmopolitan itself seems to have originated in the year 300 BC. This is when the Cynic philosopher Diogenes of Sinope famously claimed that humans were all *kosmopolites* (universal citizens) and that we should shrug off the coil of xenophobic particularism in order to behave towards one another as if we were common *citizens of the world*. Refusing to define himself by place of birth, Diogenes responded to questions regarding his communal affiliation by proclaiming "I am a citizen of the world."[11] From what we know of Diogenes and the other Cynics, their philosophy advocated a universal conception of negative liberty and universal hospitality, arguing against the dominance of arbitrary communal laws that were based on national origin alone. These ideas were further developed by the philosophy of Crates of Thebes, Chrysippus, and most importantly, through the Stoa school of Zeno of Citium. For it is Zeno who reportedly argued for a more robust form of cosmopolitanism, in which "we should regard all men as fellow-citizens and local residents, and there should be one way of life and order, like that of a herd grazing together and nurtured by a common law."[12]

Continuing for half a millennium, the cosmopolitan legacy was developed from Cynic and Old Stoa writings by the philosophical works of Marcus Cicero, Seneca and Marcus Aurelius. Unlike the Cynic philosophy of Diogenes, the Roman Stoics produced a more sophisticated exposition of cosmopolitan theory. Where Diogenes has been given credit for coining the phase *kosmopolites*, it is through middle and late Stoic philosophy that cosmopolitanism received a more comprehensive and elaborate foundation. Nevertheless, the traditions behind the development of these foundations are complicated. It would take an extensive piece of writing to detail the various theoretical nuances and transitions found throughout the chronology of Stoic cosmopolitanism. For the sake of brevity, it is sufficient to summarize Stoic cosmopolitanism as containing roughly four common themes.

The first of these themes is the idea that every human being is a member of the same species and therefore is part of a larger human community that shares a similar moral and political fate. Borrowing from earlier Cynic philosophers, the Stoics maintained that humans are members of two communities, the community of our birth and the community of humankind. As Seneca wrote, we should "measure the boundaries of our nation by the sun"[13] and although we are born into particular communities, humankind remains a single species without boundaries but those of the immortal realm. As with other Stoics, Seneca believed it is because of our common humanity that we have a universal moral purpose and a duty to respect this moral concern as mutual citizens of the world regardless of our place of birth.

The second theme shared by most Stoic philosophers is that the human species has a common capacity for human reason and communication. For the Stoic, the shared capacity for reason is the basis for a community of human beings. It is from this human ability to reason and communicate

5

that we can derive a universal respect for human worth. As Cicero wrote, the "bond of connection is reason and speech, which . . . associate men together and unite them in a sort of natural fraternity."[14] The capacity for reason has played a critical role in Stoic philosophy. As with later Enlightenment theories, the Stoics placed considerable moral significance in a shared capacity for reason and derived all political principles in relation to the universal quality of human reason. Aurelius best exemplifies the Stoic connection between reason, communication, law and political obligation when he wrote:

> If the intellectual capacity is common to us all, common too is the reason, which makes us rational creatures. If so, that reason is common which tells us to do or not to do. If so, law is common. If so, we are citizens. If so, we are fellow members of an organized community. If so, the universe is as it were a state – of what other single polity can the whole race of mankind be said to be fellow members? And from it, this common state, we get the intellectual, the rational, and the legal instinct, or whence do we get them?[15]

A third theme linking Stoic philosophy is the concept of universal natural law and teleological purpose. Despite the fact that each philosopher employed a somewhat different teleology, almost every Stoic philosopher suggested that there was a universal law of nature. Stoic teleology was generally used to illustrate the universality between humans in relation to natural law and heavenly purpose. This tradition continued far into modern political thought and can be seen to have influenced the natural law theories of John Locke and Hugo Grotius. It was not until the work of Kant and more contemporary cosmopolitans that heavenly arguments for universal natural law were abandoned, or at least replaced by other non-theistic metaphysical foundations.

The fourth theme found within the Stoic tradition is the idea that human reason should be in *harmony* with nature and universal law. The Stoics firmly believed that the human species had a unifying common purpose and that this purpose served as a universal natural law with which all human law should comply. As Cicero states, "true law is right reason in agreement with nature; it is of universal application, unchanging and everlasting; it summons to duty by its commands, and averts from wrongdoing by its prohibitions . . . We cannot be freed from its obligations by senate or people, and we need not look outside ourselves for an expounder or interpreter of it."[16] The influence of this statement in the formation of Kant's cosmopolitanism is enormous. From this statement we can see the foundation for three important Kantian cosmopolitan principles that will be further developed in the next chapter. First, morality and law should be derived and built upon one another and that they are discoverable through our capacity for reasoning. Second, this innate capacity for reason and reflection allows us to be moral beings and therefore also bestows upon all humans a universal worth. Third, the universality of human worth cannot be overruled by local commands or decrees, but must be understood as creating universal obligations and harmonious purpose between all human beings. In this regard, both Kant and the Stoics believed that all human beings are members of a universal moral community who share a similar political fate, regardless of where people come from and irrespective of local decree.

Although cosmopolitan philosophy suffered an extended period of silence after the death of Marcus Aurelius, there was a renewed interest in it between AD 1480 and 1800. Philosophers such as Bartolomé de las Casas, Francisco de Vitoria, Francis Bacon, John Locke, Denis Diderot, Hugo Grotius, Thomas Paine, F. M. A. Voltaire and, most notably for this project, Kant outlined strong commitments to various forms of cosmopolitanism within their political theory. However, there is a significant difference between the majority of later natural law theorists and the cosmopolitanism of Kant. Building on the foundations laid by Thomas Hobbes, natural law theory promoted the contractual creation of a sovereign state as the ultimate source for ethical law and human emancipation. Inherent in this type of contractrian argument is the idea that self-interested individuals contract with one another to create political institutions of mutual preservation and right. Nevertheless, contracts between individuals immediately create boundaries between contracted citizens and other non-citizens who are not considered to be obligated members of the political community. Although many natural law theorists sought limitations on state power in order to promote the universal natural rights of individual cooperators, they nevertheless did not always argue for strong principles of universal natural law that created imperative moral obligations between bounded political communities or between citizen and non-citizen.

As will be further explored in Chapter 3, it was from Kant's development of cosmopolitan theory that stronger commitments to universal principles were developed away from, and as a supplement to, the natural law tradition. Unlike the natural law tradition of *jus gentium*, Kant suggested that a higher form of *cosmopolitan law* was necessary to limit the *law of nations* and international conflicts often legitimated by political claims to absolute sovereignty. In line with Stoic universalism, Kant believed that a theory of cosmopolitan law was preferable in fostering universal human advancement and security. Although Kant held the state to be an extremely important component in the formation of moral law and a cosmopolitan constitution, he believed that "no one has more original right to possession of the earth than anyone else, and therefore all contracts short of a final cosmopolitan form of association are provisional."[17] In this regard, Kant makes a dramatic move away from the traditional law of nations by advocating an additional principle of cosmopolitan law in order to advance a legal community based on the inherent moral worth of all human beings.[18] The Kantian distinction between *international law*, the role of states and *cosmopolitan law* will be discussed in greater detail in Chapter 3. For the purpose of providing the philosophical and overall historical background for the type of Kantian cosmopolitanism that will be defended throughout this book, it is with Cicero, Seneca and Aurelius that more extrapolation is helpful here. As Martha Nussbaum has successfully demonstrated, Kant's cosmopolitanism drew greatly on the universalism found within Roman Stoic philosophy.[19]

The connection between Stoic cosmopolitanism and Kant is considerable. Nevertheless, it would be incorrect to assume that Kant's cosmopolitanism is simply regurgitating Stoic principles. Kant significantly abandons and transforms various Stoic foundations to fit his own cosmopolitan vision. Where Kant seems to mirror Stoic philosophy is in his moral assertions for a kingdom of free rational beings that are equal in humanity and treated always as having ends in themselves, no matter where the person is from.[20] Other connections are located in Kant's preferred usage of Stoic terminology, in his insistence on universal justice and law, the communal possession of the earth in common and in discussions for world citizenship.[21]

However, Kant distanced his political philosophy from the Stoics in four critical ways. First, Kant did not make exceptions to the cosmopolitan idea of a universal and unified human community and thus did not accept slavery.[22] Unlike some Stoics who saw 'barbarians' as irrational and therefore legitimately enslaved, Kant maintains that human beings are a single species of moral worth and that the Aristotelian concept of *natural slave* was a xenophobic invention with immoral implications.[23] Second, Kant did not endorse the Stoic acceptance of colonialism and expansionism. According to Kant, colonialism and any military enlargement of an empire or state was immoral and contradictory to cosmopolitan morality.

Third, Kant's cosmopolitanism sought to separate theology from moral purpose. Whereas many Stoics espoused a divine source of universal morality, Kant promoted a universal purpose derived from practical reason and his metaphysics of morals. Although many have argued that Kant is unsuccessful in completely removing divine purpose from his overall cosmopolitan project, Kant himself claimed to have done so. Whether or not we believe he was mistaken in this claim, he himself wished to draw a distinction from Stoic teleology and it is for this reason that we can suggest a perceived difference. Fourth, Kant did not share the Stoic belief that *human passions* were completely malleable and could therefore be permanently changed away from feelings of violence and hatred.[24] An underlying Stoic understanding of human nature is that human passions could be reeducated away from immoral action and influenced towards a communal love as citizens of the world. Kant did not assume that humans could always know perfect rationality, or could always be relied upon to understand cosmopolitan morality and obligation. In addition, Kant maintained that human passions were not completely malleable, but could only be partially influenced by institutional conditioning and education. According to Kant, human nature had certain basic passions that no amount of social engineering could eradicate. In this regard, there was a need for a formalized and institutionalized cosmopolitan law to appropriately reflect a universal respect for humanity. What is important in our understanding of Kantian cosmopolitanism is that we recognize the fact that Kant (and various forms of Kantianism) have altered both the Stoic and natural law tradition, advocating a much broader and more encompassing conception of cosmopolitan law. It is in relation to the normative elements involved in Kant's understanding of a cosmopolitan constitution and cosmopolitan law that the remaining chapters of this book will examine.

## II. Contemporary Cosmopolitan Themes and the Distinctiveness of a Kantian Approach to Cosmopolitanism

As was mentioned earlier, there is considerable interest within contemporary scholastic debate regarding the effects of globalization, interdependency and cosmopolitanism. Contemporary cosmopolitan arguments are generally based on an empirical understanding of global cohabitation and a corresponding moral perspective grounded on "the acknowledgment of some notion of common humanity that translates ethically into an idea of shared or common moral duties toward others by virtue of this humanity."[25] Nevertheless, despite the fact that cosmopolitanism is currently experiencing somewhat of a renaissance, there is still considerable confusion regarding what a cosmopolitan stance entails. Although cosmopolitanism is often discussed between academics, it is not always clear what cosmopolitanism is supposed to mean.

Cosmopolitanism, like any discipline, contains many facets and variations.[26] As was discussed in the last section, the legacy of cosmopolitanism finds its roots as far back as 1375 BC and has undergone many transformations. Since Diogenes first claimed that he was a *citizen of the world*, cosmopolitanism as a political theory has evolved to include, and has grown to influence, a wide distribution of subjects and disciplines. Subjects as disperse as Development Studies, International Relations, Gender Studies, Human Rights, International Law, Economics, Political Theory, Social Anthropology and Philosophy, to name a few, have embraced aspects of cosmopolitan thinking within their respective subfields. Where an interdisciplinary commonality seems to exist between them is in regard to the normative foundations behind their various cosmopolitan approaches and applications. As Thomas Pogge has suggested, most contemporary cosmopolitan theories share three general principles. First, cosmopolitanism maintains that the unit of ultimate moral concern are individual human beings. Second, cosmopolitan theories share the element that this moral concern should be equally applied, meaning that "the status of ultimate concern attaches to every living human equally."[27] Third, cosmopolitanism requires generality in its application, proclaiming that humans are the ultimate moral concern for everyone, regardless of race, nationality, social status and religious belief. As Pogge has pointed out, all cosmopolitan approaches advocate in various degrees the three normative elements of individualism, egalitarianism and universalism.

A further distinction within cosmopolitan thought can be made between what Charles Beitz has called *moral cosmopolitanism* and *institutional cosmopolitanism*. Beitz makes a distinction between institutional cosmopolitanism and the normative/moral foundations that underline any institutional framework designed to facilitate them. For Beitz, moral cosmopolitanism demands "that every human being has a global stature as the ultimate unit of moral concern."[28] As Brian Barry has pointed out, "moral cosmopolitanism leaves open the final questions of the ideal constitution of international society."[29] The distinction is related to, but separate from, institutional cosmopolitanism, which is focused on ways to implement the normative considerations of its moral counterpart. Beitz has suggested that institutional cosmopolitanism "holds that the world's political structure should be reshaped so that states and other political units are brought under the authority of supranational agencies of some kind."[30] Although both are closely related and it is difficult to imagine institutional strategies without some normative grounding, it is an important distinction to be made, for it is critical to understand that "there is no automatic move from ethical premises to any particular conclusion about the ideal world constitution."[31] In other words, moral cosmopolitanism is concerned with what should be done ethically and morally, while an institutional component is concerned with how these principles can be structured in practice or how current institutions are failing the ethical concerns of moral cosmopolitanism. There is an overlap between them, but the moral theory is prior to implementation and is meant to act as both an ethical grounding for future institutional schemes and as a moral basis for institutional evaluation.

Although the model Beitz provides makes a useful distinction for categorizing cosmopolitan moral projects from more practical-based cosmopolitan projects, the division does not provide us with clarification as to the universal scope involved in various cosmopolitan theories. We are still left with questions concerning the level of unifying and universalized community that various cosmopolitan theories advocate. It has been suggested that a further distinction is required if we are to better understand the various formulations and subdivisions involved in cosmopolitan theory. Often a further distinction is made between *weak cosmopolitanism* and *strong cosmopolitanism*, or what has also been labeled *extreme cosmopolitanism* and *moderate cosmopolitanism*.[32] This distinction is meant to illustrate the degree between various cosmopolitan perspectives and the thickness of universal morality. As the terms might suggest, a weak or moderate form of cosmopolitanism "holds only that morality is cosmopolitan in part: there are some valid principles of equal consideration with a universal scope, even though there may also be independent, nonderivative principles with a more restricted scope."[33] Conversely, strong and extreme cosmopolitanism advocates that "all moral principles must be justified by showing that they give equal weight to the claims of everyone, which means that they must either be directly universal in their scope, or if they apply only to a select group of people they must be secondary principles whose ultimate foundation is universal."[34] The distinction between

11

weak and strong cosmopolitanism is meant to connote an allowance for localized morality and obligation versus a strict adherence to a hegemonic universal morality irrespective of local sentiments. Although most contemporary cosmopolitan theories are located somewhere in the middle of the bell distribution between weak and strong, a limited number of cosmopolitan theories might be understood as located towards the ends.[35]

With a basic understanding of the distinction between a moral and institutional approach, cosmopolitan theory can be broken down into roughly four general conceptions. Although the four conceptions share elements of significant overlap, most cosmopolitan theories tend to encompass at least one of these primary forms. Gerald Delanty has defined these four conceptions as *legal cosmopolitanism*, *political cosmopolitanism*, *cultural cosmopolitanism* and *civic cosmopolitanism*.[36] In order to better understand the Kantian approach developed within this book, it is helpful to outline these four conceptions and where a Kantian position might be comparatively located.

1) *Legal cosmopolitanism* generally focuses on the concept of a system of states that are constrained by various forms of cosmopolitan and international law. Legal cosmopolitanism can have both a moral and institutional aspect with various degrees of weak or strong cosmopolitan commitments.[37] However, what is distinctive about a legal approach is the focus that is given to the creation of global law and legal obligation above state sovereignty. Another significant aspect of a legal approach has been a general recognition that states are an important and necessary component within a cosmopolitan order. Unlike world state cosmopolitanism (see below), legal cosmopolitans usually believe that properly constituted states that uphold basic cosmopolitan legal principles can serve as important mechanisms for the wellbeing of humans and for the furtherance of a cosmopolitan condition.[38] What is needed, according to legal cosmopolitans, are more robust international legal tenets that bind states to recognizable rules of conduct and sovereign legitimacy, which if properly practiced could create a cosmopolitan legal condition.

2) *Political cosmopolitanism* usually has a corresponding legal component, in that it rests on some premises of a thoroughgoing condition of cosmopolitan law, but maintains an emphasis on creating greater forms of global governance or with reforming international political institutions in line with cosmopolitan ideals. The political approach is generally concerned

12

with the creation of supranational political organizations that can generate large-scale international consensus and democratic accountability. Although political cosmopolitanism tends to focus on global institutions and global governance, the focus is often underpinned by a strong commitment to moral cosmopolitan principles.[39]

3) *Cultural cosmopolitanism* is perhaps the oldest form of cosmopolitanism, dating as far back as the philosophy of Diogenes. A cultural cosmopolitan approach generally asserts that individuals are interconnected and culturally transient beings that can identify with a multiplicity of cultural identities and obligations. From a basic understanding of manifold identities and the cosmopolitan belief in our common humanity, cultural cosmopolitans generally argue for moral duties and obligations that supercede and transgress localized ethnicity, culture and nationality. As with early Stoic philosophy, cultural cosmopolitans suggest a unifying moral duty and support this position by locating universal principles that encourage our common human culture.[40]

4) *Civic cosmopolitanism* is closely related to the cultural, legal and political approach, but places more emphasis on the idea of cosmopolitan citizenship. The degree to which universal citizenship is advocated varies greatly within civic cosmopolitanism. Some versions like the one offered by Luis Cabrera advocate a strong world civil state with corresponding rights of citizenship.[41] Other versions of civil cosmopolitanism, like the theories advocated by Jürgen Habermas, seek to create a non-national sense of global community and do not necessarily promote the idea of a world state.[42] As will be discussed in Chapter 6, civil cosmopolitans of the weaker persuasion often use human rights theory and the expansion of international legal tenets as a way to create a sense of unifying citizenship and global community without obligating themselves to a strong institutional conception of world government.[43]

Before discussing where a Kantian position might be located within current cosmopolitan debates, it is important to clarify that all of the aforementioned categories are fluid and interrelated. Most contemporary cosmopolitans work on adjoined aspects of moral and institutional cosmopolitanism, and on the various cosmopolitan principles of global justice, universal human rights, democratic law, international law, egalitarianism, individualism and universalism. Many theorists share similar moral positions, but differ in what institutional approach to take in realizing them.

Conversely, other cosmopolitans share institutional beliefs, but debate whether those institutions should be based on universal human rights or on other positive moral duties. In this respect, the four classifications are useful in relating the wide scope of cosmopolitan thought, but limited for understanding the overlapping complexities that exist between them. As with any subject as rich as cosmopolitanism, the range of debate is broad and each cosmopolitan theory has its own unique intricacies.

Nevertheless, for the purpose of this project it is important to understand that the form of Kantian cosmopolitanism argued within this book contains both a moral and institutional component. First, it is a weak form of moral cosmopolitanism, in that it advocates a minimal universal moral law while allowing for various moral principles to be derived locally by individual participants. The moral concern relates to how the world *should* be normatively understood as a coexisting whole and is meant to act as a moral compass in questions regarding global cohabitation and justice. Second, since Kant argued for a fairly formalized constitutional structure of cosmopolitan law, any form of Kantian cosmopolitanism certainly has an institutional component. In this regard, Kant's cosmopolitan law is a form of strong cosmopolitanism, in that cosmopolitan law is meant to trump local norms in favor of a universal cosmopolitan morality. In other words, the moral cosmopolitan component argues for a minimal and weak form of universal morality that respects the worth of human beings regardless of geographical location. Nevertheless, Kantian cosmopolitanism also advocates a strong institutional and legal component that demands that these minimal moral standards be recognized through the codification of cosmopolitan law, which in return demands universal application and obligation.

Because of Kant's commitment to cosmopolitan law within a federation of states (and beyond), many scholars have preferred to label Kant's cosmopolitanism as belonging to the subfield of legal cosmopolitanism. Although this classification is appropriate, the classification is often misunderstood within legal theory, creating somewhat of a misnomer. Many legal theorists of the *positivist* persuasion argue that law and morality are not connected. Positivists believe that our obligation to any form of international law is based on enforcement and convention rather than being based on strong moral sentiment.[44] In addition, *legal realists* suggest that international law is predicated on the protection of sovereign states and that the nature of the state system rules out any unified global commitment. Despite the fact that Kant certainly believed that law had a positive component and that universal law would be difficult in a world driven by state interest, Kant's cosmopolitan law is derived from moral and normative foundations. In this regard, Kant's cosmopolitan law is meant to be positive in its constitutional authority to provide order within a realist system, but this authority is justified by a naturalist consideration located within the *internal aspects* and moral foundations of cosmopolitan law. Therefore, although Kant's cosmopolitanism might well be classified as a form of legal cosmopolitanism, it should not be considered as falling into any strict category of legal positivism (what the law does), legal naturalism (the morality behind the law) or legal realism (international law as a tool for the protection of sovereignty). As Jeremy Waldron has argued, Kantian jurisprudence might best be described as a form of *normative positivism*.[45] In this sense, a Kantian position holds that there must be systematic moral reasoning underpinning international justice and law, but also that law itself, when constitutionally objectified, can have a commanding force in creating individual obligations regardless of the normative force on which it is presupposed. It will be through the discussions in following chapters that this complex relationship between cosmopolitan morality and law will be outlined and explored.

## III.   The Critiques of Cosmopolitanism and the Structure of Response

An argument advocating cosmopolitan legal principles is not one without considerable challenges and debate. Since the early Stoic conception of a universal citizen, cosmopolitanism as a political theory has historically received staunch criticism. Critics of cosmopolitanism have faulted cosmopolitan ideas largely on the fact that those ideas are morally utopian, idealistic and overly universal in a world of various ethical conceptions. Of these critics, communitarian, cultural pluralists and moral relativists have been the most prominent challengers to the cosmopolitan perspective. Moral relativists regard cosmopolitan claims as utopian in their positivist assumptions of the perfectibility of human reason and universal ethical understanding. For the cultural pluralist, cosmopolitanism replaces a plurality of values in the world with a universalism that both diminishes human diversity, but also "fosters aspirations for a universal state . . . attempting world conquest."[46] Similarly, communitarians describe cosmopolitan ideals as a threatening force to the moral goods of community and communal obligation. Communitarians fear that cosmopolitanism, with its focus on the global citizen, cannot adequately accommodate the human need to belong to immediate communities of meaning and purpose. In the communitarian argument lies an existential fear of a rootless cosmopolitan, where a person "is really no one, a man without allegiances . . . he is not, in positive terms, a friend to all, but merely not a stranger."[47]

Although we should acknowledge that some historical conceptions of cosmopolitanism are more susceptible to the communitarian and pluralist claims of authoritarian utopianism than others, this does not corrupt and make incoherent all forms of cosmopolitan theory. Furthermore, it is important to refute and satisfy pluralist, relativist and communitarian concerns of cosmopolitanism before cosmopolitan law can have any legitimate moral and legal claim on a global order. It is essential to consider the concerns of cosmopolitan critics and satisfy their most profound apprehensions. Nevertheless, where I believe cosmopolitanism is correct is in the idea that a normative international order cannot be developed and maintained independently of a general acceptance of common moral and legal principles. In contrast to some theorists such as Hedley Bull, who suggest that international order cannot be maintained directly by moral or ethical principles,[48] a Kantian position demands that stronger normative principles are needed to anchor human relations and the unavoidable coexistence of all human beings regardless of nationality, ethnicity or place of birth.

In addition, the relativist, communitarian and pluralist stance is predicated on what the international world has historically delivered and not on how a world order might organize itself; or better yet, on how the world *should* organize itself based on global cohabitation and corresponding human concerns. In order to satisfy the critics of cosmopolitanism, this book will outline and defend what I believe is the most coherent and promising form of cosmopolitanism. As we will discover, a Kantian form of cosmopolitanism, which is based closely on the works of Kant, can best capture the complexities of a pluralistic global environment while confirming a moral concern for humanity and the normative obligations that we *should* have towards one another if we are to coexist. In addition, Kant's cosmopolitan argument is not a harebrained or unrealistic argument as some like Bull have suggested, for it is based on the principle that we must in fact necessarily tolerate one another within the spherical confines of the earth. Since spherical cohabitation is an empirical fact, "the idea of cosmopolitan right is therefore not fantastic or over strained;

it is a necessary complement to the unwritten code of political and international right, transforming it into a universal right of humanity."[49]

As we will see, Kant outlines his argument for a cosmopolitan order in two ways. On the one hand, Kant makes his appeal on an empirical level, outlining the practical need for unified cosmopolitan purpose through historical examination and through the examination of international tensions that threaten our common humanity. On the other hand, Kant sets up normative a priori principles of jurisprudence, where practical reason dictates a *cosmopolitan right* to external freedom. In a fusion of empirical experience with normative principles, Kant maintains that humans cannot avoid physical contact with one another and therefore must enter into a civil order that secures mutual rights and spheres of external freedom. Nevertheless, Kant does not tell us exactly how this international order will ultimately look, or provide details as to how global institutions and economic structures will function to protect mutual cosmopolitan law. What Kant provides are the metaphysical and normative foundations within the considerations for a cosmopolitan future. It is with an attempt to flush these principles out into a coherent and defensible cosmopolitan theory that this book is ultimately concerned.

In this regard, the purpose of this book is to outline a Kantian form of cosmopolitan theory in relation to the normative requirements necessary for a constitutional global order and provide a comprehensive defense of Kant's cosmopolitan law from realist, relativist, pluralist and communitarian critiques. This will require a theoretical exploration of Kant's cosmopolitanism and the normative requirements consistent with and necessary to a Kantian-based cosmopolitan constitution. Therefore, what this book attempts is to provide a Kantian form of cosmopolitanism that not only examines Kant's cosmopolitan thought, but also engages with contemporary cosmopolitan arguments found throughout political philosophy. The goal is to provide a comprehensive outline and defense for a viable form of Kantian cosmopolitanism in order to provide a coherent theory for those concerned with global relations in an increasingly globalized world. In order to establish this grounding for a more thoroughgoing vision of Kant's cosmopolitanism, this book is divided into two parts.

Part One is comprised of two chapters. Chapter 1 outlines Kant's cosmopolitanism in general, while Chapter 2 examines the normative foundations involved in Kant's cosmopolitan constitution and cosmopolitan law. From this outline, Part Two provides a comprehensive defense and more detailed examination of the major themes and obstacles involved in

Kant's cosmopolitanism. In this part, themes concerning the relationship between Kant's federation and state sovereignty (Chapter 3), the role of diversity and culture within cosmopolitan law (Chapter 4), and a Kantian form of global distributive justice (Chapter 5) are discussed in relation to the vision of Kant's cosmopolitanism outlined in Part One. The book will conclude with a final chapter relating the various normative concepts discussed throughout this project to practical concerns often debated in contemporary international relations theory.

In Chapter 1, the basic elements that underwrite Kant's cosmopolitanism are outlined. In doing so, the chapter looks at the moral principles behind Kant's cosmopolitanism and the problem of Kant's cosmopolitan teleology, and develops a brief overview of Kant's more coherent principles of cosmopolitan law. Through these discussions, a connection is made between Kant's critical philosophy and the moral foundations of his cosmopolitanism. By framing Kant's overall cosmopolitan vision, this chapter further explores Kant's theory of history and suggests that it is based on a problematic teleology. It is from this examination that a more plausible treatment of Kant's cosmopolitan history is provided. The chapter concludes by linking the various aspects of Kant's cosmopolitanism into a single coherent narrative that will provide a basis for future redevelopment in subsequent chapters.

Based on the general overview provided in the first chapter, the purpose of Chapter 2 is to outline a Kantian form of cosmopolitan law and the legal system involved in a cosmopolitan constitution. In doing so, this chapter explores and discusses Kant's notion of cosmopolitan law, the idea of cosmopolitan right, the laws of hospitality and a revised Kantian approach to constitutional cosmopolitanism. The chapter argues beyond Kant's discussion of constitutionalism, suggesting that a written constitution not only articulates many of Kant's cosmopolitan concerns, but also provides a reasonable moral and legal foundation for an international society. The chapter focuses on the possibility of a cosmopolitan order based on jurisprudence, the necessity of a minimal consensus bound by constitutional provisions, and the corresponding legal obligations maintained by cosmopolitan law.

As was mentioned above, the aim of Part One is to outline the normative principles involved in Kant's cosmopolitanism and to discuss the various components behind Kant's cosmopolitan enthusiasm and his concept of cosmopolitan law. Based on the foundations laid out in Part One, Part Two of the book will further examine the various themes involved with Kant's cosmopolitanism and some of the main critiques leveled against it. This is done in order to provide a more comprehensive understanding of what is involved in Kant's cosmopolitanism and to provide a cosmopolitan defense from various anti-cosmopolitan and anti-Kantian arguments.

To do so, Chapter 3 examines the role of states in Kant's cosmopolitan federation and attempts to clarify the relationship between the rights of states and the concept of *cosmopolitan law*. In order to present a coherent and tenable account of a Kantian federation, this chapter explores Kant's move away from the traditional natural law concept of *jus gentium* to the idea of a *pacific federation* and its corresponding feature of *cosmopolitan law*. From this background, the chapter outlines and examines the three definitive articles of *Perpetual Peace* and their primary significance in creating a cosmopolitan order. Through this exegetical examination, the chapter seeks to resolve the debate between Kantian scholars as to whether Kant's cosmopolitanism must be understood as advocating a federation of free states or a world republic. It is from this discussion that it is argued that Kant's cosmopolitanism is best understood as a federation of free states, with the caveat that Kant maintained optimism for a continued movement toward broader multilateral and multisectoral institutions. The chapter concludes by comparing Kant's cosmopolitanism to contemporary theories. In doing so, I maintain that Kant's cosmopolitanism does not advocate the immediate destabilizing destruction of states and self-determination as some claim, but is meant as a mechanism for the lawful coexistence of various political communities constituting a judicial community of the world.

The primary concern of Chapter 4 is with the role of cultural diversity in Kant's cosmopolitan thought. In this chapter, a reformulation of Kant's epistemology of culture is defended against cultural relativists, cultural pluralists and claims from culture which deny the possibility of cosmopolitan law. This chapter argues that cosmopolitan law does not command normative shifts beyond the psychological or cultural capacities of human beings and further suggests that cultures are not static entities that should be protected from a concept of *cosmopolitan law*. The ultimate position is that a Kantian vision of cosmopolitan law does not reduce a plurality of cultures, but seeks to establish minimal cosmopolitan principles in order to allow various cultures to peacefully coexist.

Chapter 5 attempts to derive some key normative principles inherent in a Kantian scheme of distributive justice. To do so, this chapter looks at

19

Kant's conception of external freedom and social welfare, relating them to a cosmopolitan concern for global justice. The chapter argues that Kant's freedom of autonomy (co-legislation) demands a robust theory of distributive justice in order to provide a political environment that supports the *effective autonomy* of individuals in a hypothetical *kingdom of ends*. The chapter further explores a possible relationship with Martha Nussbaum's *capability theory*, suggesting that Kant's distributive principles might be best expressed through a form of the *capability approach*. Lastly, the chapter draws connections between contemporary cosmopolitan arguments for global justice and Kant's overall cosmopolitan concerns.

In order to bring the various points together, Chapter 6 articulates the major themes from the previous chapters and relates them to the Kantian model argued throughout the book. However, a large portion of the last chapter will provide a discussion of Kant's cosmopolitan theory in relation to current cosmopolitan debates. In doing so, the chapter will explore the implications of Kant's cosmopolitanism in relation to contemporary issues of globalization, global justice, humanitarian assistance and universal human rights. The point of this exercise is to illustrate how a Kantian cosmopolitan position could respond to these issues and how it might in theory and practice further a cosmopolitan condition. In providing some link between theory and practice, the argument is made that a minimal ethical/legal order might be developed from already existing and overlapping international and domestic concerns. The chapter will conclude by making a claim that we should change unjust global systems toward the metaphysical ideal of a cosmopolitan constitution and will discuss the possible positive ripple effect of a continued cosmopolitan enthusiasm.

## IV. METHODOLOGY: KANT THE COSMOPOLITAN AND A KANTIAN FORM OF COSMOPOLITANISM

However, before examining Kant's cosmopolitanism in more detail, it is important to clarify the methodology underpinning this project. It has often been argued that there are two basic methodological approaches that can be taken when exploring Kant's cosmopolitanism. Both models have been used as separate scholarly activities or have been used together in various degrees in order to clarify and expand Kant's philosophy. The first approach is to employ strict exegesis in an attempt to understand Kant's cosmopolitanism by directly analyzing his use of words, logical structure and the relationship between various aspects of his philosophy.

Undoubtedly, this exercise can be extremely useful in resolving logical incoherence (or as in most cases highlighting it) and with providing a synoptic reading of the works of Kant.

The other approach is to reconstruct aspects of Kant's cosmopolitanism in order to establish a coherent and defensible argument for Kantian cosmopolitanism. This method can demand significant dedication to exegesis, but also allows for flexibility in reconstructing and altering Kant's philosophy in order to advance a more consistent, defensible and contemporary position. The relationship between these two methodologies and their use is important to clarify. This is because both methodological approaches, when haphazardly or unclearly mixed together, can often create misappropriated "Kantian" hybrids that potentially lack textual support and can often confuse the reader as to what is meant to be taken as belonging to Kant and what is meant to be understood as reconstruction.

Therefore, because this form of misappropriation can cause considerable confusion, it is important to clarify the approach one is taking when examining Kant's cosmopolitanism. To be clear, I believe it is important to try to remain faithful to both the context of Kant's work as well as the textual material. However, I also believe that there is heuristic value in allowing for the redevelopment of Kant's cosmopolitanism when it is properly substantiated in relation to strong exegetical evidence. In other words, I do not believe that exegesis and reformulation are mutually exclusive as long as one makes it clear what is being attributed to Kant and what is being presented as a conscious reformulation of what might be broadly considered as a Kantian position. For I believe it is possible to present both a faithful reading of Kant's cosmopolitanism while also openly exploring an alternative reconstruction that consciously attempts to capture his best-known philosophical tenets. However, to do so properly, it is important to be as forthright about one's approach as possible. Therefore, it is important for me to highlight the fact that the methodology used throughout this book will approach the works of Kant from this mixed perspective. This is initially done through outlining and examining Kant's cosmopolitan vision directly from primary and secondary sources. By doing so, an exegetical account of what Kant said about cosmopolitanism, and what other scholars say that Kant said, is outlined. Based on that exegetical discussion, this book then reexamines and reinterprets ambiguous or underdeveloped aspects of Kant's cosmopolitanism in order to provide what could be considered a more coherent and thoroughgoing formulation of Kantian cosmopolitanism. In other words, the first aspect of this methodology requires a certain dedication to exegesis and to mapping out the various exegetical debates within Kantian scholarship. The second aspect then attempts to reconcile, reinterpret, reformulate and reconstruct a vision of cosmopolitanism that not only provides for a more coherent Kantian-based cosmopolitan vision, but one that is also better equipped to respond to contemporary cosmopolitan debates.

Although I believe it is useful to maintain a methodology that allows for exegesis on the one hand and the heuristic value of reconstruction and reformulation on the other, it is often the source of some contention within Kantian scholarship and it is worth explaining my reasoning further. As was alluded to above, strict exegetical scholars of Kant's philosophy often protest the way some contemporary political theorists use the works of Kant as a basis for their political theory. Critics are concerned with a perceived use of generous interpretation and are critical of using these lax readings of Kant in order to suit contemporary debates. Although I agree that some interpretations are irresponsible misappropriations of Kant, I also believe it is problematic to absolutely restrict any reformulation or extrapolation of Kant's theories. This is especially true if one takes Kant's theory of human progress seriously. For as Kant himself suggests, human enlightenment is not the act of discovery by one person alone, but is a process of development through countless generations of human involvement and reexamination. If we were to solely approach the study of Kant as narrow exegesis, to outline what Kant said, the historical context of his work and the logical coherency of his internal philosophy, it would significantly limit his contribution to human knowledge. Although radical interpretations are often made and this might lead a contemporary theorist away from what Kant may have "actually" had in mind, it does not necessarily suggest that constructing a more contemporarily robust form of Kantian cosmopolitanism from Kant's best-known tenets and principles is always an unjustified exercise. As Otfried Hoffe claims, "one can still make use of Kant in order to go beyond Kant."[50] For as Kant suggests in *The Contest of Faculties*, no theory can assume to be complete and it is only through a continued reexamination by future generations that any work can hope to find some level of reasonable satisfaction.

In this regard, this book should be seen as providing an exegetical examination of Kant's cosmopolitan theory as well as normatively engaging with it. As stated above, this will require that in the first instance, Kant's cosmopolitan theory be outlined as faithfully as possible. Nevertheless, when Kant's cosmopolitanism is vague, incomplete, incoherent or insufficient, other cosmopolitan arguments or philosophical interjections will be utilized in order to resolve these issues. An example of this methodology is illustrated in Chapter 5, where there is an attempt to develop a Kantian conception of global distributive justice. Since Kant does not fully develop a theory of distributive justice, let alone global distributive justice, the chapter constructs a scheme of global distributive justice in light of Kant's overall discussions of social welfare and justice. By examining the underlining normative concerns involved in Kant's discussions, the chapter extrapolates and constructs further normative principles of distributive justice on a cosmopolitan level. Although the distributive scheme moves away from strict textual exegesis, it is nevertheless extrapolated from Kant's conception of justice and is based on Kant's overall cosmopolitan concerns. What is critical, and something that I have tried to be clear about throughout this book, is to explicitly highlight when an idea is being attributed to Kant exegetically and when my argument is a reconstruction of a broadly Kantian position. Although this book will in no way provide a complete and exhaustive analysis of any conception of Kantian cosmopolitanism, it is my hope that it will form the heuristic groundwork for future thoughts and understandings of Kant's theory and its consanguinity to international relations.

Nevertheless, before moving forward it is necessary to clarify one last issue related to the aforementioned topic. The issue is related to the complexity involved in linking Kant's critical philosophy to his political theory. It should be mentioned that there is an inherent difficulty with focusing on an examination and extrapolation of Kant's cosmopolitan theory, which arises from the fact that Kant's political theory evolves from his more complex philosophical principles. In order to understand Kant's political theory, it becomes increasingly important to place it within the context of his critical philosophy and vice versa. This is due to the fact that Kant wrote many of his political works after *The Critique of Pure Reason* and saw his political theory as a logical extension of his overall philosophy. Therefore, in order to construct a convincing form of Kantian cosmopolitanism, it is often necessary to have a sense of the interrelation between his critical philosophy and his interspersed political works. However, there is no simple way to summarize or encapsulate Kant's critical philosophy and the transition to his political theory.[51] The critical works are both massive in substance as they are in technical subtlety. When focusing on Kant's political theory, it becomes difficult not to get bogged down in Kant's more technical philosophical principles.

Nevertheless, since the focus of this book is with advancing a form of Kantian cosmopolitanism, concentrating on a form of Kant's legal cosmopolitanism in particular, I must limit my analysis to the realm of Kant's political theory. Therefore, any discussion of Kant's critical philosophy will be brought out where it is relevant to the cosmopolitan theory I outline. Although this will often do a great injustice to the nuances of Kant's argument, I have done my best to relate the major critical themes while maintaining a focus on Kant's cosmopolitanism.

To my knowledge, there is no thorough analysis or extrapolation of a Kantian form of cosmopolitanism and its connection to contemporary cosmopolitan debates. Although various scholars have discussed detailed aspects of Kant's cosmopolitanism, from a more exegetical account,[52] to Kant's use of metaphysics and duty,[53] to Kant's principles for perpetual peace,[54] there does not seem to be any exhaustive attempt to tie the various complexities of Kant's cosmopolitan vision into a comprehensive picture. In addition, many contemporary cosmopolitans construct their more elaborate institutional models on some form of Kantian premise without detailed consideration of what this basic cosmopolitan condition entails. For anyone interested in Kant's cosmopolitanism, we are decidedly stuck with the puzzlement of what a Kantian form of cosmopolitanism advocates. This problem is exacerbated by the fact that Kant provided little explanation of his cosmopolitan vision. What Kant provided was the metaphysical and normative foundations for a future philosophical movement toward a cosmopolitan order. The task of this book is to provide a more comprehensive understanding of Kant's cosmopolitanism and to draw out the normative implications of this Kantian vision within contemporary international political theory.

## NOTES

1. This wonderfully poignant quote has wrongly been attributed to the Victorian writer Herman Melville by many reference dictionaries and by such noted politicians as Hilary Clinton. However, the quote is actually that of Henry Melvill "Partaking in Other Men's Sins," *The Golden Lectures* (London: Chapter House, 1855), p. 454.
2. Immanuel Kant, "Perpetual Peace," in Hans Reiss (ed.), *Kant's Political Writings* (Cambridge: Cambridge University Press, 1970), p. 107. [8:360]
3. Immanuel Kant, *Grounding for the Metaphysics of Morals*, J. Ellington (trans.) (Cambridge, MA: Hackett Publishing Company 1981), p. 30. [4:421]
4. Martha Nussbaum, "Patriotism and Cosmopolitanism," *The Boston Review*, 19 (5) (1995), p. 3.

5. I borrow the phrase cosmopolitan enthusiasm from Georg Cavallar, *Kant and the Theory and Practice of International Right* (Cardiff: University of Wales Press, 1999).

6. I am assuming that the effects of globalization are in fact forcing communities to relate with one another in both positive and negative ways that is historically unique. For a detailed discussion of globalization and its implications, see, D. Held, A. McGrew, D. Goldblatt, & J. Perraton, *Global Transformations* (Cambridge: Polity Press, 1999).

7. Garrett Wallace Brown, "Globalization is What we Make of it: Globalization Theory and the Future Construction of Global Interconnection," *Political Studies Review*, vol. 6, no. 1 (2007), pp. 42–53.

8. Immanuel Kant, *The Metaphysics of Morals*, M. Gregor (ed & trans.) (Cambridge: Cambridge University Press, 1996), pg. 121. [6:352–3]

9. The ebb and tide of cosmopolitan thinking seems as old as humanity itself. Although we do not know exactly when cosmopolitan thinking began, we can categorize western cosmopolitan thought into roughly eight historical periods, Old Stoa (500–206 BC), Middle Stoa (206–51 BC), Late Stoa (51 BC–AD 180), Renaissance Neostoicism, The School of Salamana (AD 1440–1620), The Enlightenment (AD 1500–1800), and what I would argue is two renewed stages arising from the end of World War II (Post-AD 1945–55) and Post-Soviet/Globalization (1990–present). For a good history of cosmopolitan thought, see Derek Heater, *World Citizenship and Government: Cosmopolitan Ideas in the History of Western Political Thought* (New York: St. Martin's Press, 1996).

10. Huge Harris, "The Greek Origins of the Idea of Cosmopolitanism," in *The International Journal of Ethics*, vol. 38, no. 1 (1927), pp. 1–10.

11. Diogenes Laertius, *The Lives of Eminent Philosophers*, Vol. II, R. Hicks (trans.) (Cambridge, MA: Loeb Classical Library, 1925).

12. These words are attributed to Zeno by Plutarch in "On the Fortune of Alexander," in A. Long D. Sedley (eds), *The Hellenistic Philosophers*, vol. I (Cambridge: Cambridge University Press, 1987), p. 429.

13. Seneca, *De Otio*, A. Long & D. Sedley (eds) (Cambridge: Cambridge University Press, 1987), p. 431.

14. Cicero, *De Officiis*, M. T. Griffin & E. M. Atkins (eds) (Cambridge: Cambridge University Press, 1991), Book I (50), pg. 21.

15. Marcus Aurelius, *The Meditations* (New York: Hackett, 1983), Sect. 14.

16. Cicero, ibid.

17. Sharon Anderson-Gold, *Cosmopolitanism and Human Rights* (Cardiff: University of Wales Press, 2001), pg. 13.

18. More detail and explanation regarding the Kantian move away from *jus gentium* to cosmopolitan law is provided in Chapter 3. For another discussion on this topic, see Daniele Archibugi, "Immanuel Kant, Cosmopolitan Law and Peace," *European Journal of International Relations*, vol. 1 (4), 1995.

19. Martha Nussbaum, "Kant and Cosmopolitanism," in *Perpetual Peace: Essays on Kant's Cosmopolitan Ideal*, J. Bohman & M. Lutz-Bachmann (eds) (Cambridge, MA: MIT Press, 1997).

20. Ibid., pg. 36.

21. Klaus Reich, "Kant and Greek Ethics," *Mind*, 48 (1939), pp. 338–54.

22. Some feminists have challenged whether Kant included women in his cosmopolitan

equation. These arguments are based on some of Kant's side comments on the irrationality of women. However, I don't believe Kant's personal bias, if the feminist critique is correct, has any effect on how we have to understand Kant's overall philosophy. Although Kant may have held views of women that reflected the chauvinism of his day, these beliefs do not represent inherent problems with his cosmopolitanism in general and we can simply include women as rational agents worthy of equal respect.

23. Christine M. Korsgaard, "Aristotle and Kant on the Source of Value," in *Ethics*, 96 (April 1986), p. 486–505.
24. Nussbaum, "Kant and Cosmopolitanism."
25. Catherine Lu, "The One and Many Faces of Cosmopolitanism," *Journal of Political Philosophy*, vol. 8 (2) (June 2000), pg. 245.
26. For a fairly comprehensive bibliography of cosmopolitan movements, see D. Archibugi and M. Koening-Archibugi, "Globalization, Democracy and Cosmopolis: A Bibliographical Essay," in D. Archibugi (ed.), *Debating Cosmopolitics* (London: Verso, 2003), p. 273–91.
27. Thomas Pogge, "Cosmopolitanism and Sovereignty," *Ethics*, 103 (1992), p. 49–50.
28. Ibid., pg. 49. Quoted by Charles Beitz in "International Liberalism and Distributive Justice: A Survey of Recent Thought," *World Politics*, 51 (1992), p. 287.
29. Brian Barry, "International Society From a Cosmopolitan Perspective," in D. Maple & T. Nardin (eds), *International Society* (New Jersey: Princeton University Press, 1998), pg. 143.
30. Charles Beitz, "Cosmopolitan Liberalism and the State System," in C. Brown (ed.), *Political Restructuring in Europe: Ethical Perspectives* (London: Routledge, 1994), pg. 124.
31. Barry, "International Society From a Cosmopolitan Perspective," pg. 145.
32. Samuel Scheffler uses the terminology of moderate and extreme cosmopolitanism. However, the definition seems to be synonymous with weak and strong cosmopolitanism. This is because Scheffler states that extreme cosmopolitanism requires that all moral commitments, even localized sentiments for the family, must be justified in relation to a particular cosmopolitan ideal or principle without exception. This is different from a moderate cosmopolitan position, which allows for the acceptance that some special obligations can be held independently and in mutual compatibility with cosmopolitanism. See Samuel Scheffler, *Boundaries and Allegiances* (Oxford: Oxford University Press, 2001), pp. 115–19.
33. David Miller, "The Limits of Cosmopolitan Justice," in D. Mapel & T. Nardin (eds), *International Society* (New Jersey: Princeton University Press, 1998), pg. 166.
34. Ibid.
35. As with any discipline as broad as cosmopolitanism, it is often difficult to know exactly where any variation is located in relation to one another. However, a good example of a possible weak form of cosmopolitanism can be seen in the arguments of someone like Chandran Kukathas who suggests an extremely minimal universalism between groups. A strong contemporary conception of cosmopolitanism can be located in works such as those of Charles T. Taylor, who advocates a single world state with a strong overarching unifying liberal morality. See respectively, Chandran Kukathas, *The Liberal Archipelago: A Theory of Diversity and Freedom* (Oxford: Oxford University Press, 2003) and Charles T. Taylor, *Toward World Sovereignty* (Lanham, MD: University Press of America, 2002).

36. Gerard Delanty, *Citizenship in a Global Age* (Buckingham: Open University Press, 2000).

37. For a more comprehensive discussion of legal cosmopolitanism and its various formulations, see Garrett Wallace Brown, "Moving from Cosmopolitan Legal Theory to Legal Practice: Models of Cosmopolitan Law," *Legal Studies*, vol. 28, no. 3 (2008), pp. 430–51.

38. Contemporary theorists such as Allan Buchanan and Fernando Teson are examples of legal cosmopolitan arguments. See Allan Buchanan, *Justice, Legitimacy and self-determination: Moral Foundations for International Law* (Oxford: Oxford University Press, 2004), and Fernando Teson, *A Philosophy of International Law* (Boulder, CO: Westview, 1998).

39. Theorists such as David Held, Richard Falk, Patrick Hayden and Daniele Archibugi are active contemporary examples of a political cosmopolitan approach. See David Held, *Democracy and the Global Order: From the Modern State to Cosmopolitan Democracy* (Cambridge: Polity Press, 1995), Richard Falk, *On Humane Governance: Towards a New Global Politics* (Cambridge: Polity Press, 1995), Patrick Hayden, *Cosmopolitan Global Politics* (Aldershot: Ashgate, 2005) and Daniele Archibugi & D. Held (eds), *Cosmopolitan Democracy: An Agenda for a New World Order* (Cambridge: Polity Press, 1995).

40. Contemporary cultural cosmopolitanism is best expressed in the political theories of Timothy Brennan, Jeremy Waldron and Martha Nussbaum. See Timothy Brennan, *At Home in the World: Cosmopolitanism Now* (Cambridge: Cambridge University Press, 1997), Jeremy Waldron, "What is Cosmopolitan?" *Journal of Political Philosophy*, vol. 8, no. 2 (2000) and Martha Nussbaum, *Cultivating Humanity* (Cambridge: Cambridge University Press, 1998).

41. Luis Cabrera, *Political Theory of Global Justice: A Cosmopolitan Case for the World State* (New York: Routledge, 2004).

42. Jürgen Habermas, *The Post National Constellation*, M. Persky (trans.) (Cambridge, MA: MIT Press, 2001). Also see Jürgen Habermas, *The Divided West*, Ciaran Cronin (ed. & trans.) (Cambridge: Polity Press, 2006), especially part IV.

43. Contemporary examples of *civic cosmopolitanism* in the weak form can be seen within the works of Thomas Pogge, Jack Donnelly and Charles Jones. See Thomas Pogge, *World Poverty and Human Rights* (Cambridge: Polity Press, 2002), Jack Donnelly, *International Human Rights* (Boulder, CO University of Colorado Press, 1998) and Charles Jones, *Global Justice: Defending Cosmopolitanism* (Oxford: Oxford University Press, 1999). It is also important to point out that many cosmopolitans who advocate universal human rights are also legal cosmopolitans in the sense that human rights should form a legal minimum for any system of cosmopolitan civil order.

44. Legal Nihilists take legal positivism a step further by denying the existence of international law since there are no enforcement mechanisms with compulsory jurisdiction.

45. Jeremy Waldron, "Kant's Legal Positivism," *Harvard Law Review*, vol. 109 (1996), p. 1535. A more detailed discussion of Kantian cosmopolitan law is provided in Chapters 1, 2 and 3.

46. Martin Wight, *An Anatomy of International Thought*, *Review of International Studies*, 13 (1987), pg. 226. As paraphrased by Catherine Lu, "The One and Many Faces of Cosmopolitanism," pg. 251.

47. John Bryant, "Nowhere a Stranger: Melville and Cosmopolitanism," *Nineteenth Century Fiction*, 39 (#3) (1984), pg. 278. Also quoted in Catherine Lu, "The One and Many faces of Cosmopolitanism."

48. Hedley Bull, *The Anarchical Society* (London: Macmillan, 1977). Bull suggests that the world cannot be constituted anything beyond a modus vivendi. Generally understood, a modus vivendi is an order based on the power relationships of self-interested associations and subject to alteration on those grounds. In contrast, a normative society is a cooperative order that recognizes the trumping priority of certain common ethical principles. In a normative order, individuals pursue their self-interest in relation to those mutually agreed principles versus motivation on the exclusive considerations of self-interest and power balance.

49. Kant, "Perpetual Peace," pg. 108. [8:360]

50. Otfried Hoffe, *Kant's Cosmopolitan Theory of Law and Peace* (Cambridge: Cambridge University Press, 2006), pg. 16.

51. Hans Reiss has described the task of summarizing Kant's critical philosophy as "virtually impossible." Found in Reiss, *Kant's Political Writings*, Introduction, pg. 16. Steven Korner also states a problem with summarizing Kant's philosophy, but gave what I consider to be the most successful attempt in his book entitled *Kant* (Harmondsworth: Penguin, 1955).

52. Hoffe, *Kant's Cosmopolitan Theory of Law and Peace*.

53. Katrin Flikschuh, *Kant and Modern Political Philosophy* (Cambridge: Cambridge University Press, 2000).

54. J. Bohman & M. Lutz-Bachmann (eds), *Perpetual Peace: Essays on Kant's Cosmopolitan Ideal* (Cambridge, MA: MIT Press, 1997).

# Part One

# CHAPTER I

# Kant's Cosmopolitanism

"It makes no difference whether a person lives here or there, provided that, where he lives, he lives as a citizen of the world." – Marcus Aurelius

## INTRODUCTION

In *Idea for a Universal History with a Cosmopolitan Purpose*, Immanuel Kant defines cosmopolitanism as being "the matrix within which all the original capacities of the human race may develop."[1] In the broadest sense, Kant's cosmopolitanism can be understood as being concerned with the cultivation of a global environment within which everyone can fully develop his or her human capacities. Kant expands on what establishing this matrix entails when he proclaims that, "the greatest problem for the human species, the solution of which nature compels him to seek, is that of attaining a civil society, which can administer justice universally."[2] There are two important distinctions that should immediately be made from these passages when understanding Kant's cosmopolitanism. One distinction involves understanding the components embroiled in creating a matrix of cosmopolitan law. This includes formulating what is to be meant by universal justice, a global civil society and the moral value assigned to human capacities. The other involves synthesizing these principles with Kant's assertion that nature compels us to administer justice universally and that all human beings have original capacities that nature obliges us to fully develop. In this regard, there exist two strands in Kant's cosmopolitanism. One is concerned with what some might consider a naturalistic teleology and the other is concerned with the formal principles involved in creating universal justice and cosmopolitan law.

The distinctions are important, for whereas Kant's cosmopolitan theory of history sought to discover various motivations behind the formation of a cosmopolitan order, cosmopolitan law was specifically dedicated to inaugurating principles of jurisprudence necessary for a condition of universal justice to exist. Although both concepts are linked, they sustain two distinctive functions within Kant's cosmopolitanism and should not be lumped tightly together as has been traditionally done.

What the two quotes also help to highlight is that there are three interrelated elements involved in both aspects of Kant's cosmopolitanism. First, individuals represent the unit of ultimate moral concern equally and that our human capacities can only be fully developed within a condition of universal justice. Second, the attainment of universal justice requires the broader cultivation of a cosmopolitan civil society, one based solely on our humanity alone, without reference to nationality, localized political affiliation or place of birth. Third, the sole concern of cosmopolitan law is with establishing this matrix of universal justice and with formulating the necessary fundamental normative principles that underwrite a cosmopolitan constitution. It is in this sense that there is a connection between Kant and the quote used at the beginning of this chapter by Marcus Aurelius. The connection stems from a shared cosmopolitan belief that it makes no difference where a person lives, as long as that person is also understood as embedded within the larger human community. The foundations of that larger community should be based on a conception of universal justice and the establishment of a global condition where the development of everyone's capacities is to be considered as if they were equal citizens of the world.

Although many cosmopolitan scholars have invoked Kant's moral philosophy and aspects of his cosmopolitan theory as the foundational basis for their own arguments, they have often disagreed on the exact nature of Kant's cosmopolitanism. This is because there is considerable ambiguity and complication involved in the development of Kant's cosmopolitan matrix. The purpose of this chapter is to help clarify some of these ambiguities by outlining the basic elements that underwrite a Kantian form of cosmopolitanism. In doing so, this chapter will look at the ethical principles behind Kant's cosmopolitanism, the problem of Kant's cosmopolitan teleology, and develop a brief overview of Kant's more coherent principles of cosmopolitan law. Although the focus of this book will remain on Kant's notion of cosmopolitan law as the basis for any coherent construction of Kantian cosmopolitanism, this chapter will provide a link with Kant's critical philosophy while also rendering a possible alternative to his problematic teleology. To do this, the chapter is divided into four sections. In Section I, a connection is made between Kant's critical philosophy and the moral foundations of Kant's cosmopolitan vision. The second section will then outline Kant's cosmopolitan theory of history and suggest that it is based on a problematic teleology. It is in this section that a more plausible treatment of Kant's cosmopolitan history is provided. The third section discusses the concept of cosmopolitan law and couches it in Kant's overall theory of universal justice. The aim of the fourth section is to tie the various aspects of Kant's cosmopolitanism into a single coherent narrative that will provide a basis for deeper exploration and redevelopment in subsequent chapters.

## I. MORAL FOUNDATIONS OF KANT'S COSMOPOLITANISM

The easiest way to capture the essence of Kant's moral philosophy is to state his philosophical intention. It is generally accepted that Kant's goal was to give meaning to human experience without relying on pure rationalism or empiricism. Although this is stated very broadly, it does capture Kant's basic intent, which was to provide philosophical meaning to both the realm of scientific and empirical experience, but also to metaphysical concepts such as the *idea of morality*. In opposition to David Hume's empiricism, Kant believed that the forces of nature were not to be discovered by experience alone, but also through *a priori* constructions which gave significant human meaning to these experiences. This does not mean that Kant looked unfavorably on empiricism, for Kant was extremely influenced by Newtonian science and was considered to be a knowledgeable source on the scientific method. What Kant stressed in his critical philosophy was the necessary element of independent principles of human reason, which were prior to experience and which gave order to what he called "the experience of nature." In other words, the critical philosophy of Kant was an attempt to establish a system of *a priori* principles for the purpose of understanding the external world. This understanding could only be one from the human mind, which gives meaning not only to our empirical experiences, but also provides meaningful order to the world around us.

It is in Kant's discussions of morality that his epistemological considerations transfer into political foundations. The question for Kant was how to

33

understand the idea of morality beyond the realm of empirical experience, where the idea of morality has the ability to provide guiding principles that can be confirmed by practical reason. For Kant, the idea of morality starts with the *transcendental deduction* and the inherent assumption that individuals are free to make moral decisions. If humans are not free to determine the imperative force behind moral values, then morality no longer represents a self-imposed duty, but rather a meaningless coerced action. In order for morality to have subjective imperative, individuals must be understood as having the capacity for self-prescribed duty. The idea of morality, in order to remain internally consistent, must contain this corresponding imperative action. These moral decisions are not made in the context of determined causes alone, but find imperative weight principally through choices of our *free will*. In order to justify the idea of having a moral choice, human beings must be considered not only as phenomenal beings, but also as noumenal beings that are free. The idea of morality demands the *freedom of will* to make reasoned judgements, which in turn enable humans to make meaningful moral judgements that act in accordance with self-imposed duties. According to Kant, the capacity to self-legislate is the power to be autonomous moral agents and represents the ultimate source of human dignity. Thus, "by acting in accordance with moral principles prescribed by his own reason, man asserts his independence from the natural world and establishes what is distinctively human in his nature."[3]

Nevertheless, morality is different from other cognitive decisions because the latter command action in relation to self-imposed belief or agreed-upon social rules. Kant understands that choices as profoundly important as moral decisions must be conceived in relation to whether the moral duty can also be conceived as universally valid. It is in regard to determining what are correct rules of moral action that the idea of morality metaphysically necessitates practical synthetic *a priori* judgements of the *categorical imperative* which states, "act only according to the maxim whereby you can at the same time will that it should become a universal law."[4] It is from variations of the categorical imperative that Kant derives two important principles of cosmopolitan universality. One derivative affirms that we should "act in such a way that you treat humanity, whether in your own person or in the person of another, always at the same time as an end, and never as a means."[5] Another derivative maintains that legislative maxims are only valid if they "can at the same time have for their object themselves as universal laws of nature."[6] In other words, since everyone has the capacity to be moral lawgivers, it is therefore rational to treat all humans with respect and a sense of universal human dignity. Kant consequently defines our human capacity for freedom as an innate right when he states, "freedom (independence from being constrained by another's choice) insofar as it can coexist with the freedom of every other in accordance with a universal law, is the only original right belonging to every man by virtue of his humanity."[7] This original right translates into the maxim that individuals should thus never be used simply as means, but should be understood as having ends in themselves. We determine the validity of this maxim by understanding that we could never justify the violation of this right, for one could never rationally demand the violation of this maxim as a universal law of nature.

As Linklater has pointed out, the moral theory of Kant has two significant implications in regard to its transition to the realm of political theory. The first relates to the transcendental deduction and a moral claim that "human beings do not submit to a morality which has its source outside them."[8] The second implication relates to the categorical imperative and the principle that because individuals are moral beings, they must also have an "awareness of participating with others in a law-making community."[9] Kant himself describes this principle as a universal principle of hypothetical community when he suggests that humans should act "as if one were through his maxims always a law-making member in the universal kingdom of ends."[10] The implications derived from these principles are complex but simply summarized. Human beings should be allowed to exercise their capacity to be moral beings and that by exercising this equal capacity, we must come to understand our political and legal structures as vehicles for the development of our mutual co-legislation and external freedom.

It is therefore from a combination of the transcendental deduction and the categorical imperative that Kant formulates his *principle of universal justice* and *public right*. Kant's justice and the corresponding condition of public right are defined as "the sum of conditions under which the choice of one can be united with the choice of another in accordance with a universal law of freedom."[11] From the short discussion above, we can understand Kantian justice as an attempt to facilitate a civil condition where autonomous agents can socially coexist in accordance with universal freedom, which is for Kant the capacity of co-legislation and the voluntary subjugation to moral laws legislated by themselves. Nevertheless, there is an important distinction that should be made between the categorical imperative as used in Kantian ethics and his principle of universal justice. Whereas the first formulation of the categorical imperative describes how universal laws of morality can be determined, the principle of universal justice is concerned with what legitimate restrictions to individual freedom should exist in order to create a condition of universal public right. In this regard, justice necessitates that a legal condition of public right should exist so that "the freedom of the individual is limited in such a way as to secure the equal freedom of all."[12] The justification for this restriction of freedom is derived through the categorical imperative and a universal respect for the dignity of human beings as ends in themselves. The fact that we should see humans as moral decision makers and therefore also as having ends in themselves is derived from the transcendental deduction and the idea of morality.

The broader cosmopolitan implications of Kant's critical and moral philosophy are nicely encapsulated in the *Critique of Pure Reason*. The following quote not only represents Kant's first transition point from his critical writings to his political writings, but also provides an outline of his entire cosmopolitan project. In addition, the quote illustrates the transition of the categorical imperative into a scheme of constitutional public right. Kant's guiding principle of the categorical imperative is outlined as a shared idea of equal and universal justice when Kant suggests:

> A constitution allowing the *greatest possible human freedom in accordance with laws which ensure that the freedom of each can coexist with the freedom of all the others* (not one designed to provide the greatest possible happiness, as this will in any case follow automatically), is at all events a necessary idea which must be made the basis not only of the first outline of a political constitution but of all laws as well. It requires that we should abstract at the outset from present hindrances, which perhaps do not arise inevitably out of human nature, but are rather occasioned by neglect of genuine ideas in the process of legislation . . . Even if the latter should never come about, the idea which sets up this maxim as an archetype, in order to bring the legal constitution of mankind nearer and nearer to its greatest possible perfection, still remains correct. For no one can or ought to decide what the highest degree may be at which mankind may have to stop progressing, and hence how wide a gap may still of necessity remain between the idea and its execution. For this will depend on freedom, which can transcend any limit we care to impose.[13]

There are five important elements that should be taken from Kant's moral theory to the realm of Kantian cosmopolitan theory. First, the source of ultimate moral concern is located within individuals as having ends in themselves and with their equal capacity to be free and autonomous lawgivers within a universal *kingdom of ends*.[14] Second, the normative purpose of all civil law is to provide a constitution that can universalize a condition of equal freedom where "the freedom of each can coexist with the freedom of all the others."[15] In this sense, the concept of public right is an egalitarian principle of formal jurisprudence, since it affirms the equal restriction of everyone's external freedom in order to promote a mutually consistent level of equal freedom between individuals.[16] Third, the concept of cosmopolitan justice is universal, since it demands the universal restriction of freedom in order to maximize the equal freedom of everyone, in all places and at all times. Fourth, Kant's theory of justice is an *a priori* ideal and is meant to provide the normative grounding to which all external laws are to be legislated. Kant believes that an ideal constitution can be discovered through the use of metaphysical philosophy and should be seen as providing a moral compass toward which the establishment of universal justice is possible. In this regard, Kantian justice is also meant to provide an ideal standard from which all existing civil legislation is to be judged. Finally, despite the fact that present hindrances demonstrate a difficulty with manifesting a cosmopolitan ideal, this does not mean that it is not what humankind should strive for or that it is necessarily an impossible undertaking.

All of these principles essentially express the same conviction in Kant's thought, namely that global justice necessitates "a condition in which each individual's external freedom is restricted so as to make it consistent with the freedom of all others in the framework of a common law or system of laws."[17] For it is only within a condition of public right that humans can enjoy an environment of secured external freedom and the possibility to fully develop their moral capacities. As Kant argues, "such is the requirement of pure reason, which legislates *a priori*, regardless of all empirical ends."[18] It is from the philosophical backdrop provided in this section that a further extrapolation of a cosmopolitan framework of law will be made in Section III. However, before discussing cosmopolitan law, it is necessary to understand how Kant saw the ultimate formulation of a cosmopolitan matrix as a result of human history. It is in the next section that an outline of Kant's theory of history is provided and what implications this has for his cosmopolitanism.

## II. COSMOPOLITANISM, GLOBALIZATION AND KANT'S PROBLEMATIC THEORY OF HISTORY

The most useful way to understand Kant's cosmopolitan theory of history is by examining the teleological implications of *Idea for a Universal History with a Cosmopolitan Purpose* and *Perpetual Peace*. Critics of Kant have accused the ambitiously titled essays as proof that Kant maintained a spurious conception of human perfectibility with a correspondingly idealistic and impalpable teleology. Although critics are right to point out some inherent difficulties involved in Kant's vision of history, a different interpretation of these aspects can be provided that can salvage Kant's cosmopolitan enthusiasm without being obliged to the notion that nature mechanically compels humans toward a universal purpose. For we can interpret an alternative view of Kantian history that is more modest than Kant perhaps may have delineated. It is through an examination of Kant's theory of history that we can begin to understand the role of nature in Kant's cosmopolitan theory and determine how we might reinterpret this theory in order to make it more tenable.

As was pointed out at the beginning of the chapter, Kant maintained that "the greatest problem for the human species, the solution of which nature compels him to seek, is that of attaining a civil society, which can administer justice universally."[19] Kant further grounds the development of universal justice and the corresponding condition of perpetual peace in what is often seen as a naturalistic teleology:

> Perpetual peace is *guaranteed* by no less than the great artist *Nature* herself (*natura daedala rerum*). The mechanical process of nature visibly exhibits the purposive plan of producing concord among men, even against their will and indeed by means of their very discord.[20]

This passage generates a difficult conundrum for any consistent account of Kantian cosmopolitanism. This is because the passage seems to directly contradict Kant's critical philosophy and the necessary element of independent *a priori* principles of human reason. The most problematic element within this quote is the seemingly determined and mechanical "intention of nature" and the corresponding guiding force of what Kant later describes as "providence."[21] If humans are in fact determined by a natural purpose and therefore "guaranteed" to action by the mechanical forces of providence, then this has dangerous implications for Kantian ideas of free will and moral autonomy. As Karl-Otto Apel has pointed out, if Kant's theory of history is teleological in the sense that it is determined, then it puts "nearly every presupposition of the Kantian sketch into question."[22] In relation to some implications involved in Kant's cosmopolitan vision, the problem arises that nature's *providence* not only seems to provide the motivation to adopt a cosmopolitan constitution, but also guarantees all the means for its inevitable construction.

To this end, Kant makes four teleological comments about human evolution and the way in which history can be understood as having a cosmopolitan purpose. First, Kant believes that nature has enabled humans to "live in all the areas they have settled" and has fashioned humans so that they can adapt to the most inhospitable conditions.[23] Second, Kant explains that nature has driven humans "in all directions by means of war," so that they willingly inhabit even the most inhospitable regions of the earth.[24] Third, nature has compelled all humans to develop legal relationships in order to avoid war and thus to live in communities of law. Fourth, "nature has chosen war as a means of attaining this [civil] end" and the forces of war will continue until legal relationships are broadened and a cosmopolitan matrix is ultimately procured.[25] As Kant clearly states, "the distress produced by the constant wars in which the states try to subjugate or engulf each other must finally lend them, even against their will, to enter into a cosmopolitan constitution."[26]

However, Kant claims that war is not the only mechanism that nature employs to create an inevitable "concord among men." Although Kant never used the term *globalization* specifically, he did believe that the world was becoming increasingly interconnected and that the forces of nature were organized in such a way that it would eventually produce a cosmopolitan condition. As Kant suggests, "trade between nations . . . [creates] peaceful relations with one another, and thus achieves mutual understanding, community of interests and peaceful relations, even with the most distant of their fellows."[27] However, Kant notes that the growth of commerce is also dialectical in the sense that it can have inadvertent consequences.[28] In the case of Kant's understanding of globalization, although commerce can establish communities of mutual interest, it can also "provide the occasion for troubles in one place on our globe to be felt all over it."[29] In relation to nature's use of war, Kant maintained that "the spirit of commerce sooner or later takes hold of every people, and it cannot exist side by side with war."[30] Therefore, providence employs a carrot and stick method to motivate humanity toward a cosmopolitan condition. Humans are forced to socially relate with one another through forces of global commerce and mutual interest while also being continuously threatened by the global effects and ramifications of destructive war. Kant stresses the "unsocial sociability" involved in human nature and how this natural antagonism is actually the "intention of nature" when he claims that it is a "purposive plan of producing concord among men, even against their will and indeed by means of their very discord."[31]

What is often considered dubious about Kant's understanding of globalization is that he seems to argue that nature has created the dialectics involved with interconnectedness as a way to force humans to seek peace and a universal condition of justice. In this regard, "it is the unintended consequences of global interconnectedness that propel human beings toward peace, so long as they can solve the problems that this form of order poses."[32] Nonetheless, a problem ensues from the fact that Kant's globalization does not simply supply the empirical circumstances of human experience that are to inform a possible cosmopolitan solution. As we have seen, Kant's concept of globalization also appears to entail much more. For as many ascribe to Kant, global interconnectedness is not simply an empirical fact of experience, it is the "intention of nature" and compels us to resolve problems associated with globalization in order for humanity to fully develop a cosmopolitan matrix and the predetermined natural capacities of the human species.

Despite the fact that textual evidence might often support the notion that Kant is grounding his cosmopolitanism in a naturalistic teleology, there is another way to interpret Kant's intended use of historical prognosis. This is because we can interpret a Kantian vision of history that is divorced from what Karl Popper called teleological "futurism."[33] To do so, Kant's history must be understood as hermeneutic in the sense that human experiences have inadvertently brought us to where we are and that these experiences highlight the various empirical considerations from which a metaphysics of morals must take into account. In this regard, history is comprised of the empirical considerations that Kantian metaphysics must attempt to understand *as if it is possible* to derive a moral purpose behind human existence. As Apel has similarly suggested, "a morally grounded ought demands that we think hypothetically and fallibly about progress in history – that is, in terms of a possible historical process to which morally informed practice can be tied."[34] This does not mean however that the purpose of history is actually determined or guaranteed, but only that a metaphysics of morals can provide a hypothetically possible vision of historical progress from which conflicts in history might be understood as resolvable through the establishment of a cosmopolitan matrix. It is from the fact that we cannot fully understand the forces of history that we can suggest the possibility that human beings could be reflective moral participants towards this cosmopolitan ideal. Apel has understood this interpretation of Kant as a form of *reflective judgement*, where history provides practical considerations from which it is our moral concern to attempt to resolve.

Allen Wood has offered a similar interpretation of Kant's theory of history. According to Wood, "the right way to describe his [Kant's] approach is to say that he proceeds from considerations of theoretical reason, projecting the "idea" (or *a priori* rational concept) of a purely theoretical program for making comprehensible sense of the accidental facts of human history."[35] In other words, Wood suggests that Kant's natural teleology is "heuristically motivated . . . for obtaining and systematizing theoretical knowledge about history."[36] In doing so, Kant only attempts "to make sense of human history as a process involving an unconscious and unintended teleology of nature" in order to derive possible "regulative principles of reason,"[37] and not as a means to provide predictive evidence about how "this end will actually come about."[38]

What these interpretations suggest is that a tenable conception of Kantian cosmopolitanism must reject the inherent complications involved in understanding Kant's theory of history as promoting a determined natural teleology. Whether or not Kant's theory of history was actually meant as a scheme of reflective judgement as Apel claims, or as a "perverted" form of dialectical science as charged by Popper, any practical construction of Kantian cosmopolitanism must distance itself from the possible teleological ramifications of "guaranteed" human progression. Nevertheless, as Apel has noted, adopting this interpretation of Kant's vision of history might be in contrast to what Kant may have actually believed. Furthermore, utilization of this interpretation requires a thorough examination of the teleological evidence. The reinterpretation of Kant's historical dimension in relation to the possibility of moral progress is a colossal undertaking and this subject has been given a more thorough treatment elsewhere.[39] However, there are two areas connected to Kant's vision of history where application of this reinterpretation could be helpful in understanding a vision of Kantian cosmopolitanism.

The first area where determined empirical considerations inform Kant's cosmopolitanism is in relation to the development of human capacities. As was suggested in the last section, human capacities relate to the transcendental deduction and to the metaphysical idea of morality. The base for Kant's discussion of moral agency stems from the empirical fact that humans generally live in moral communities and that when we speak of moral actions we usually speak in terms of people being either morally right or morally wrong. The language of morality implies freedom of will and the ability of individuals to make autonomous moral choices. This is because when someone has acted wrongly from a moral point of view the implication is that the person could have and therefore should also have acted differently. For Kant, humans have the power to be moral agents and this capacity for moral reasoning is a universal attribute of the human species.

Nevertheless, Kant also affirmed that morality is not an action of pure reason outside of social context. This is because Kant understood that human capacities can be only fully developed within a civil society and that human reason cannot mature without social interaction and instruction. In addition, the capacity for moral agency is only valid when determined in relation to social context and when it can be conceived as consistent with a possible universal natural law. Otherwise, moral actions cannot be conceived as a subjective power inherent to the human condition, but as anomalistic impulses outside of cognitive influence or beyond the spectrum of practical and social considerations. It is for this reason that Kant claims that human capabilities can only be fully developed within a social condition of civil public right and justice. For it is only within a just social arrangement that individual capacities will be held as having an end in themselves, so that "the choice of one can be united with the choice of another in accordance with a universal law of freedom."[40]

Despite the fact that humans have the capacity for moral agency, this does not mean that all humans believe in the same moral norms or that they will always act upon their own moral judgements. This is due to the empirical fact that a plurality of ethical perspectives exists in the world and that not every individual has developed the equal capacity to relate morally toward others.[41] Consequently, it is a fact of human existence that antagonisms exist between various societies and that there are degrees to which individuals formulate moral imperatives. Antagonism in itself is not the problem, for Kant firmly believes that it is through antagonistic relationships that the exchange of ideas and the evolution of the human species is possible. Nonetheless, if this condition of natural antagonism is to be understood as having a historical purpose for humanity, it must also be thought as having a universal purpose for humanity. As Kant explains, "this purpose can be fulfilled only in a society which has not only the greatest freedom, and therefore a continual antagonism among its members, but also the most precise specification and preservation of the limits of this freedom in order that it can coexist with the freedom of others."[42] It is in this regard that the practical concern for cosmopolitanism is with creating a global environment where various individuals can mutually develop their capacities without the consequences of conflict that have been witnessed throughout history. Therefore, the cosmopolitan ideal of history is meant to illustrate that if antagonism and human agency are to be both understood as having a universal human end, we should also reflectively conclude that they must accord with universal principles of right which can guarantee the development of these purposeful ends.

This leads to the second area where determined empirical considerations inform Kant's metaphysics and the cosmopolitan prescription for a political boundary limited only by the spherical shape of the earth. The significance of the symbolism of earth's sphere is paramount to Kant's cosmopolitanism, because it provides the only natural political boundary for Kant's use of practical reason. In fact, the idea of confined global space in conjunction with a diverse global population provides for Kant's insistence that humans should enter into a cosmopolitan order. In this regard, the spherical confine of the globe provides the empirical conditions that inform his metaphysics of morals while also providing the motivation behind why we should establish cosmopolitan law. Since the world is not an infinite plane, but a sphere where individuals must necessarily occupy a finite space next to one another, reason dictates the establishment of a system of public right. As Kant proclaimed, "the peoples of the earth have thus entered in various degrees into a universal community and it has developed to the point where the violation of rights in *one* part of the world is felt *everywhere*."[43] However, this does not mean that humans are in fact actual members of a universal community, but that empirical conditions are such that we can metaphysically infer that humans are embroiled in something like an actual community of mutual interest. From this empirical consideration, reason dictates that we should theorize about mutual interests and universal public right from a global perspective. As Katrin Flikschuh has suggested of Kant's position, it "includes all those who because they cannot avoid occupying a place on earth, claim such a right to such a place."[44] In this regard, the bounded sphere of the earth acts as "an unavoidable constraint of nature within the limits of which finite rational beings must resolve conflicts of external freedom and justice."[45]

The elimination of Kant's naturalistic teleology does not require the rejection of his cosmopolitan enthusiasm or weaken the force of logic that underpins its relevance. This is because we can understand history as providing empirical considerations from which our normative reflection must seek to resolve. In the case of globalization and human evolution, humans have found themselves inextricably interconnected where history has proven a need to peacefully adjudicate disagreement between cohabitants of a spherically bounded world. In a fusion of empirical experience with normative principles, Kant maintains that humans cannot avoid physical contact with one another and therefore should enter into a civil order that secures mutual right and the conditions for human capabilities to develop. In this regard, Kantian cosmopolitanism is an attempt to come to terms with the plurality of various societies in some sort of minimally recognized framework of cosmopolitan law. It is in the next section that a brief description of cosmopolitan law and universal justice is furnished before a more detailed discussion of Kant's legal cosmopolitanism is offered in the subsequent chapters.

## III. Cosmopolitan Jurisprudence and the Foundation for a Cosmopolitan Matrix

The formalization of Kant's cosmopolitan matrix rests on two related ideas of jurisprudence. The first involves Kant's concept of a universal condition of public right, or as it is referenced in the context of global relations, *cosmopolitan right*. As was mentioned before, the condition of public right is linked directly to Kant's theory of justice, namely, "the sum of the conditions under which the choice of one can be united with the choice of another in accordance with a universal law of freedom."[46] Mary Gregor defines the jurisprudence behind the concept of public right as simply "the sum of laws that need to be publicized in order to produce a rightful condition, one in which individuals, nations and states can enjoy their rights."[47] In this regard, Kant's jurisprudence is both concerned with the creation of a legal framework of mutually negative restraints on external freedom (justice), while also concerned with positive *laws of publicity* which are necessary in order to promote a condition of cosmopolitan right.[48] In the global context, cosmopolitan right refers to an equal right of all individuals to inhabit the earth, the subsequently legal condition of mutual public right and the formulation of consistent legal obligations that are based solely on our humanity alone.

The second area of Kant's jurisprudence involved in the formalization of a cosmopolitan matrix relates to cosmopolitan law and universal justice. As Kant argued, a condition of public right cannot exist unless the very idea of rightful coexistence is grounded and propagated within a greater framework of cosmopolitan law and universal public right. In this

44

case, cosmopolitan law refers to the framework of global law that must exist in order for any mutually consistent condition of right to be possible. As Kant maintained in *Perpetual Peace*, a cosmopolitan legal condition must not only be concerned with the rightful relations between individuals within states, but also with the rightful relations that should exist between state actors and their rightful treatment of all human beings.[49] It is through this legal condition that both justice and perpetual peace should be maintained, for they are codependent and one cannot exist exclusive of the other.[50]

In order to formalize this cosmopolitan legal condition, Kant advances a tripartite system of jurisprudence divided into *domestic law, international law* and *cosmopolitan law*. As the tripartite suggests, a judicial system of public right is to be maintained through the three corresponding forms of rights and law, which in tandem create a universal condition where "the freedom of each can coexist with the freedom of all the others."[51] However, Kant believed that the tripartite system of jurisprudence could not guarantee a condition of right when operated solely as independent cells. As Kant suggests, "the problem of establishing a perfect civil constitution is subordinate to the problem of a law governed external relationship with other states, and cannot be solved unless the latter is also solved."[52] This is because a thoroughgoing condition of public right cannot exist when certain violations of international right persistently threaten to undermine already established micro systems of domestic justice. In other words, since the world has become inextricably linked and interconnected, "if the principle of outer freedom limited by law is lacking in any one of these three possible forms of rightful condition, the framework of all the others is unavoidably undermined and must finally collapse."[53] It is from this reality of global interconnectedness that reason dictates the establishment of cosmopolitan law and a universal condition of public right.

As mentioned above, the framework of universal justice demands three corresponding forms of law and rightful condition: domestic justice and internal state law; international justice and international law; and global justice and cosmopolitan law. Within Kant's legal tripartite framework, domestic law involves the rights and duties that should exist between citizens and their governments (citizen to citizen, state to citizen). As is outlined in greater detail in Chapter 3, domestic justice is the cornerstone of Kant's overall cosmopolitan vision. This is because Kant believed that states represent the most rational form of social organization from which individual capacities could fully be allowed to develop.[54] Nonetheless, Kant also firmly believed that only a republican constitution is suitable to secure and maintain justice both internally and externally. This is because well-constituted states have the ability to function as both the providers of justice and human development, while poorly constituted states have historically been the greatest violators of public right and human dignity.

For Kant, the first principle of global justice rests on the secured justice of state law and public right. According to Kant, a well-constituted state is based on three *a priori* principles; "the freedom of every member of society as a human being; the equality of each with all the others as subject; and the independence of each member of a commonwealth as a citizen."[55] Based on this domestic foundation, international law should be primarily concerned with the rightful condition that must exist between various state actors as representative entities (state to state). As was stated before, Kant believed that domestic justice could not flourish without the state also being secured in its external relations through a legal condition of international right. In order to secure international right, Kant suggests that a federation of independent states should be established in which the members uphold the various interlocking levels of justice in order to form a unified system of universal law. These principles of right are to be cemented into universal law not by a world government, but by the willing concomitants of various communities and states that are dedicated to preserving this condition of universal public right.

However, Kant's cosmopolitanism is concerned with more than the strict prerogative of international relations. This is because Kant's political theory is preoccupied with the moral worth and rightful condition of all human beings everywhere. To this end, cosmopolitan law is ultimately concerned with establishing a universal rightful condition that should exist between all humans and all states, regardless of national origin or state citizenship (state to all humans, humans to all humans, especially non-citizens). Although the subsequent chapters will provide a more detailed explanation of cosmopolitan law and Kant's cosmopolitan constitutionalism, it is nevertheless necessary to make clear that Kant's cosmopolitan law was primarily concerned with the hospitable treatment of everyone by everyone, whether as individuals or as political entities. By hospitality Kant means "the right of a stranger not to be treated with hostility when he arrives on someone else's territory."[56] This hospitable treatment was not merely a philanthropic principle, but "a principle having to do with rights."[57] In addition, cosmopolitan right applied to visiting foreigners and to the inhabitants of newly discovered lands. For cosmopolitan hospitality strictly forbids foreign powers from exploiting native inhabitants or from using their territory without the explicit consent of the native population.[58] As Charles Covell suggests, cosmopolitan law "was the body of public international law . . . constituting the juridical framework for the intercourse of men and states, considered in their status as bearers of the attributes of citizenship . . . that extended to embrace all mankind."[59] In this regard, "the idea of a cosmopolitan right . . . is a necessary complement to the unwritten code of political and international right, transforming it into a universal right of humanity."[60]

## IV. COSMOPOLITAN JURISPRUDENCE AND THE DEVELOPMENT OF A KANTIAN COSMOPOLITAN MATRIX

The first order of Kantian cosmopolitanism is to provide a legal framework that prevents any violation of public right and establishes a universal system of justice. Nevertheless, the establishment and propagation of a cosmopolitan matrix goes beyond Kant's legal foundation to include the optimistic cultivation of a broader sense of shared community, where everyone is considered as if they were mutual citizens of the world. It is in this realm that principles of cosmopolitan law and hospitality are meant to provide the grounding for a broadened sense of global community. As Kant suggests, we "stand in a community [confined by the global sphere] of possible interaction, that is, in a thoroughgoing relation of each to all others of offering to engage in commerce with any other, and each has the right to make this attempt."[61] Although current circumstances may restrict the free movement of commerce and relations, "this possible abuse cannot annul the right of citizens of the world to try to establish community with all, and to this end, to visit all regions of the earth."[62]

In this regard, cosmopolitan law goes beyond mutual security and is also meant as the legal foundation for continued interconnection and development that may eventually bring human beings closer to understanding each other as mutual citizens. However, this does not necessarily mean that they are actually citizens in the sense usually used in discussions of political obligation and national citizenship. For Kant himself defines cosmopolitan right simply as a means for a future cosmopolitan enthusiasm by suggesting that "hospitality does not extend beyond those

conditions which make it possible for them to attempt to enter into relations with native inhabitants. In this way, continents distant from each
other can enter into peaceful mutual relations which may eventually be
regulated by public laws, thus bringing the human race nearer and nearer
to a cosmopolitan constitution."[63] What this quote highlights is Kant's
optimism that by creating a minimal system of cosmopolitan law which
governs actions both within the *pacific federation* and externally with
other communities, individuals will gradually engage with one another to
the point where critical distinctions of tension disintegrate. In this sense,
cosmopolitan law, and its corresponding feature of cosmopolitan right,
is meant to provide the basic legal mechanism necessary for individuals
to peacefully and rightfully associate, trade, communicate and exchange
ideas without conflict or mistreatment. As a result, this basic cosmopolitical order fits nicely with Kant's overall philosophical project in that it
"provide[s] important guarantees for the security and property of persons,
but more importantly it create[s] sufficient safety for them to proceed to
perfect their moral lives."[64]

Furthermore, the provision of hospitality illustrates the Kantian notion
for the equal freedom of individuals to be unfettered in the process of
communication and political emancipation.[65] For it is only through "the
freedom to make public use of one's reason" that broader social change
and global civil advancement can hope to be achieved.[66] This in turn also
reflects Kant's beliefs regarding enlightenment and a possible human evolutionary progression toward a cosmopolitan condition. As Kant himself
proclaims, "the public use of man's reason must always be free, and it
alone can bring about enlightenment among men."[67] We can understand
Kant as addressing all of humanity when he further claims that a violation
of this freedom "would be a crime against human nature, whose future lies
precisely in such progress."[68]

Cosmopolitan law therefore acts as the protective mechanism for the
possibility of continued transnational deliberation and dialogue. As James
Bohman has suggested, Kant's enlightenment and the successful propagation of a cosmopolitan sense of community requires an "unrestricted
audience" from which transnational dialogue can foster.[69] It is through
cosmopolitan law and its corresponding principle of a cosmopolitan
right to hospitality from which various individuals can engage with one
another to communicate, criticize, remonstrate, debate, evince, expostu-
late and to have their own conceptions measured by critical examination.
Since I have argued that a coherent form of Kantian cosmopolitanism

should not rely on a naturalistic teleology, a construction of Kantian cosmopolitanism must rely on mechanisms of public deliberation and reasoned dialogue as a means to further cosmopolitan enthusiasm. As Sharon Anderson-Gold has suggested, "public reason is then ultimately the basis for the development of a cosmopolitan community."[70]

Consequently, we can understand cosmopolitan law and the right to hospitality as containing two distinctive features of public right and deliberation underwriting Kant's cosmopolitan enthusiasm. The first stipulates that every human being should enjoy the right of free movement in order to associate, trade and communicate. Following from this, the second principle of public right demands that all individuals should have the freedom to reason freely with one another without dogmatic external hindrances or the fear of prosecution. Kant stresses that an ability for public reason is paramount to human advancement when he writes, "these rights of man must be held sacred . . . there are no half measures here . . . for all politics must bend the knee before right, [if] politics may hope in return to arrive, however slowly, at a stage of lasting brilliance."[71]

Nevertheless, it is difficult to understand how we should apply Kant's cosmopolitan enthusiasm in the modern context.[72] The difficulty arises from the fact that human relationships need to reach a certain stage of maturity in order to adopt and implement cosmopolitan law. However, reaching this stage of maturity requires an already existing amount of hospitality and mutual relations from which this sense of community can flourish. Although this does not create a strict "chicken and egg" dilemma, it does call into question how we are to determine exactly where human relationships stand as far as the practical application of a Kantian system of cosmopolitan law. Some have suggested that Kant's minimal requirement for global hospitality is absolutely necessary if human beings are to engage in a continued process of mutual education toward a sense of cosmopolitan community.[73] Many contemporary scholars have suggested that cosmopolitan right is synonymous with current discussions of universal human rights and that the language of human rights has developed to a point where Kant's cosmopolitanism is conceivable.[74] Some contemporary cosmopolitans have argued that humans currently exist at a point in our development and maturity where human interdependence has made cosmopolitan law a necessarily viable alternative to the existing global order.[75] Finally, many contemporary cosmopolitans argue that the legal foundations for a cosmopolitan condition are already in some sense visible and that what is needed is a continued dedication to "cosmopolitan law enforcement"[76] and to emerging principles of "political cosmopolitanism."[77]

The practical and empirical considerations that give substance to these issues are complex and multifaceted. Nevertheless, we can say with a reasonable amount of certainty that we no longer live in a world of community isolation. Humanity has evolved, for whatever reasons, into an extremely interdependent, culturally transient and globalized environment. If this environment of global interdependence is to have a greater chance to peacefully evolve, it is important to find recognizable ethical and juridical principles that not only facilitate greater cooperation, but that also protect the valuable pluralist and autonomous concerns of various communities impacted by global cohabitation. For although we can claim that humans have reached a level of interdependence that has forced us to "relate" with one another, this very same interdependence does not necessarily mean that how we "relate" with one another could be labeled as developing a sense of shared humanity. It is in this sense that the normative principles behind Kant's cosmopolitan law are both relevant to contemporary global issues, even perhaps necessary, if we are going to tackle the problems associated with the benefits and burdens of confined global cohabitation. It is from this need to think normatively about global cohabitation that the remaining chapters seek to further develop a vision of Kantian cosmopolitan law.

## V. CONCLUSION

The quote by Marcus Aurelius used at the beginning of this chapter maintains that "it makes no difference whether a person lives here or there, provided that, where he lives, he lives as a citizen of the world."[78] The ethical concern implicit within the quote refers to how human beings *ought* to treat one another and to what degree we *should* feel a sense of broadened communal membership. For Marcus Aurelius, an adequate communal obligation stems from our humanity alone, without reference to state, national or ethnic membership. From this, our sense of communal membership and obligation must stem from something inherent about our mutual existence in this world as *living* human beings. In alignment with the spirit of Aurelius, the version of Kant's cosmopolitanism outlined throughout this chapter is meant to provide the philosophical and moral foundations that are to underpin the development of this cosmopolitan community.

As has been discussed, Kant's cosmopolitanism is firmly grounded in his moral philosophy and the recognition of human beings as moral agents deserving of universal respect and dignity as co-legislators within a *kingdom of ends*. Therefore, individual human capacities represent the ultimate unit of moral concern equally and it is the prerogative of Kant's cosmopolitanism that these capacities should be allowed to fully develop within a condition of universal public right. It was from this moral platform that it is possible to understand Kant's cosmopolitanism as being preoccupied with providing the normative principles that are meant to ground the motivation, the formation and the maintenance of a cosmopolitan matrix. In addition, the attainment of this cosmopolitan matrix requires the cultivation of a cosmopolitan civil society; one based solely on our humanity alone, grounded in a system of cosmopolitan law. Although Kant is both ambiguous and at times inconsistent as to what forces are behind the formation of this cosmopolitan matrix, I have argued that it is still possible to maintain a defendable enthusiasm for taking Kant's cosmopolitanism seriously. It is in this vein that the subsequent chapters will provide a more detailed analysis of cosmopolitan law, the cosmopolitan federation, the place for cultural diversity within cosmopolitan law, a possible form of Kantian global distributive justice and how a connection between Kantian theory and real world application might be understood as possible.

## NOTES

1. Immanuel Kant, "Idea for a Universal History with a Cosmopolitan Purpose," in H. Reiss (ed.), H. B. Nisbet (trans.) *Kant's Political Writings* (Cambridge: Cambridge University Press, 1970), p. 51. [8:28]
2. Ibid., p. 45. [8:22]
3. Andrew Linklater, *Men and Citizens in the Theory of International Relations*, 2nd edn (Basingstoke: Macmillan, 1990), pp. 98–9.
4. Immanuel Kant, *Grounding for the Metaphysics of Morals*, J. Ellington (trans.) (Cambridge, MA: Hackett Publishing Company, 1981), pg. 30. [4:421]
5. Ibid., p. 36. [4:429]
6. Ibid., p. 42. [4:437]
7. Immanuel Kant, *The Metaphysics of Morals*, M. Gregor (ed. & trans.) (Cambridge: Cambridge University Press, 1996), p. 30. [6:237]
8. Linklater, p. 101.
9. Ibid., p. 102.
10. Kant, *Grounding for the Metaphysics of Morals*, p. 40. [4:434]
11. Kant, *The Metaphysics of Morals*, p. 24. [6:230]
12. Charles Covell, *Kant and the Law of Peace: A Study in the Philosophy of International Law and International Relations* (New York: Palgrave, 1998), p. 49.

13. Immanuel Kant, Appendix, "Transcendental Logic II, Dialectic I, Ideas in General," in J. M. D. Meiklejohn (trans.), *The Critique of Pure Reason* (New York: The Colonial Press, 1900). [3:247]

14. The *kingdom of ends* is a metaphysical ideal of justice understood as "a systematic union of different rational beings through common laws" which is determined by "universal validity." A participant in the *kingdom of ends* is someone who "legislates in it universal laws while also being themselves subject to such laws." For these quotes, see Kant, *Grounding for the Metaphysics of Morals*, pp. 39–45. [4:433-440]. I also discuss principles of distributive justice that can be derived from this ideal in Chapter 5.

15. Ibid.

16. Thomas Pogge, "Kant's Theory of Justice," *Kant-Studien*, 79 (1988).

17. Allen Rosen, *Kant's Theory of Justice* (New York: Cornell University Press, 1993), p. 9.

18. Immanuel Kant, "On the Common Saying, This May be True in Theory, But it Does not Apply in Practice," in Hans Reiss (ed.), H. B. Nisbet (trans.) *Kant's Political Writings* (Cambridge: Cambridge University Press, 1970), p. 73. [8:290]

19. Kant, "Idea for a Universal History with a Cosmopolitan Purpose," p. 45. [8:22]

20. Kant, "Perpetual Peace: A Philosophical Sketch," in Hans Reiss (ed.), H. B. Nisbet (trans.), *Kant's Political Writings* (Cambridge: Cambridge University Press, 1970), p. 108. [8:360–1]

21. Ibid. [8:361–2]

22. Karl-Otto Apel, "Kant's Toward Perpetual Peace as Historical Prognosis from the Point of View of Moral Duty," in J. Bohman and M. Lutz-Bachmann, *Perpetual Peace: Essays on Kant's Cosmopolitan Ideal* (Cambridge, MA: MIT Press, 1997), p. 81.

23. Kant, "Perpetual Peace," pp. 109–10. [8:363]

24. Ibid., p. 110.

25. Ibid., p. 111. [8:364]

26. Kant, "On the Common Saying: This May be True in Theory, But it Does not Apply in Practice," p. 90. [8:310–11]

27. Kant, "Perpetual Peace," p. 111. [8:364]

28. I use the term dialectic in the Habermasian form. Namely that global interconnectedness both promotes more interconnectedness (thesis) while also creating new and unforeseen forces of opposition (antithesis) that ultimately are to be resolved through a synthesis of resolution. In Kant's case, synthesis of human history will be the result of a teleology, which culminates in a cosmopolitan condition.

29. Kant, *The Metaphysics of Morals*, p. 121. [6:353]

30. Kant, "Perpetual Peace," p. 114. [8:368]

31. Ibid., p. 108. [8:360–1]

32. James Bohman & Matthias Lutz-Bachmann (eds), *Perpetual Peace: Essays on Kant's Cosmopolitan Ideal* (Cambridge, MA: MIT Press, 1997), p. 8.

33. Karl Popper, *The Poverty of Historicism* (London: Routledge, 1957).

34. Apel, p. 83.

35. Allen W. Wood, "Kant's Philosophy of History," in Pauline Kleingeld (ed.), *Toward Perpetual Peace and Other Writings on Politics, Peace and History* (New Haven: Yale University Press, 2006), p. 245.

36. Ibid., p. 256.

37. Ibid., p. 254.

38. Ibid., p. 257.
39. Karl-Otto Apel, *Understanding and Explanation: A Transcendental-Pragmatic Perspective* (Cambridge: MIT Press, 1984); Allen W. Wood, "Kant's Compatibilism," in Wood (ed.), *Self and Nature in the Philosophy of Kant* (Ithaca: Cornell University Press, 1984), pp. 73–101. Also see Wood's article in note 35.
40. Kant, *The Metaphysics of Morals*, pg. 24. [6:230]
41. A more thorough discussion of culture, pluralism and their relationship with Kantian cosmopolitanism is provided in Chapter 4.
42. Kant, "Idea for a Universal History with a Cosmopolitan Purpose," p. 45. [8:22]
43. Kant, "Perpetual Peace," pp. 107–8. [8:360]
44. Katrin Flikschuh, *Kant and Modern Political Philosophy* (Cambridge: Cambridge University Press, 2000), p. 179.
45. Ibid.
46. Kant, *The Metaphysics of Morals*, p. 24. [6:230]
47. Mary Gregor, "Kant's Approach to Constitutionalism," in A. Rosenbaum (ed.), *Constitutionalism: The Philosophical Dimension* (New York: Greenwood Press, 1988), p. 71.
48. As Kant argues, "all maxims which require publicity if they are not to fail their purpose can be reconciled both with right and with politics." Kant, "Perpetual Peace," p. 130. [8:386]
49. Ibid., p. 126. [8:381–2]
50. I have provided an extensive discussion of Kant's federation, the role of states, and the interplay between domestic, international and cosmopolitan law in Chapter 3. Therefore, I will not go into any great detail here, but will sustain a more general focus in order to provide the foundation behind Kant's cosmopolitan jurisprudence as a whole.
51. Kant, *The Metaphysics of Morals*, p. 24. [6:230]
52. Kant, "An Answer to the Question 'What is Enlightenment?," in Hans Reiss (ed.), H. B. Nisbet (trans.), *Kant's Political Writings* (Cambridge: Cambridge University Press, 1970), p. 47. [8:24]
53. Kant, *The Metaphysics of Morals*," p. 89. [6:311]
54. Jeremy Waldron, "Kant's Theory of the State," in Pauline Kleingeld (ed.), *Toward Perpetual Peace and Other Writings on Politics, Peace and History* (New Haven: Yale University Press, 2006).
55. Kant, "On the Common Saying: This May be True in Theory, But it Does not Apply in Practice," pg. 74. [8:290]. Also see *The Metaphysics of Morals*, p. 91. [6:314]
56. Kant, "Perpetual Peace," p. 105. [8:357–8]
57. Kant, *The Metaphysics of Morals*, p. 121. [6:352]
58. Ibid., p. 122. [6:353]
59. Covell, p. 141.
60. Kant, "Perpetual Peace," p. 108. [8:360–1]
61. Kant, *Metaphysics of Morals*, p. 121. [6:352]
62. Ibid. [6:353]
63. Kant, "Perpetual Peace," p. 106. [8:358]
64. Linklater, p. 99.
65. I will provide a more thorough discussion of the rights derived from cosmopolitan right and hospitality in the next chapter. For my purposes here, I will focus on only

two rights, the right to freedom of travel and the right to engage in the public use of reason and communication.

66. Kant, "An Answer to the Question 'What is Enlightenment?'," p. 55. [8:36–7]
67. Ibid.
68. Ibid., p. 57. [8:39]
69. James Bohman, "The Public Spheres of the World Citizen," in Bohman & Lutz-Bachmann (eds), *Perpetual Peace: Essays on Kant's Cosmopolitan Ideal* (Cambridge, MA: MIT Press, 1997).
70. Sharon Anderson-Gold, *Cosmopolitanism and Human Rights* (Cardiff: University of Wales Press, 2001), p. 40.
71. Kant, "Perpetual Peace," p. 125. [8:380]
72. I discuss the relationship between theory and practice in modern context in greater detail in Chapter 6.
73. Martha Nussbaum, *Cultivating Humanity* (Cambridge, MA: Harvard University Press, 1997).
74. Sharon Anderson-Gold, *Cosmopolitanism and Human Rights*, op. cit.
75. David Held, "Cosmopolitanism: Globalization Tamed?," *Review of International Studies*, 29 (2003), pp. 465–80.
76. Mary Kaldor, *Global Civil Society: An Answer to War* (Cambridge: Polity Press, 2003).
77. Patrick Hayden, *Cosmopolitan Global Politics* (Burlington: Ashgate, 2005).
78. Marcus Aurelius, *The Meditations* (New York: Hackett, 1983), section 3.

# CHAPTER 2

# Kant's Cosmopolitan Law and the Idea of a Cosmopolitan Constitution

"Ethics is Hospitality. Ethics is thoroughly coextensive with the experience of hospitality." – Jacques Derrida

## INTRODUCTION

The study of ethics is usually understood as being concerned with princi-ples of good conduct that are associated with a system of standards which govern given social organizations. In some cases, the study of ethics seeks to discover these principles from an already existing social order. In other cases, ethics is concerned with formulating normative principles of good conduct from which to establish additional juridical or social standards for communal living. In relation to the study of global ethics, Jacques Derrida has suggested that universal hospitality is a necessary, yet also his-torically "perverted," concept that must become thoroughly coextensive with an experience of hospitality if humanity is to ever hope to realize a cosmopolitan condition.[1] This, according to Derrida, is because hos-pitable behavior is the foundation behind propagating an experience of good social conduct and therefore plays a prominent role in inaugurating any move towards a future cosmopolitan ethic. In many regards, Kant's cosmopolitanism makes a similar claim. If the development of a cosmo-politan condition is to be actualized in practice, then hospitable conduct between states, nations, individuals and associations will be the predomi-nant mechanism from which a system of continued ethics can flourish.[2] This explains why Kant often defines cosmopolitan right as being analo-gous with a condition of universal hospitality and a condition of peace. For it is only from a baseline of mutual security, hospitable conduct and a condition of respected public right that the experience of ethical interchange can blossom into a more pronounced and standardized system of cosmopolitan order.

Nevertheless, many scholars have offered critiques of Kant's cosmopolitan law and its corresponding feature of universal hospitality. Philosophers such as Derrida, Seyla Benhabib and Georg Cavallar have all questioned whether the principles of Kant's cosmopolitan law are hospitable enough, suggesting that they might be too weak and minimalist to truly create a cosmopolitan condition where everyone is treated as a citizen of the world.[3] Conversely, Hegelian and international relations theorists such as Martin Wight have argued that Kantianism is inordinately demanding of a common morality and therefore so fantastically universalistic that it is rendered both untenable and extremely dangerous to a plurality of global beliefs.[4] Adding more confusion to how to understand Kant's conception of cosmopolitan law, many cosmopolitan scholars such as Onora O'Neill and Charles Jones have debated about how to interpret Kant's cosmopolitan right and whether it is better understood as a duty-based theory or as a legal theory of right-based entitlements.[5]

What this confusion illustrates is a need to clarify the jurisprudence involved in Kant's cosmopolitanism. As will be illustrated, Kant's cosmopolitan law is more robust than Derrida has assumed, while also not guilty of establishing the "nightmarish hegemony" feared by Wight.[6] Furthermore, both O'Neill and Jones have looked at Kant's cosmopolitanism too narrowly, for Kant's theory contains both rational duties to establish a global ethic while also advocating rightful legal claims to the performance of those duties and obligations. Due to the fact that there is general confusion surrounding the nature of Kant's cosmopolitan law, the purpose of this chapter is to outline a Kantian form of cosmopolitan law and the juridical system involved in creating a cosmopolitan constitution. In doing so, it will explore and discuss Kant's cosmopolitan law, the idea of cosmopolitan right, the laws of hospitality and a revised Kantian approach to constitutional cosmopolitanism. By a revised approach to Kantian constitutionalism, this chapter will argue beyond Kant's constitutionalism, suggesting the establishment of an actual written constitution that can facilitate an experience of mutual citizenship while also providing a minimal ethical foundation for a civil cosmopolitan order.

In order to provide an outline for this form of Kantian cosmopolitan law and the principles underpinning a cosmopolitan constitution, this chapter is divided into three sections. The first section will examine Kant's idea of cosmopolitan law and explore its relationship in creating a condition of cosmopolitan public right. From this background, Section II develops and extrapolates the inherent principles of cosmopolitan right found within Kant's laws of hospitality and discusses how these principles are meant to act as legal obligations under a scheme of cosmopolitan law. Section III builds upon the first two sections by examining the jurisprudence behind the establishment of a cosmopolitan constitution and argues that the idea of an actual written constitution is an effective component in grounding a cosmopolitan legal condition.

## I. Cosmopolitan Law and a Condition of Cosmopolitan Right

In the *Metaphysics of Morals*, Kant defines right as "the sum of the conditions under which the choice of one can be united with the choice of the other in accordance with a universal law of freedom."[7] Under this definition of right, the idea of a universal law of freedom is meant to ground two related normative principles of cosmopolitan jurisprudence and public right. The first normative principle is that a rightful condition of cosmopolitan law must be reflective and protective of an "innate right" to freedom. As Kant claims, "freedom (independence from being constrained by another's choice), insofar as it can coexist with the freedom of every other in accordance with a universal law, is the only original right belonging to every man by virtue of his humanity."[8] In this regard, human beings should have the right to be free to determine their lives as long as their actions can conform to a universal system of freedom and mutual right. As will be discussed in the next section, Kant links this innate right to universalized freedom to the laws of cosmopolitan hospitality which are meant to act as the ethical minimums for grounding global coexistence and public right.

The second principle of cosmopolitan right dictates that "all human beings are originally (prior to any act of choice that establishes a right) in a possession of land that is in conformity with right, that is, they have a right to be wherever nature or chance (apart from their will) has placed them."[9] What this passage suggests, is that all human beings are originally located somewhere on earth and that this is not a matter of choice (a decision of moral will), but simply a matter of physical existence and circumstance.[10] However, since individuals will take control of land as a believed entitlement and this can affect and be affected by the claims

57

of others, reason dictates that any right to land can only be provisional unless grounded within a mutually recognized system of universal law. Therefore, a rightful cosmopolitan condition under law must contain the prerequisites of equal freedom and a rightful place of secured existence within a world that is held in common. These principles are synthetic a priori truths related to a condition of right and do not exist as facts, "but as a concept of reason which alone yields a principle making it possible for individuals, families, nations or states to use land compatibly with principles of right."[11] What is needed to effectively ground these principles into a thoroughgoing system of public right is cosmopolitan law, which must be firmly rooted to a priori principles of right and be universally understood as forming mutual obligations between all human beings.

Although cosmopolitan right must be grounded systematically on a priori principles of freedom and a condition of public right, Kant also requires that these principles must be universally recognized as law. In this sense, a rightful condition is connected to his theory of justice and an authorized use of civil coercion. As Kant claims, "if a certain use of freedom is itself a hindrance to freedom in accordance with universal law (i.e. wrong), coercion that is opposed to this (as a hindering of a hindrance to freedom) is consistent with freedom in accordance with universal laws, that is, it is right."[12] As was discussed in the last chapter, Kantian justice is concerned with what legitimate restrictions to individual freedoms should exist in order to create a condition of universal public right. In this regard, a rightful condition demands the regulation and enforcement of laws that are designed specifically to allow the greatest freedom of everyone in accordance with maintaining universal law. Coercion is justified if it is grounded and enforced in relation to the concept of universal right and freedom. As Mary Gregor has suggested, "the conclusion Kant draws is that only in a 'rightful condition,' in civil society, can anyone's right be conclusive, secured or guaranteed."[13] In relation to cosmopolitan right, "cosmopolitan law imposes legal obligations both on individuals and on states, and in so doing becomes an attempt to provide a legal foundation for the rights of the individual regardless of the state which he or she belongs – hence for veritable rights of citizens of the world."[14] However, we can ask what obligations and legal commands are the members of a Kantian federation accepting as legally binding and imperative. It is in the next section that the principles of cosmopolitan right and hospitality are extrapolated and discussed.

## II.  COSMOPOLITAN RIGHT AND THE LAWS OF HOSPITALITY

Scholars have long debated the meaning and juridical purpose behind Kant's hospitality and its relationship with formulating a condition of cosmopolitan right. As Kant defines it, hospitality is "the right of a stranger not to be treated with hostility when he arrives on someone else's territory."[15] Sharon Anderson-Gold has argued that cosmopolitan hospitality can be easily linked to a modern conception of universal human rights as enumerated in the United Nations Universal Declaration of Human Rights.[16] Others like F. H. Hinsley have taken a more skeptical view, suggesting that cosmopolitan hospitality is little more than the basic protections needed for expanding global commerce and trade.[17] Philosophers such as Derrida have insinuated that Kant's hospitality does not demand enough for the protection of asylum seekers and therefore negates Kant's own concern for individual freedoms while also placing too many prerogatives in the hands of state actors.[18] Lastly, scholars such as Onora O'Neill have argued that it is misguided to discuss Kant's cosmopolitanism as embodying the language of human rights, but that it is more appropriately understood through the categorical imperative and universal moral duties that can be derived from Kant's critical philosophy.[19] Nevertheless, despite the depth of opinion, there is a critical problem involved with all of these interpretations. The problem is that none of these positions has unraveled the meaning behind Kant's laws of hospitality and taken them seriously. In fact, when surveying the literature, there has been little attempt to develop the specific freedoms and duties that are lurking implicitly within Kant's discussion of cosmopolitan right. In O'Neill's particular case, she seems to ignore many of Kant's political writings, focusing mainly on the *Metaphysics of Morals* and his critical philosophy. Although she has skillfully highlighted the point that cosmopolitan right only makes practical sense when placed within a system of universal obligation, she seems to have overlooked the fact that Kant's laws of hospitality take her concerns into account by mirroring rights of hospitality with corresponding positive duties of legal obligation.[20] In other words, not only does Kant suggest that we have cosmopolitan duties to fellow human beings based on our common humanity, but also that this duty must be inscribed as a legal obligation to uphold these rights within a system of cosmopolitan law. It is because of the fact that there is a general misconception and lack of scholarship on this aspect of Kant's theory that the remainder of this section intends to extract, recapitulate and make coherent Kant's laws of hospitality.

As was outlined in Chapter 1, the primary concern of cosmopolitan law is with the creation of a cosmopolitan "matrix within which all the original capacities of the human race may develop."[21] As was also discussed, cosmopolitan right can be understood as a condition of global public right, where there is a "restriction of each individual's freedom so that it harmonizes with the freedom of everyone else."[22] In order to slowly develop and maintain a condition of cosmopolitan right, Kant suggests the establishment of universal laws of hospitality. This condition of "public right is the distinctive quality of the external laws which make this constant harmony possible."[23] We can understand Kant as grounding cosmopolitan right and the laws of hospitality as a necessary right under cosmopolitan law, when he states, "a thoroughgoing community of all nations on the earth that can come into relations affecting one another is not a philanthropic principle but a principle *having to do with rights*."[24] As Charles Covell aptly points out, "for Kant, the right to hospitality was an authentic legal right. It was moreover, a right that he thought of as belonging to all human beings without exception."[25] Kant further elaborates on this right and ties it back to an a priori right to the earth in common when he suggests that "no-one originally has any greater right than anyone else to occupy any particular portion of the earth . . . [Thus a] right to the earth's surface . . . the human race shares in common."[26]

Accordingly in direct relationship to the juridical principles necessary to create a condition of cosmopolitan right, Kant attaches coterminous laws of hospitality, defined broadly as "the right of a stranger not to be treated with hostility when he arrives on someone else's territory."[27] However, the laws of hospitality are not as simplistic and impotent as some thinkers like Derrida and Cavallar have often assumed. For throughout his discussion of cosmopolitan right, Kant subtly elaborates on five universal freedoms and corresponding duties that can be understood as necessary under cosmopolitan right and the law of hospitality. Although he did not systematically outline these freedoms, they can be extrapolated from his discussions within the *Metaphysics of Morals* and his various political writings. He himself suggested that we should make such an attempt to extrapolate the meaning of these laws when he wrote, "as for cosmopolitan right, I pass over it here in silence, for its maxims are easy to formulate and assess on account of its analogy with international right."[28]

In the spirit of Kant's invitation to formulate principles of cosmopolitan right, we can comprehend that the first law of hospitality demands the *freedom of exit and travel*. These principles can be derived from Kant's discussion of cosmopolitan right within both the *Doctrine of Right* and *Perpetual Peace*. As Kant states, individuals have "a right of citizens of the world to try to establish community with all, and to this end, to visit all regions of the earth."[29] Kant further argues that all humans can claim a right to such travel, arguing that "[humans] may only claim a right to resort, for all men are entitled to present themselves in the society of others by virtue of their right to communal possession of the earth's surface."[30] Although Kant does not specifically suggest that hospitality necessitates a right to freely exit one's locality, it is reasonable to assume that this condition must be a premise to the right of global travel, for someone could not travel without the assumption that they were able to exit their current location. In addition, it is clear within Kantian ethics that any unequal and arbitrary physical restraint on individual freedom is tantamount to coercion and is not sanctioned under the Kantian concept of public right and freedom. Since an arbitrary restriction from exiting a given territory is an immediate restriction to the freedom to travel, we can assume that such coercion is a violation of universal justice and the laws of hospitality.

The second law of hospitality specifies a *freedom from hostility and from negligence resulting in death* when engaged in global travel. Kant outlines this basic negative freedom when he suggests "[someone] can be turned away, if this can be done without causing his death, but he must not be treated with hostility, so long as he behaves in a peaceable manner in the place he happens to be in."[31] Although this statement is rather ambiguous in that it could be interpreted as standing in contradiction to the first law of hospitality, it must be placed into context in order for it to be understood properly. In the context of *Perpetual Peace*, we can understand Kant to be suggesting that a right to residence can be denied and that any unlawful act can result in banishment. Nevertheless, given an individual's lawful behavior and a continued behavior that is consistent with the following duties of hospitality, the right to travel cannot be denied. As was previously quoted in relation to a right to travel, all humans have "a right to resort and are entitled to present themselves in the society of others by virtue of their right to communal possession of the earth's surface."[32] Additionally, individuals are to be free from hostile behavior and from "inhospitable conduct" that would result in immanent harm to body or property. Kant outlines some examples of what constitutes inhospitable harm that should be forbidden as *enslaving stranded seafarers*, the *plundering of property*, slavery for repayment of debt, starvation or forced *famine*, *treachery*, *physical violence* and actions that would immediately cause significant harm to body and property.[33]

Based on this right to "present [oneself] in the society of others," the third law of hospitality demands an additional *freedom of communication and to engage in public reason*. As Kant plainly states, all individuals should have "the freedom to make public use of one's reason."[34] This freedom is not only necessary for Kant's overall enlightenment project, but is also a necessary element for a continued global dialogue and the possible movement toward understanding each other as mutual citizens of the world. The use of public reason has a significant position within Kant's thought because it is a necessary mechanism that allows for humanity to rightfully associate, trade, communicate and exchange experiments in living without conflict. Covell has reached a similar conclusion, suggesting that "the stranger was entitled to attempt to enter into relations with native inhabitants . . . [And] the right of men to hospitality carried with it the possibility of the whole human race being able to progress towards eventual union under a lawful cosmopolitan constitution."[35] Kant further articulates the importance of a freedom to share ideas when he writes, "freedom of the pen is the only safeguard of the rights of the people."[36] Although this last quote was written in the context of domestic right, it clearly illustrates Kant's concern for free access to information in relation to the creation of an overall condition of public right. Based on Kant's discussions of enlightenment, free communication, free access to information, a right to engage in public reason and that these principles are collectively necessary for the promotion of a condition of public right, we can justifiably extend these principles into the realm of cosmopolitan right.

Since humans have "a right to present themselves in the society of others," the fourth law of hospitality stipulates a *freedom to engage in commerce and the use of the world in common*. As Kant writes:

> Since possession of the land, on which an inhabitant of the earth can live, can be thought only as a possession of a part of a determinate whole, and so possession of that to which each of them originally has a right, it follows that all nations stand originally in a community of land, though not of rightful community of possession and so of use of it, or property in it; instead they stand in a community of possible physical interaction, that is, in a thoroughgoing relation of each to all the others

of offering to engage in commerce with any other, and each has the right to make this attempt without the other being authorized to behave toward it as an enemy because it has made this attempt.[37]

What this passage highlights is the Kantian concept of the earth in common and an equal right to make use of its property through commerce and physical interaction. Kant further suggests that, "since the earth is a globe, [humans] cannot disperse over an infinite area, but must necessarily tolerate one another's company. And no-one originally has any greater right than anyone else to occupy any particular portion of the earth."[38] In relation to commerce, Kant builds upon this idea by suggesting, "[humans] stand in a community of possible interaction, that is, in a thoroughgoing relation of each to all the others of offering to engage in commence with any other, and each has the right to make this attempt."[39] In other words, since humans are interlocked within a community of possible and actual interchange, the laws of hospitality are not only meant as a right to engage in hospitable international commerce, but also meant to establish regulative principles of commerce and trade to assure continued hospitality. In this regard, although individuals, nations and associations have a legal right to engage in commerce, these exchanges must also conform to legal principles of public right and justice in a world in common. These legal conditions are further elaborated in the fifth and final law of hospitality.

The fifth law of hospitality is related to the previous right to commerce by suggesting that fair and equal commerce demands a *freedom from false, misrepresented, extorted or fraudulent contracts*. According to Kant, the law of hospitality is a necessary component for the possible evolution of cosmopolitan order, for it is concerned "with those conditions which make it possible for [individuals] to attempt to enter into relations with native inhabitants. In this way, continents distant from each other can enter into peaceful mutual relations which may eventually be regulated by public laws, thus bringing the human race nearer and nearer to a cosmopolitan constitution."[40] However, this condition necessitates a lack of "inhospitable conduct" when engaging with others. In relation to settlement and community relations, the law of hospitality demands that "settlement may not take place by force but only by contract, and indeed by a contract that does not take advantage of the ignorance of those inhabitants."[41] From this it can be garnered that Kant is restricting external relations so that all dealings must conform to the fair principles of hospitality and contract so as to allow the potentiality for a future civil condition. In this regard, both visitor and inhabitant must conform to a fair and balanced relationship of commerce and contract. For it is only from a sense of mutual cooperation and benefit that a broad sense of cosmopolitan public right can be secured.

Although cosmopolitan right and the corresponding laws of hospitality place considerable negative limits on the extent to which individuals, states and communities can treat fellow human beings, it must be understood that Kant's discussion of cosmopolitan right is originally confined to the realm of hospitality. This is clearly evidenced by the title of the third definitive article of *Perpetual Peace* where Kant claims that "Cosmopolitan Right Shall be Limited to Conditions of Universal Hospitality."[42] In this regard, Kant assigns two caveats within the law of hospitality, stipulating that any visiting individual must obey local laws and that any further claim to domestic citizenship must be secured through an additional contract. As Kant states, there is not a "right to make settlement on the land of another nation (ius incolatus); for this, a specific contract is required."[43] From these caveats, Derrida is correct to suggest that Kant's hospitality "excludes the right of residence" thus limiting "it to the right of visitation."[44] However, Derrida is incorrect to immediately assume that this restriction somehow weakens the protective force of cosmopolitan hospitality. This is because Kant does not suggest that residence and migration is forbidden, but simply that any permanent claim to residency is subject to an additional "friendly agreement" between that individual and local inhabitants. As will be argued momentarily, the requirement for this additional "special contract" represents an important element in creating a mutually consistent condition of cosmopolitan right. In addition, Kant clearly states that an individual cannot be "turned away" if this could not "be done without causing his death."[45] Moreover, as was stated under the second law of hospitality, individuals are to be free from "inhospitable conduct" that would result in immanent harm to body and or property. In this case, Derrida's concern regarding the possible rejection of asylum seekers under Kantian hospitality is not as clearly evident as he seems to assume, since Kant's hospitality strictly forbids rejection if death and/or immanent harm to body or property would be the result of such deportation.[46] Since in many cases asylum seekers face torture and/or death if extradited, it could be argued that this deportation would be tantamount to "inhospitable conduct" and would therefore be a negligent violation of the laws of hospitality.

However, as alluded to above, it is important to understand how we should interpret Kant's distinction between *a right to visitation*

(*Besuchsrecht*), *a right to reside* (*Gastrecht*) and his requirement for an additional "special contract." This is because, like Derrida, many scholars have questioned whether this additional condition contradicts Kant's overall concern for cosmopolitan citizenship[47] and whether cosmopolitans are misguided in their attempt to base their more sophisticated cosmopolitical models on a foundation laid by Kant's laws of hospitality.[48] As Cavallar argues, "reliance on Kant in this respect is not justified," since Kant holds too "narrow [an] understanding of hospitality rights."[49] Nevertheless, one concern with the positions held by Derrida, Benhabib and Cavallar is that they all seem to assume that Kant's laws of hospitality represent the final vision of what constitutes a cosmopolitan condition. However, this assumption is questionable, since the laws of hospitality were never intended to be the final representation of what would constitute a thoroughgoing condition of cosmopolitan justice. In fact, what seems more plausible is to suggest that the laws of hospitality only represent the minimal conditions that are necessary for peaceful interaction to occur, which may eventually, with consistent application, evolve into a more thoroughgoing condition of cosmopolitan law. In this regard, Kant's distinction between *Besuchsrecht* and *Gastrecht* is a limiting condition of basic reciprocity, which is meant to delineate a mutually consistent condition for peaceful interaction and communication between foreign visitor and local inhabitant. This condition is not to be understood as a final condition of cosmopolitan right, but should be seen as a minimal legal condition that allows for a future discussion regarding cosmopolitan justice to take place equally between peoples of the world. This is because by requiring a "special contract," which is based on a principle of hospitable reciprocity, Kant seeks to establish the first legal iteration in a move to ground all future legal relations. In this regard, the laws of hospitality are meant to underpin a system of mutually consistent legal relations in two ways. First, hospitality was meant to offer an amount of negative protection for various inhabitants of the world from the imperialistic and "inhospitable conduct" of so-called "civilized states."[50] Second, the laws of hospitality, and the additional requirement for a "special contract," were meant to create a necessary level of extra-legal and legal expectation, so as to allow space for peaceful communication about future regulatory laws to take place. Kant himself suggests this much, when he claims that the laws of hospitality only represent "those conditions which make it *possible* for [individuals] to attempt to enter into relations with native inhabitants. In this way, continents distant from each other can enter into peaceful mutual relations which may *eventually* be regulated by public laws, thus bringing the human race nearer and nearer to a cosmopolitan constitution."[51]

As Kant suggests in both the *Metaphysics of Morals* and *Perpetual Peace*, the claim to cosmopolitan right should be understood as a matter of legal right and therefore should act as an ethical guide for establishing corresponding duties and obligations under cosmopolitan law. It is in relation to furthering this cosmopolitan condition that the laws of hospitality can be seen as a first stage in establishing the practice of a more robust cosmopolitan legal order. For example, in direct relation to cosmopolitan right and the laws of hospitality, there is a corresponding duty on the part of federated members not to fraudulently engage in extorted or misrepresented contracts. This obligation is not only in relation to foreign visitors, but is also obligatory in any external relations with foreign inhabitants.[52] This could be seen to have broad implications for the regulation of global markets and with resolving many global inequalities associated with globalization.[53] In this regard, individuals, states and associations are obligated to deal in good faith with each other and a failure to do so results in a violation of cosmopolitan right, nullifying all extraneous contracts. Therefore, as well as establishing a simple duty to allow free travel, federated members must also attempt to establish relationships of fair trade and interaction without hostility. Finally, there exists something like a *duty of reasonable care* for all individuals, especially non-citizens, so that visitation or rejection from a territory does not lead to their death, inhospitable treatment or immanent harm to body and property. In this respect, a condition of cosmopolitan right and hospitality not only protects individual negative freedoms, but also establishes positive duties to all human beings in connection with travel, trade, contracts, settlement and asylum. It is in the next section that the laws of hospitality and cosmopolitan right are placed into the framework of Kant's cosmopolitan law and the construction of a cosmopolitan constitution.

## III. KANTIAN CONSTITUTIONALISM AND THE IDEA OF A COSMOPOLITAN CONSTITUTION

In *The Critique of Pure Reason*, Immanuel Kant writes that "a constitution allowing the greatest possible human freedom in accordance with laws which ensure that the freedom of each can coexist with the freedom of all the other, is at all events a necessary idea which must be made the basis not only of the first outline of a political constitution but of all laws as well."[54] By constitution, we can understand that Kant does not specifically mean a written political document, but rather is alluding to the underlying normative principles that underwrite a juridical condition of mutual public right. In this regard, a constitution refers to the totality of laws that should be publicized so as to create a rightful condition of mutual freedom between individuals, states and associations. What is to be *constituted* within a Kantian system of laws is the idea that the mutual protection of individual freedom is paramount for the creation of a condition of universal justice and that all subsequent laws should reflect a commitment to this corresponding universal condition of public right. Kant defines the relationship between public right and his constitutionalism as:

> The sum of laws which need to be promulgated generally in order to bring about a rightful condition is *public right*. – Public right is therefore a system of laws for a people, that is, a multitude of human beings, or for a multitude of peoples, which, because they affect one another, need a rightful condition under a will uniting them, a constitution (constitutio), so that they may enjoy what is laid down as right.[55]

We can understand Kant to mean that these principles should not only be the concern of domestic constitutions, but also a requirement of all laws, which should ultimately culminate in a cosmopolitan constitution. Since humanity has an "original possession of the earth in common" and since we are bounded by spherical cohabitation, any domestic and international constitution "will always remain provisional unless this contract extends to the entire human race."[56] As Kant elaborates, "so if the principle of outer freedom limited by law is lacking in any one of these three possible forms of rightful condition [domestic, international and cosmopolitan], the framework of all the others is unavoidably undermined and must finally collapse."[57]

As was previously mentioned, Kant does not specifically advocate the creation of a written cosmopolitan constitution. For Kant, constitutionalism seems to refer mainly to a condition of right under a mutually recognized collection of laws. This legal condition can include both codified law and extra-legal principles of convention that act to underpin a universal condition of right. In fact, within his argument for a *foedus pacificum* Kant makes only one direct reference to a written constitution. From this discussion Kant seems to disfavor the possibility of a drafted cosmopolitan constitutional document. In qualifying an obligation to the *foedus pacificum*, Kant maintains that the alliance is not to be "a federation (like that of the American states) which is based on a constitution and can therefore not be dissolved," but a federation of voluntary association.[58] Despite the fact that Kant is misinformed about the permanent rigidity of the US Constitution,[59] he also seems to underestimate the contractarian benefits that are analogous with an objectified written constitution and its ability to formalize the normative principles of voluntary association. In addition, under close inspection, it would seem that Kant is not so much against the idea of a written constitution per se, as he is skeptical of creating a legal document that cements a structure of federal government which cannot be "renounced" or "renewed from time to time."[60] In this regard, what Kant seems to dislike is the category of a *rigid* written constitution that would contain no ability for member states to either secede or reconfirm their contractual obligations.[61] What this highlights is the importance of voluntary contractualism behind Kant's federation and the idea that political obligation is grounded by a moral self-commitment and concomitance to universal principles of law and membership. This contractual element fits well with both Kant's morality and his transcendental belief that "human beings do not submit to a morality which has its source outside them."[62] Furthermore, voluntary association is also consistent with Kant's argument against a world republic and his claim that "such a state is in turn even more dangerous to freedom, for it may lead to fearful despotism . . . distrust must force men to form an order which is not a cosmopolitan commonwealth under a single ruler, but a lawful federation under a commonly accepted international right."[63]

What is not clear from the above discussion is whether Kant would reject a minimalist constitutional document that enumerated the normative principles of international and cosmopolitan right. The reason for suggesting a constitutional document as a possibility is the fact that Kant certainly argued that the federation would have some form of written treaty and further suggests that this document would be different from contemporary definitions of what a treaty usually entailed.[64] In fact, the essay *Perpetual Peace* is written in the style of a treaty, borrowing common terminology as well as adopting the formal structure of many treaties of the time. Nevertheless, other than the treaty's normative content and a corresponding demand for perpetual peace, Kant does not specifically outline how this document would come about or how it would be practically different from other treaties. Consequently, Kant does not tell us about how the treaty of a *foedus pacificum* would be drafted, its structure, the legal authority it would ultimately procure, or how the treaty would seek renewed obligation and/or rejection once inaugurated. Although Kant certainly found various written constitutions to be "remarkable" documents of voluntary republicanism, he did not link these examples to any illuminating relationship with his own political theory. As a result, it is impossible to know exactly how Kant would feel about the idea of a written cosmopolitan constitution, for he simply did not write enough on the subject for us to reasonably speculate.

Regardless of this gap in Kant's theory, it is still possible for a reconstructionist account of Kantian cosmopolitanism to argue that a formalized written cosmopolitan constitution could provide additional coherency to his theory and should therefore be considered as a critical component in grounding a condition of cosmopolitan right. However, in order to remain faithful to Kant's opposition to a world government and the establishment of coercive global institutions, it is necessary to examine any cosmopolitan constitution as a minimal document that only outlines the normative and juridical principles of both international and cosmopolitan right. By looking at a Kantian constitution from the perspective of a contractual agreement to normative principles of right, it might be possible to understand the creation of a constitutional document that does not formulate any system of institutional government. In this regard, a cosmopolitan constitution simply outlines the normative principles that underpin the legal requirements of voluntary association, legal obligation and federal membership.

It is at this point that constitutional theory is most useful and relevant to the vision of Kantian cosmopolitanism that is being proposed. Generally understood, legal constitutions are an expressed superstructure erected to secure the rules of organization and the further maintenance of those rules themselves.[65] In this sense, a constitution is an objectification of norms and expected social rules, designed in an expressed form to facilitate universal obligation. Furthermore, constitutions can be seen as a conscious contract between mutually agreed participants, outlining the terms and conditions of a juridical order while also providing possible limitations to the reach of those conditions. In relation to Kant, a constitution can be understood as a possible instrument to secure the requirements of the *foedus pacificum*. This is because a constitution can outline the normative principles of law that act as the basis for membership, while also defining various rights which act as limitations to the power of the federation itself. These legal limitations are designed not so that the federation is completely static, for additional voluntary obligations are not prohibited, but are provisions so that change is a result of expected procedures which all the members have recognized as legitimate. In this case, the constitution exists because members of the federation have made a conscious decision that a cosmopolitan order is beneficial not only to their own interests, but to others who seek to peacefully coexist in a bounded sphere where human beings must necessarily tolerate one another.[66] This dedication has significant relevance to Kant's cosmopolitan ethic and to a corresponding experience of global hospitality which legitimates the system. Since "living as members of a society, dependent for the satisfaction of most of our needs on various forms of cooperation with others, we depend for the effective pursuit of our aims clearly on the correspondence of the expectations concerning the actions of others on which plans are based with what they will really do."[67]

Nevertheless, many constitutional scholars might reject the idea that this document qualifies as an actual constitution, suggesting that a constitution by definition must outline governmental institutions and the corresponding restrictions to these institutions. Otherwise it fails to determine how a system of rule formation and alteration is to be legitimated. Nevertheless, it is unconvincing to suggest that a constitution cannot be legitimate or an actual constitution because it refuses to describe the structure of government and the way institutions have to operate.[68] Although it is true that constitutions generally outline governmental institutions and then place restrictions upon them, it does not mean that a constitution must have this governmental component in order to qualify as the supreme law from which all other laws must be in compliance.[69] What is being suggested by a cosmopolitan constitution is that states form a contract to abide by the federal constitution and obligate themselves to the promotion and protection of a condition of public right enumerated by the document. The fact that the constitution does not outline a world government does not weaken the force or authority of the document because the associated members would sign on and therefore believe in the objectified and universalized authority of the constitution. It would, in a Kantian sense, represent a moral law to which members were co-legislators and thus self-determining authors subscribing to the imperative of self-proscribed moral law.

As was briefly mentioned in the introduction of this chapter, many cosmopolitans believe that there is a direct relationship between the experience of mutual global hospitality and the propagation of a cosmopolitan order. This is because historical developments and perceptions of

70

experience largely form our social obligations to both national and to any eventual global identity. If a sense of world citizenship is to be advanced, it will largely be the result of positive experiences of global interaction and the formation of norms based on the fulfillment of certain mutual expectations. One element that a cosmopolitan constitution provides is the expressed normative content behind principles of cosmopolitan law and a corresponding expectation for mutual obligation through contractual agreement. As is clearly stated by Kant, what is needed is "a will uniting them, a constitution," so that individuals can enjoy a common will, understood as a believed and expected condition of mutual public right.[70] This cosmopolitan will is not the result of a purely external source, like a global authority, but a will derived through moral reflection and the self-committed imperative to objectify the authority of this will into universal law.

Nevertheless, a cosmopolitan constitution does more than enumerate the normative principles of public right, for it also becomes a symbolic entity itself, acting as the supreme reference point for a common sense of global identity. In this regard, a cosmopolitan constitution could also provide the juridical basis for what Jürgen Habermas has referred to as *constitutional patriotism*. According to Habermas, the term refers to a sense of obligation that is derived by a belief in the procedures and juridical principles that underpin a constitution. This sense of patriotism can be separate from a national or ethnic identity and can act as an additional level of patriotic identification beyond localized political obligations. The idea of constitutional patriotism is based on the premise that "a legally constituted status of citizen depends on the supportive spirit of a consonant background of legally non-coercible motives and attitudes of a citizenry oriented toward the common good."[71] In other words, if a sense of cosmopolitan citizenship is to develop it will do so only through the beliefs of individuals and their non-coerced willingness to broaden their identity formation so as to incorporate humanity itself. As Habermas states, cosmopolitanism will remain untenable unless "populations can be shifted onto the foundation of constitutional patriotism" and a belief in "a common ethical-political dimension that would be necessary for a corresponding global community and its identity formation."[72] What a cosmopolitan constitution would provide is the normative framework from which the formation of a broadened global identity can take place and further supplies a vehicle from which a self-imposed sense of common motive is secured.

In many regards Kant's cosmopolitanism wishes to establish such a sense of patriotism towards a cosmopolitan constitution. According to the Kantian model that will be outlined in Chapter 3, the federation would be the result of a small number of republics who accept to be governed in the pursuit of their self-interest by the priority of common interest-trumping norms and universal law. As Kant suggests, cosmopolitanism cannot be coerced, but must be the result of international norm building and a recognized need for juridical principles that "will gradually spread further and further."[73] However, it is important to make some distinctions in relation to the study of constitutionalism and the idea of a Kantian cosmopolitan constitution that is being suggested. The Kantian constitution that is being proposed has various distinct characteristics that might distinguish it from what is usually understood in the study of constitutions.

First, my Kantian cosmopolitan constitution derives its status and authority from both its original enactment and by the acceptance of its principles by joining members. In this regard, states voluntarily contract themselves to abide by the cosmopolitan constitution and understand that membership can therefore be accepted or rejected based on performance of their obligations. In this sense, the constitution "provides the standards against which obligatory performance can be measured."[74] Second, and in relation to the above, the cosmopolitan constitution would clearly outline the requirements for membership and the general principles which member states must accept as obligatory. Third, in light of Kant's requirement for the possibility to "renounce" the federation, the constitution would have an explicit clause that allows for members to legally withdraw from the federation. This clause is necessary to reinforce a sense of self-determination and identity formation within the *foedus pacificum*. It is from a self-held belief in cosmopolitan law and its objectification within a formal constitution that a sense of constitutional patriotism can be fostered. For it is only through identification and acceptance that a genuine sense of obligation can be garnered.[75] In this sense, any feature of *positive law* within the constitution is derived from a self-commitment to be governed in the pursuit of their self-interest by the priority of a system of universal law. Fourth, a Kantian cosmopolitan constitution is a mixture of what is usually called natural law and positive law. Since membership is dependent on continued compliance to cosmopolitan law, Kant's cosmopolitan law is meant to be positive in its constitutional authority to persuade compliance and obligation. However, the authority is justified by a naturalist consideration located within the internal aspects, moral foundations and a priori principles of cosmopolitan law. Jeremy Waldron has argued that the dual nature of Kant's jurisprudence is best understood as a form of *normative positivism*.[76] What Waldron suggests is that a Kantian position is one where moral reasoning is meant to ground both the fabrication and *internal aspects* behind the systematic maintenance of law, but also that this law itself when constitutionally codified has a commanding force in creating individual obligations regardless of its normative content. Mary Gregor has made a similar conclusion regarding Kantian jurisprudence, proposing that "since people do not always do what they can recognize that they ought to do, civil society would be necessary to restrain them from interfering with one another's claim."[77] What both Waldron and Gregor are suggesting is that Kantian jurisprudence must have a corresponding component of positive law based on a system of accepted legal obligations that states, individuals and associations understand as having a commanding force.

So what can we understand a Kantian cosmopolitan constitution to contain? An appropriate starting point is to look at Kant's own treaty of *Perpetual Peace* and how this document can act as the basis for a cosmopolitan constitution. From what is outlined in *Perpetual Peace*, it is reasonable to assume that a cosmopolitan constitution would contain the articulation and extrapolation of both the *Preliminary* and *Definitive Articles*. In tandem, these articles are meant to frame the various prohibitive laws against state behavior, the terms of federal membership and the restrictions to the institutional complexity of the federation itself. The next two sections will develop upon both sets of articles and affix these principles to the idea of a possible cosmopolitan constitution.

### A. The Preliminary Articles for a Cosmopolitan Constitution

There are six *Preliminary Articles* that function as "prohibitive international laws." These laws delineate what state actions are prohibited within the federation so as to create a condition of public right and security. In essence, the preliminary articles seek to ground the federation on measures of good faith, self-determination and non-interference.[78] The *Preliminary Articles* are as follows:

1. "No conclusion of peace shall be considered valid as such if it was made with a secret reservation of the material for a future war."
2. "No independently existing state, whether it be large or small, may be acquired by another state by inheritance, exchange, purchase or gift."

3. "Standing armies (*miles perpetuus*) will gradually be abolished altogether."
4. "No national debt shall be contracted in connection with external affairs of the state."
5. "No state shall forcibly interfere in the constitution and government of another state."
6. "No state at war with another shall permit such acts of hostility as would make mutual confidence impossible during a future time of peace."

As Kant makes evident, Articles 1, 3 and 6 are meant to describe the necessary principles for the maintenance of good faith between federated members and external states. The first article suggests that misrepresented, fraudulent or any "mental reservation with a view to reviving pretensions" is tantamount to contract nullification and will not be considered valid by federated members. This implies that states must join in good faith and that any intended failure to comply with the articles of the treaty could result in a loss of membership. For the purpose of devising a cosmopolitan constitution, any failure to comply in good faith with any article of the constitution can be seen as unconstitutional and therefore grounds the legal basis for federal exclusion. Furthermore, Article 3 forbids states to maintain standing armies and suggests that an effort between federated states for arms reduction is a necessary element for an experience of good faith and continued membership compliance. Nevertheless, it is important to explain the fact that Kant was not suggesting that states could not maintain a force for self-protection. This is because Kant is very clear that a state must be able to defend itself and its population from external attack. By standing army, Kant was referring to armies with long-range striking capability with no other purpose then conducting foreign wars. In this regard, member states could have protective forces and military agreements with federated members for mutual defense, but under the cosmopolitan constitution, no single state could amass large forces with the purpose of threatening federated or non-federated members. Lastly, Article 6 further elaborates on Articles 1 and 3 by demanding that if circumstances are such that a state is forced to engaged in warfare, all federated members would conduct these operations in such a manner that future negotiations and peace could still be secured. In other words, federated states must resist warfare, but when attacked must conduct war in such a manner that it could be seen as a justified defense of the *foedus pacificum*. In addition, warfare by federated members must be carried out in such a way that it does not permanently destroy any long-term relations with the inhabitants of a state and therefore ruin the possibility of future cooperation.

Articles 2 and 4 refer to maintaining mutual security and an obligation to respect the self-determination of states. Article 2 demands that states are self-determining and cannot be obtained without the willful consent of its population. In this regard, the Kantian constitution would forbid state accession without the expressed consent of the inhabitants. Article 4 makes three interesting and related demands. First, it demands that states cannot use foreign loans as a means to bankrupt and ruin other states. Second, it forbids states from amassing large national debts to fund military operations. Third, it forbids the loaning of money to states if that money is to be used to procure armaments and military power. States cannot borrow money for the purpose of military spending, while loaning states are also forbidden to allow other states to borrow money with the implicit goal of bankrupting and/or destroying the economic stability of a state. In this regard, Article 4 strictly limits economic practices that might be used by federated members as a means for international brinkmanship or as a policy to exert economic and/or military pressure on other states.

Lastly, Articles 3 and 5 cement an obligation to non-interference in the internal constitutions of other federated member states as well as external non-federated states. As aforementioned, Article 3 forbids standing armies designed specifically to invade and interfere with other states. The supposition behind the article is put more straightforwardly by Article 5, which disallows the interference of internal state constitutions by external states or by any other federated members. These articles provide negative protections, outlining what is prohibited so as to create a condition where states can enjoy equal security and right. These articles are normatively grounded in Kant's public right, but are also pragmatic necessities for the creation of a positive experience of universal obligation and mutual security.[79]

### B.  The Definitive Articles for a Cosmopolitan Constitution

Whereas the preliminary articles outline the legal restrictions to which states must obligate themselves while members of the federation, the definitive articles enumerate stronger terms for membership and the normative conditions upon which the federation stands. The three definitive articles demand that membership be strictly restricted to republics, that the *foedus pacificum* will be a federation of free states (not a world republic) and that all federated members will adopt and abide by cosmopolitan law and the laws of hospitality. Since a more detailed discussion of the relationship between state sovereignty and the definitive articles is provided in Chapter 3, this section will focus on the extent to which the definitive articles could be seen as determining the composition of a possible cosmopolitan constitution.

In regard to providing substance to a cosmopolitan constitution, the first definitive article places conditions on the types of states that can be considered for membership, by strictly demanding that "The Civil Constitution of Every State shall be Republican."[80] In this regard, membership is reserved for republics that reflect a domestic condition of internal justice and are recognized by other federated members as constituted as such. As has been discussed elsewhere, domestic justice and the internal make-up of federated states are critical to the sustainability of the *foedus pacificum*. This is because Kant believes that only republican states can maintain a priori principles of justice both internally and externally. For Kant, the republican make-up of federated members is necessary because they represent the only form of constitution that can approximate "the freedom of every member of society as a human being, the equality of each with all the others as a subject and the independence of each member of a commonwealth as citizen."[81] As Kant argues, these are "laws by which a state can alone be established in accordance with pure rational principles of external human right."[82]

It is generally believed that constitutions function primarily to limit government and the extent to which democratic majorities may exercise their will at the expense of minority opinions.[83] It is in this regard that the second article acts largely as a restriction to any transnational institutions that could evolve within the federation by stipulating that "The Right of Nations shall be based on a Federation of Free States."[84] In other words, the federation is not to have a centralized government, like a world state, but must remain a federation of independent and free states bounded together by voluntary contract and a self-commitment to principles of international and cosmopolitan right. By this, the second article provides constitutional restrictions on the institutional complexity of the federation, thus limiting the power and authority that any multilateral and transnational bodies could attempt to acquire. The cosmopolitan constitution fulfills a limiting role toward a world government by strictly forbidding it, forcing the institutional complexity of the federation to be voluntary and based solely on multilateral or multisectoral networks.

A final condition of federal membership is that by joining the *foedus pacificum*, states obligate themselves to uphold cosmopolitan laws of hospitality and, in doing so, dedicate themselves to the protection and facilitation of cosmopolitan right. As was previously detailed in Section II, the laws of hospitality would act as a set of cosmopolitan rights that would be considered to have full legal status within the federation. States that wished to join the federation must abide by the laws of hospitality and must conform to and reform internal law so that it is in compliance with cosmopolitan law. Any violation of cosmopolitan right by member states would be an unconstitutional breach of contract that would result in the loss of federal membership. In addition, by obligating themselves to the laws of hospitality, members are also binding themselves to the fulfillment of these laws when dealing with all foreign individuals, including interactions with non-federated individuals, nations and associations.

The constitution as outlined above includes many aspects that are analogous to what is commonly understood as representative of modern constitutions. As with the structure of most constitutions, the cosmopolitan constitution proposed in this chapter satisfies three contractarian criteria. First, it explicitly outlines what bodies are to be considered as participants to the contract and seeks expressed consent from them. Second, the terms of constitutional membership are delineated in good faith and in a spirit of mutual consensus and understanding. Third, the constitution enumerates a time frame from which reasonable expectations for compliance are to be mutually generated. In the last case, the constitution is perpetual; assuming consent until a participant legally withdraws from the *foedus pacificum*. However, the cosmopolitan constitution also contains additional elements that are ordinarily associated with drafted constitutions. As we have seen, the cosmopolitan constitution places limitations on the institutional complexion of the federation, while also representing itself as the supreme body of law to which all state law must comply. Lastly, the cosmopolitan constitution includes something like a bill of rights as represented by its laws of hospitality. These cosmopolitan rights represent legal claims for hospitable treatment by all member states while also imposing restrictions on how member states can treat all human beings regardless of nationality.

Nevertheless, before concluding it should be mentioned that a cosmopolitan constitution does not necessarily have to be limited to these articles and/or to the minimum laws of hospitality that have been outlined. This is because member states could willingly choose to adopt additional conditions that would be involved with membership and/or expand the definition of cosmopolitan right and hospitality to include more freedoms.[85] This voluntary expansion of cosmopolitan right and the laws of hospitality is compatible and congruent with Kant's principles of justice and right. What this chapter has attempted to provide is the bare skeletal foundation for a cosmopolitan constitution and outline the basic normative principles of public right behind the creation of a minimal cosmopolitan condition. Although the constitution as discussed in this chapter does not allow the formation of a world government, this does not mean that it excludes the possibility of cooperative multisectoral networks. As will be detailed in Chapter 3, Kant was particularly careful to separate his normative principles of right from any detailed prescriptions for the institutional make-up of a cosmopolitan order. This is because Kant understood that he could not foresee the exact practical complexions involved in securing a future international consensus. In this light, Kant's cosmopolitanism has no particular predictive institutional complexion, only the requirement that the process must be the result of a free consensus in line with a priori principles of universal public right. Consequently, a Kantian cosmopolitan constitution should be seen as attempting to establish the rules of the game to create a legal condition necessary to facilitate an order of consensual cooperation, enlightenment, coexistence and individual toleration. How complex this cooperative system will ultimately become will be solely determined by the will(s) of various federated states and their shared belief in broadening a condition of cosmopolitan public right.

## IV. CONCLUSION

The beginning of this chapter started with a quote by Derrida, which asserted that ethics and hospitality could no longer be thought of as mutually exclusive. As Derrida argues, ethics and hospitality must be sustained as being thoroughly coextensive. This is due to the fact that what is to be considered ethical, will be determined through experiences of mutual hospitality and corresponding expectations for a future of similar good conduct. As Derrida, Habermas and others have suggested, any move toward a cosmopolitan order will have to include a broadened sense of hospitality that promotes the ethical interchange of good conduct and mutual respect.

As was mentioned before, Kant also held this view. Nevertheless, for Kant the empirical experience of ethical treatment is only half the story. This is because Kant also believed that current inhospitable circumstances provided enough motivation for us to strive toward inaugurating cosmopolitan law. Since humans are unavoidably located next to each other and must necessarily live side by side, human reason dictates that without ethical interchange current circumstances of intolerance will perpetuate. What reason tells us a priori, is that in order for anyone to experience a sense of ethical right, it would have to be done within a system of mutually understood legal rights and obligations. However, since historical experiences have not completely delivered peaceful exchange, right necessitates an additional legal condition, a cosmopolitan condition understood as a minimal set of genuinely agreed constraints governing what all people can reasonably expect in the course of living alongside one another. In this regard, Kant's cosmopolitanism is an attempt to further facilitate the hospitable toleration of various peoples and a future of cooperation by mutual restraints of universal law and justice. This necessary condition is true a priori, regardless of, and in addition to, what historical circumstances have so far produced.

However, there has often been confusion regarding what a Kantian system of cosmopolitan law would entail and/or what minimal obligations would be required by a cosmopolitan legal order. In an attempt to clarify the confusion, the last two chapters have examined the jurisprudence underpinning Kant's cosmopolitan law and have reconstructed these normative principles into a basic outline for a cosmopolitan constitution. In doing so, this chapter has attempted to untangle the implied laws of hospitality found throughout Kant's writings and to further connect them to a juridical system of cosmopolitan law. Although I have in no way exhausted the subtle nuances and implications involved in a possible Kantian cosmopolitan constitution, I believe that I have provided some important groundwork toward the exploration of a cosmopolitan constitution and its possible relationship to a future global order.

From the normative foundations outlined thus far, Part Two of this book will provide a more detailed examination and defense of some of the major themes and obstacles involved in the vision of Kantian cosmopolitanism that have been outlined thus far. As has previously been stated, Kant's cosmopolitanism has historically received staunch criticism from realists, pluralists, communitarians and relativists. These criticisms I believe largely rest on various misunderstandings regarding what universal principles a Kantian cosmopolitan condition supposedly requires. In order to clarify these misunderstandings, Part Two will examine three critical issues surrounding Kant's cosmopolitanism. The next three chapters will provide a thorough examination of the role of states within Kant's federation, the role of cultural diversity within a universal system of cosmopolitan law, and how the development of a global system of distributive justice might be possible. By examining these critical concerns, it will be possible to better satisfy those who remain skeptical about the relevance and desirability of a Kantian cosmopolitan order and to clarify its position within the future study of international relations theory.

## NOTES

1. Jacques Derrida, "On Cosmopolitanism," M. Dooley & M. Hughes (trans.), *On Cosmopolitanism and Forgiveness* (London: Routledge, 2002). By historically perverted, Derrida seems to be suggesting that history has often witnessed states making claims to principles of hospitality while also systematically engaging in imperialistic and globally inhospitable behavior.
2. Hospitality can be loosely defined as the cordial and generous reception of guests that is both receptive and open minded to their particular ways of living.
3. Jacques Derrida, "Foreign Question," R. Bowlby (trans.), *Of Hospitality* (Stanford: Stanford University Press, 2000); Seyla Benhabib, *The Rights of Others: Aliens, Residents and Citizens* (Cambridge: Cambridge University Press, 2004); Georg Cavallar, *The Rights of Strangers* (Aldershot: Ashgate, 2002).
4. Martin Wight, *International Theory: The Three Traditions*, G. Wight & A. Roberts (eds) (Leicester: Leicester University Press, 1991).
5. Onora O'Neill, 'Transnational Justice,' in D. Held (ed.), *Political Theory Today* (Oxford: Polity Press, 1995), pp. 276–304; Charles Jones, *Global Justice: Defending Cosmopolitanism* (Oxford: Oxford University Press, 1999).
6. Martin Wight, "An Anatomy of International Thought," *Review of International Studies*, 13 (1987), p. 226. I have dealt more thoroughly with this argument in both Chapters 3 and 4.
7. Immanuel Kant, *The Metaphysics of Morals*, M. Gregor (ed. & trans.) (Cambridge: Cambridge University Press, 1996), p. 24. [6:230]
8. Ibid., p. 30. [6:237]
9. Ibid., p. 50. [6:262]
10. Ibid.
11. Mary Gregor, "Kant's Approach to Constitutionalism," in A. Rosenbaum (ed.), *Constitutionalism: The Philosophical Dimension* (New York: Greenwood Press, 1988), p. 82.
12. Kant, *The Metaphysics of Morals*, p. 25. [6:232]
13. Gregor, "Kant's Approach to Constitutionalism," p. 79.
14. Daniele Archibugi, "Immanuel Kant, Cosmopolitan Law and Peace," *European Journal of International Relations*, vol. 1 (4), 1995, p. 449.
15. Immanuel Kant, "Perpetual Peace: A Philosophical Sketch," in Hans Reiss (ed.), H. B. Nisbet (trans.), *Kant's Political Writings* (Cambridge: Cambridge University Press, 1970), pp. 105–6. [8:357–8]
16. Sharon Anderson-Gold, *Cosmopolitanism and Human Rights* (Cardiff: University of Wales Press, 2001).

17. F. H. Hinsley, *Power and the Pursuit of Peace* (Cambridge: Cambridge University Press, 1963).
18. Derrida, "On Cosmopolitanism."
19. Onora O'Neill, *Faces of Hunger: An Essay on Poverty, Justice and Development* (London: Allen & Unwin, 1986).
20. To be fair, O'Neill is mostly concerned with human development and the satisfaction of basic needs and does not specifically discuss cosmopolitan hospitality. However, I believe this oversight to be an error and I will now attempt to draw out the laws of hospitality. In relation to O'Neill's concerns, I have provided my own Kantian suggestion regarding the normative foundations for a scheme of distributive justice and human development in Chapters 5 and 6.
21. Immanuel Kant, "Idea for a Universal History with a Cosmopolitan Purpose," in Hans Reiss (ed.), H. B. Nisbet (trans.), *Kant's Political Writings* (Cambridge: Cambridge University Press, 1970). p. 51. [8:28]
22. Immanuel Kant, "On the Common Saying: This May be True in Theory, But it Does not Apply in Practice," in Hans Reiss (ed.), H. B. Nisbet (trans.), *Kant's Political Writings* (Cambridge: Cambridge University Press, 1970), p. 73. [8:290]
23. Ibid.
24. Kant, *The Metaphysics of Morals*, p. 121. [6:352]
25. Charles Covell, *Kant and the Law of Peace: A Study in the Philosophy of International Law and International Relations* (New York: Palgrave, 1998), p. 143.
26. Kant, "Perpetual Peace," p. 106. [8:358]
27. Ibid. [8:357–8]
28. Kant, "Perpetual Peace," p. 128. [8:384]
29. Kant, *The Metaphysics of Morals*, p. 121. [6:353]
30. Kant, "Perpetual Peace," p. 106. [8:358]
31. Ibid.
32. Ibid.
33. Ibid., pp. 106–7. Also see footnotes. [8:358–60]
34. Kant, "An Answer to the Question: 'What is Enlightenment?'," in Hans Reiss (ed.), H. B. Nisbet (trans.), *Kant's Political Writings* (Cambridge: Cambridge University Press, 1970), p. 55. [8:36–7]
35. Covell, p. 143.
36. Kant, "Theory and Practice," p. 85. [8:304]
37. Kant, *The Metaphysics of Morals*, p. 121. [6:352]
38. Kant, "Perpetual Peace," p. 106. [8:358]
39. Kant, *The Metaphysics of Morals*, p. 121. [6:352]
40. Kant, "Perpetual Peace," p. 106. [8:358]
41. Kant, *The Metaphysics of Morals*, p. 122. [6:353]
42. Kant, "Perpetual Peace," p. 105. [8:357]
43. Kant, *The Metaphysics of Morals*, p. 121. [6:353]
44. Derrida, "On Cosmopolitanism," p. 21.
45. Kant, "Perpetual Peace," p. 106. [8:358]
46. This is not to say that Derrida is categorically wrong in questioning Kantian hospitality, for it may be the case that the laws of hospitality do not protect asylum seekers to Derrida's satisfaction under closer scrutiny. My point is that there seems to be room for interpretation and broader application within the laws of hospitality than Derrida

immediately suggests and that they may indeed satisfy an obligation to protect asylum
seekers.

47. Benhabib, *The Rights of Others*, pp. 36–8.
48. Cavallar, *The Rights of Strangers*, p. 323.
49. Ibid., p. 394.
50. Kant, "Perpetual Peace," p. 106. [8:358]
51. Ibid. Emphasis is mine.
52. Kant, "Perpetual Peace," pp. 106–7. [8:358–60]
53. A broader discussion of these implications is provided in Chapter 6.
54. Immanuel Kant, Appendix, "Transcendental Logic II, Dialectics I, Ideas in General,"
    in J. M. D. Meiklejohn (trans.), *The Critique of Pure Reason* (New York: The Colonial
    Press, 1900). [3:247]
55. Kant, *The Metaphysics of Morals*, p. 89. [6:311]
56. Ibid., p. 53. [6:266]
57. Ibid., p. 89. [6:311]
58. Kant, *The Metaphysics of Morals*, p. 120. [6:351]
59. Although the US constitution does not require renewal, it can be legally dissolved as
    the supreme law of the land with a majority vote of congress and the subsequent rati-
    fication by two-thirds of all fifty states.
60. Kant, *The Metaphysics of Morals*, p. 115. [6:345]
61. Constitutional rigidity is a rather ambiguous concept with various complexities
    within legal theory. Nevertheless, it is meant here generally in that a rigid constitu-
    tion is one so designed that "it is hard to alter . . . seldom altered and or cannot be
    amended or altered as a supreme law." This includes being unable to legally withdraw.
    K. C. Wheare, *Modern Constitutions* (Oxford: Oxford University Press, 1951), p. 23.
62. Andrew Linklater, *Men and Citizens in the Theory of International Relations*, 2nd edn
    (Macmillan: Basingstoke, 1990), p. 101.
63. Kant, "Theory and Practice," p. 90. [8:311]
64. Kant, "Perpetual Peace," p. 104. [8:355–6]
65. F. A. Hayek, *Law, Legislation and Liberty* (London: Routledge, 1973), p. 134.
66. Kant, "Perpetual Peace," p. 104. [8:355–7]
67. Hayek, p. 36.
68. For a more detailed argument regarding the versatility of what can be considered a
    constitution see Cecile Fabre, *Social Rights Under the Constitution: Government and the
    Decent Life* (Oxford: Oxford University Press, 2000), especially Chapter 3, pp.
    67–79.
69. Thomas Gray, "Constitutionalism: An Analytic Framework," in J. Pennock & J.
    Chapman (eds), *Constitutionalism* (New York: New York University Press, 1979), pp.
    189–209.
70. Kant, *The Metaphysics of Morals*, p. 89. [6:311]
71. Jürgen Habermas, *Between Facts and Norms*, W. Rehg (trans.) (Cambridge: Polity
    Press, 1996), p. 499.
72. Jürgen Habermas, *The Post National Constellation*, M. Pensky (trans.) (Cambridge,
    MA: MIT Press, 2001), pp. 76 & 109.
73. Kant, "Perpetual Peace," p. 104. [8:356]
74. William Andrews, *Constitutions and Constitutionalism* (Princeton: Van Nostrand Co.,
    1968), p. 21.

75. Habermas, *Between Facts and Norms*, p. 499.
76. Jeremy Waldron, "Kant's Legal Positivism," *Harvard Law Review*, vol. 109 (1996), p. 1535.
77. Gregor, "Kant's Approach to Constitutionalism," p. 71.
78. Covell, p. 102.
79. It is interesting to note that many modern peace treaties contain almost every aspect of these preliminary articles, in that most peace treaties demand good faith by arms reduction, clauses protecting self-determination, non-interference demands, anti-military loan restrictions and limits to weapons of mass destruction.
80. Kant, "Perpetual Peace," p. 98. [8:348]
81. Kant, "Theory and Practice," p. 74. [8:290]. A connection between Kant's republicanism and a possibility to understand it as being synonymous with liberal democracies is discussed in Chapter 3.
82. Ibid.
83. Charles McIlwain, *Constitutionalism: Ancient and Modern* (Ithaca: Cornell University Press, 1947), p. 21. It should be noted that this limiting function is not a necessary requirement of constitutionalism, only that many constitutions maintain articles that do in fact limit government. See Cecile Fabre, *Social Rights Under the Constitution*.
84. Kant, "Perpetual Peace," p. 102. [8:354]
85. An argument for the possibility for a greater system of distributive justice and its incorporation into the cosmopolitan constitution is made in Chapter 5.

# Part Two

# CHAPTER 3

## *State Sovereignty, Federation and Kant's Cosmopolitanism*

"Far along the world-wide whisper of the south-wind rushing warm,
With the Standards of the people plunging thro' the thunder-storm;
Till the war-drum throbb'd no longer, and the battle flags were furl'd.
In the parliament of man, the Federation of the World.
There the common sense of most shall hold a fretful realm in awe,
And the kindly earth shall slumber, lapt in universal law." – Alfred Tennyson

### INTRODUCTION

There is an undeniable semblance between the poem of Alfred Tennyson and the cosmopolitan philosophy of Immanuel Kant. Although Kant was hardly an aficionado of poetry, it would be difficult to imagine him unable to appreciate the cosmopolitan vision for perpetual peace expressed within Tennyson's work. The semblance comes from a shared belief that the consistent ravishing of conflict will provide a motivation for humanity to finally realize the common destruction caused by war and seek a truly lasting peace. As Tennyson implies, it is through "common sense," or in Kant's terminology *practical reason*, that universal principles could be understood and created. From this premise, Tennyson insinuates that the world should be organized into a kind of lawful federation, where various states are united by a dedication to peaceful coexistence and mutual security. Lastly, Tennyson contends that if humans are to enjoy a perpetual world peace, then some form of universal law must be established in order to codify mutual recognition and to regulate the peaceful coexistence of various peoples.

In spite of the prima facie similarities, it would be disingenuous to suggest a categorical homology between Kant's *Perpetual Peace* and

87

Tennyson's poem. Unlike Tennyson, Kant did not explicitly advocate a federal parliament or recommend any institutions for world government. On the contrary, Kant was often critical of a world government and the creation of a world state. Alternatively, what Kant suggests is that a federation between states should be established in which the members acknowledge principles of universal law. These principles were to be cemented into universal law not by an external authority, like a world government, but through the republican make-up of each state and the contractual agreement for *public right* ratified by any cooperating member.

Nevertheless, like the subtle differences that exist between what Tennyson and Kant advocated, there is considerable contention between academics regarding the exact nature of Kant's cosmopolitanism in relation to the role of states. Some international relations theorists suggest that Kant yearned to create a society of world citizens independent from states.[1] Similarly, Hegelians insist that Kant abandons the moral significance of localized state obligations and the communal good of political self-determination, replacing them with a universalized moral hegemony.[2] Even Kantian scholars debate whether Kant truly envisioned a global federation of free states or a world republic.[3] Others have suggested that Kant's political philosophy requires strict maintenance of state sovereignty and that this is in direct contrast to his aspirations for cosmopolitan reform.[4] Adding to the confusion, international lawyers have often suggested that Kant's cosmopolitan law is nothing more than a supplement to contemporary understandings of international law, merely stipulating how states should treat visiting foreign-nationals and that it has nothing to do with regulating a world federation.[5]

The purpose of this chapter is to examine the role of states in Kant's cosmopolitan federation and to clarify the relationship between the rights of states and the concept of cosmopolitan law. In order to present a coherent and tenable account of a Kantian federation, this chapter is divided into four sections. In Section I, Kant's move away from the traditional natural law concept of *jus gentium* to the idea of cosmopolitan federation and cosmopolitan law is outlined. In doing so, I will discuss the historical context of Kant's cosmopolitanism and the paradigm shift produced by Kant's contribution to international relations theory. From this background, Section II examines the three definitive articles of *Perpetual Peace* and their primary significance in creating a cosmopolitan order. From this, an argument is furthered that the internal justice of a state confers political legitimacy and the acceptability for state membership within a cosmopolitan federation. For this, Kant's distinction between *international right* and *cosmopolitan right* is further developed, arguing that a Kantian form of cosmopolitanism advocates a new level of cosmopolitan law which holds supremacy over the idea of absolute state sovereignty. Section III seeks to resolve the debate between some realist and Kantian scholars regarding whether Kant's cosmopolitanism must be understood as advocating a federation of free states or a world republic. Through this discussion, it will be argued that Kant's cosmopolitanism is best understood as a federation of free states, with the caveat that Kant maintained optimism for a continued movement toward broader multilateral and multisectoral institutions. The fourth section will conclude by comparing this Kantian vision to contemporary theories offered by international relations theorists. In doing so, I will maintain that Kantian cosmopolitanism does not advocate the immediate destabilizing destruction of states and self-determination as many have claimed, but is best understood as a mechanism for the lawful coexistence of various political communities as a judicial community of the world.

## I.  Kant's Move from Natural Law to Lawful Cosmopolitanism

In order to understand how the idea of a Kantian federation and the corresponding formation of cosmopolitan law depart from both contemporary international relations theory and from theories contemporaneous to Kant, it is important to know something about the traditions from which Kant is departing. Through an examination of how Kant departed from the natural law tradition, while emphasizing from what theories he drew inspiration, we can dispel a claim made against Kant's efforts for an international federation while also highlighting some ambiguities involved in his cosmopolitan vision. A brief contextual analysis helps to refute the concern that Kant wants to abandon state entities altogether and that he had aspirations for a universal state. As will be discussed below, Kant wants to challenge the natural law doctrine supporting state sovereignty while also dismissing arguments advocating the creation of a world state. In this regard, Kant's international theory tries to navigate a middle passage between the idea that states can act as the ultimate protectors of human freedom, while also aware of the fact that states are often the primary violators of this very freedom. By understanding in which ways Kant abandons the idea of state sovereignty, while also examining what alternatives he accepted and rejected, we can locate the international problems that Kant sought to remedy and the areas that a reconstructivist argument must improve upon in order to make a Kantian cosmopolitan federation coherent.

In the context of eighteenth-century European politics, Kant inherited an international order based on the concept of absolute sovereignty that was fastened into common practice by the Treaty of Westphalia (1648). This treaty can be understood as establishing a state-centered system that was based on principles of equal state sovereignty and the absolute right to internal self-determination without external interference. In essence, the Treaty of Westphalia solidified a Hobbesian anarchical global system dominated by state self-interest and motivated by the maintenance of a *balance of power* without any overarching coordination by international institutions or organizations.

Kant was highly critical of the Westphalia model, claiming as he did that a "permanent universal peace by means of a so-called *European balance of power* is a pure illusion."[6] For Kant, the Westphalia model only sought to justify and regulate the rules of warfare, providing nothing to help eliminate war or to provide for the lawful coexistence of various states. Understanding that the Treaty of Westphalia often sanctioned the use of war for political means, Kant refused to refer to the treaty as an important aspect of international law as was commonly done,[7] but consistently insisted that it legitimated a world devoid of law, tantamount to Thomas Hobbes' constant *state of war*. In order to provide for a lasting peace away from a Hobbesian state of war, Kant advocated the establishment of a lawful federation of states anchored to perpetual peace by a commitment to universal law and the acknowledgement of a public right to external freedom and universal coexistence.

However, Kant's ambitions for perpetual peace were uniquely different from those of his contemporaries. This is because the prevailing theoretical doctrines of the time offered little alternative to the Hobbesian paradigm. The dominant theoretical doctrine of international relations in Kant's lifetime was natural law theory and the corresponding principle of *jus gentium*. Although Kant was familiar with the natural law tradition, teaching several courses on the subject, he was reticent to fully accept the doctrine. In fact, Kant was highly critical of many celebrated natural law theorists, complaining that Hugo Grotuis, Samuel Pufendorf and Emeric de Vattel were "sorry comforters" unwilling to challenge the doctrine of *jus gentium* and the lawless supremacy awarded to state sovereignty.[8]

In line with his critique of the Treaty of Westphalia, Kant argued that the doctrine of *jus gentium* sought only to regulate war between major European states and was unable to provide for a truly lasting peace by creating a lawful community of states grounded on principles of external right and universal law.

Although displeased with the failures of the natural law tradition and *jus gentium*, Kant did understand the value of using three of its major tenets as his starting point. Kant recognized that individual states were the central actors in international relations and that any cosmopolitan theory would have to deal immediately with how to establish a lawful system of rights between existing states and between the individual members of those states. In addition, Kant recognized that conditions for the justified use of war had to be distinguished from those which violated universal principles of external freedom and coexistence. In this regard, Kant recognized that the justified use of war was warranted in certain extreme circumstances and that states had the right to defend themselves against tyrannical regimes.[9] Finally, Kant agreed with certain natural law theorists who argued that individuals are by nature sovereign entities and that their freedom must be universally respected in the same way that sovereign states were supposed to be universally respected under international law.

Despite his disagreement with certain authors, Kant did believe that a few natural law theorists were attempting to broaden the scope and universality of the three tenets of *jus gentium*. Notably absent from Kant's list of sorry comforters is Christian Wolff and his seminal work *The Law of Nations Treated According to a Scientific Method*. In this work, Wolff argued that individuals belong to a single global community and that states should be held accountable to this notion of global society. As Wolff maintained, the earth should be organized into "a kind of democratic form of government. For the supreme state is made up of nations as a whole, which as individual nations are free and equal to each other."[10] Nevertheless, Kant seems to be uncomfortable with Wolff's prescription for a world government, suggesting that Vattel was correct to abandon this aspect in his translation and adaptation of Wolff's work. As Kant writes, "such a [world] state is in turn even more dangerous to freedom, for it may lead to fearful despotism . . . distrust must force men to form an order which is not a cosmopolitan commonwealth under a single ruler, but a lawful federation under a commonly accepted international right."[11] What Kant seems to have taken from Wolff is the acceptance that human beings are equal to each other and that this equality can only be assured if states are organized into some form of lawful global community. Where Kant departs from Wolff is in his insistence that international institutions should not "interfere in the constitution and government of another state" and that world government is a threat to freedom.[12]

The critique of *jus gentium* and Kant's argument against Wolff's advocacy for a world government illustrates a source of possible tension within Kant's international theory. On the one hand, Kant wishes to create a judicial environment which eliminates absolute sovereignty and the injustices often committed by states under this claim. On the other hand, Kant wants to create a universal order without the establishment of a world government or any formal coercive institutions to secure legal obligation. It seems that for Kant, there is a belief that global justice cannot be secured either through traditional natural law models or through the idea of a world government. In this regard, the former model is too weak to control states from violating human freedoms both internally and externally, while the latter has the equal potential to become overly coercive and unjust. Therefore, the task for Kant's cosmopolitanism was to resolve the tension of preserving a place for states while also providing a tenable alternative to both the Hobbesian and world state paradigms.

A starting point for a Kantian alternative can be found through the examination of two major influences within Kant's political theory. While Kant found the natural law tradition to be sufficiently unable to provide for a lawful community of states, he did draw considerable influence from the perpetual peace projects of Abbé de Saint-Pierre and Jean-Jacques Rousseau.[13] Saint-Pierre argued for the establishment of a federation of free states based on the rule of law and the creation of an international court of justice. In addition, Saint-Pierre abandoned the natural law concept of *jus gentium*, suggesting that the only justification for war is when external enemies directly threaten the peaceful federation of states. In his writings on Saint-Pierre, Rousseau also seems to advocate a federation of states with a minimal institutional complexion. In *Abstract and Judgement of Saint-Pierre's Project for Perpetual Peace*, Rousseau considers the merits of establishing an international congress consisting of state representatives, where international concerns could be debated through parliamentarian rules of order.[14] However, Kant rejects both Saint-Pierre and Rousseau's advocacy for coercive international institutions. Alternatively, Kant believes the most promising aspect of Rousseau's treatment of Saint-Pierre to be the emphasis placed on the relationship between domestic policy and how states behave in the international environment. Rousseau firmly held that "well constituted states"[15] would be more tolerant of similarly organized states and more willing to form cooperative international relationships with them. As we will see in the next section, Kant further develops this idea from Rousseau and that the domestic constitution of international actors has a critical role in Kant's theory of international relations. This is because Kant's concept of a federation of free states is predicated on the first definitive article of *Perpetual Peace* and the condition that "the Civil Constitution of Every State shall be Republican."[16]

Although there are many ambiguities in Kant's international theory, three factors remain fairly consistent in relation to the writings of his contemporaries. First, Kant is clearly disenchanted with the natural law tradition and with the lawless international system propagated by the Westphalian model. Second, Kant firmly maintains that perpetual peace and the idea of international right can only be secured through a consistent commitment to universal law and a corresponding resolution for public right. Third, Kant clearly rejects Wolff's, Saint-Pierre's and Rousseau's institutional design for international organizations with coercive power. In an attempt to provide an alternative to these theories, Kant redirects international relations theory away from the Hobbesian paradigm to a model that focuses on domestic justice as the necessary first principle for a cosmopolitan order. According to Kant, a federation based on republican states provides two conditions necessary for a lawful community of states and the possibility of international and cosmopolitan right. The first condition is based on Kant's assumption that republican governments do not fight one another.[17] Kant believes that a federation of republican states would greatly diminish international conflicts and war.[18] Where international tensions might continue to exist, they would not occur between like-minded republican states, but between the federation and states that directly threaten the pacific alliance. The second condition is based on Kant's assertion that republican states represent the only form of government that can provide justice internally and externally. By focusing on the relationship between domestic justice and international policy, Kant is attempting to circumvent the need for a coercive world government. This is premised on the notion that an equality of freedom is already secured through each individual state constitution. It is from this position that Kant accepts Rousseau's belief that republican states are more willing to cooperate with similarly constituted states and to establish cosmopolitan principles of global justice which mirror their own internal constitutions.

However, an examination of the various influences within Kant's work will never provide a definitive solution to the ambiguities within his theory. All an historical analysis can furnish is some background to help explain how Kant altered international relations theory and how we might better understand the role of states within Kantian cosmopolitanism. In addition, by looking at how Kant revised the theories of his time, the realist position that Kant promoted an overarching world state becomes a questionable conclusion. As has been shown, Kant is critical of a world state while also remaining equally critical of the unjust global system legitimated by claims to state sovereignty. It is from the backdrop provided in this section that a further discussion of Kant's federation will be provided in the next section.

## II.  THE DEFINITIVE ARTICLES OF PERPETUAL PEACE AND THE JURISPRUDENCE OF KANT'S COSMOPOLITANISM

The idea for a federation of free states based on a system of corresponding rights stems directly from Kant's overall theory of justice and his metaphysics of morals. The foundation for this system of rights is a variation of Kant's categorical imperative and his *Doctrine of Right*, namely: "right is . . . the sum of the conditions under which the choice of one can be united with the choice of another in accordance with a universal law of freedom."[19] According to Kant, reason itself dictates that humans have an obligation to leave the *state of nature* and establish a "civil condition" to which the maintenance of external freedom and coexisting public right can be managed. Since the world is not an infinite plane, but a sphere where individuals must necessarily occupy a finite space next to one another, reason dictates the establishment of a system of public right. As Kant proclaimed, "the peoples of the earth have thus entered in various degrees into a universal community and it has developed to the point where a violation of rights in *one* part of the world is felt *everywhere*."[20] From this empirical consideration, reason dictates that restraints on external freedom ought to be universally applied and mutually consistent, limiting external freedom equally between all members of the earth.[21] Mary Gregor defines the jurisprudence behind the concept of public right as, "the sum of laws that need to be publicized in order to produce a rightful condition, one in which individuals, nations and states can enjoy their rights."[22]

In order to provide a rightful condition that maintains symbiotic cohabitation between human beings and the states of the world, Kant advances a tripartite system of jurisprudence divided into *domestic law, international law* and *cosmopolitan law*. As the names of the tripartite distinction suggest, a judicial system of public right is to be properly maintained through three corresponding forms of rights and law, which together create a universal condition where "the freedom of each can coexist with the freedom of all the others."[23] The first rightful condition involves domestic law and the establishment of rights and duties that are to exist between citizens and their government (citizen to citizen, state to citizen). The second form of public right involves international law and the necessary establishment of a rightful condition that should exist between the various governments of the world as representative entities (state to state). The third rightful condition involves the establishment of cosmopolitan law and the rightful condition that should exist between all humans and all states, regardless of national origin or state citizenship (states to all humans, especially non-citizens). It is no surprise that there is a direct link between the tripartite as outlined in the *Metaphysics of Morals* and the three definitive articles of *Perpetual Peace*, since each section of Kant's treatise deals directly with the establishment of the aforementioned rightful conditions: 1. The Civil Constitution of Every State shall be Republican (citizen to citizen, state to citizen); 2. The Right of Nations shall be based on a Federation of Free States (state to state); 3. Cosmopolitan Right shall be limited to Conditions of Universal Hospitality (states to all humans, especially non-citizens).

The purpose of the following three subsections is to provide a brief outline of Kant's concept of domestic, international and cosmopolitan law respectively. From this discussion, the argument will be made that the definitive articles correspond to the categorical imperative and represents an attempt to create a rightful condition of universal law without the need for an overarching world government. It is in Section III that I will attempt to resolve the debate regarding the nature of Kant's cosmopolitanism and to further refute the argument that it necessarily advocates the eradication of states altogether.

### A. *Domestic Law, Popular Sovereignty and Domestic Justice*

As was mentioned at the end of Section I, an extremely important element of Kant's federation of free states is the first definitive article of

Perpetual Peace and the condition that "the Civil Constitution of Every State shall be Republican."[24] As was suggested earlier, Rousseau was a source of inspiration for Kant and provided the grounding for his theoretical shift away from the natural law tradition. In following Rousseau's emphasis on domestic politics and justice, Kant altered the Hobbesian paradigm by focusing on domestic justice as a precondition for establishing a global civil condition of public right. Kant predicates the foundation of the federation on domestic law and republicanism because he firmly believes that a republican constitution is the only form of government that can secure and maintain justice both internally and externally.[25]

In many ways there is a direct connection with contemporary liberal democratic theory and Kant's use of republican terminology. Although Kant specifically dismisses democracies as "despotism," this opinion is largely based on Aristotelian concepts of direct democracy and the belief that democracies cannot maintain a meaningful separation of powers.[26] As Kant insists, states can have various configurations (anything from dictatorships to democracy), but that there are only two forms of government, republican or despotic. For Kant, a republican form of government separates the executive and the legislative branch, whereas a despotic form of government does not. In addition, a well-constituted republic strives to approximate three universal principles; the "freedom for all members of society," the "dependence of everyone upon a single common legislation" and "legal equality as citizens."[27] In contrast to despotism, a republican form of government locates these principles through an idealized "united general will of the people" and a dedication to its citizens by dividing power between the legislative, the executive and the judicial branch.[28] In this regard, Kant's discussions of republicanism come considerably close to contemporary understandings of liberal democracy and representative government. As has been suggested by many scholars, Kant's conception of republicanism is closely synonymous with current understandings of representative democracies, and it is from this resemblance that their interchange has been deemed warranted.[29]

Georg Cavallar, among others, has suggested that the first definitive article of *Perpetual Peace* and Kant's treatment of republicanism within the *Metaphysics of Morals* directly confirm a transition away from the concept of absolute state sovereignty to what has been called *popular sovereignty*. According to Cavallar, "state sovereignty is relative in the sense that it is dependent upon popular sovereignty. It is also relative in the sense that Kant accepts it as provisionally legitimate."[30] In this regard, the domestic legitimacy of the state directly influences whether or not a state is considered a sovereign and whether it should be considered to have a legitimate claim as a global representative. As Cavallar points out, Kant is adamant in his conviction that republicanism is the only form of government that "can be derived from the idea of an original contract."[31] A republican contract is legitimate precisely because it represents the "united will of the people" and is derived from the fact that sovereignty lies with the people.[32] Although the united general will is not meant as a practical legislative mechanism as some interpretations have suggested, it does represent the metaphysical ideal of what a sovereign should exemplify in its mutual relations with all cohabitants of the earth. In this regard, the idea of a united general will is meant to act as both a moral guide for determining whether a state is to be considered as a representative sovereign or as a despotic state, and also to make the determination that an existing order must accommodate the fact that the world is shared in common.[33]

Nevertheless, it would be a mistake to insinuate that Cavallar's interpretation of popular sovereignty is beyond a question of doubt. This is because considerable ambiguities exist in Kant's treatment of sovereignty. Although Cavallar does capture a predominant theme within the Kantian concept of sovereignty, there are textual counterpoints where the concept of sovereignty is claimed as necessary regardless of the form of government involved. One such counterexample is located in Kant's discussion of the state of nature and his premise that any state authority is better than a lack of state authority. As Kant argues, "any legal constitution, even if it is only in a small measure *lawful*, is better than none at all."[34] From this, Kant is expressing the importance of having an absolute sovereign to maintain stability and to allow for an environment where the progression of human morality is at least possible. Moreover, Kant's discussion of justice does not allow individuals to revolt against a state, because he believes that a return to the state of nature is worse than living under a despotic regime.[35] Kant reiterates his commitment to this stance when he writes, "man is an animal who needs a master . . . to force him to obey a universally valid will under which everyone can be free."[36] Therefore, without a state to force a civil order and the compliance to law, the human condition will revert to the state of nature where the possibility of public right and moral progression is impossible. Although a state may be despotic, it still maintains order and at least allows for the possibility of reform towards the metaphysical ideal of popular sovereignty.

Some Kantian scholars have suggested that Kant's willingness to accept any form of sovereignty, even a tyrannical regime, represents an inherent perplexity in his notion of justice and its extrapolation to international relations.[37] The complication is based on the clear fact that Kant upholds a republican government as the only constitution that can ideally maintain internal and external justice. From this premise, a tension arises from the fact that Kant is also willing to allow for the maintenance of unjust states, if a removal of those states meant a return to the state of nature. However, these ambiguities in Kantian sovereignty are not necessarily fatal to his overall argument. This is because there are distinctions that can be made between a legal order and a sovereign based on public right and justice. For Kant, the condition of public right presupposes the existence of a legal order and a legal order is a necessary first step in reforming states toward justice. As Kant writes in the *Doctrine of Right*:

> The *spirit* of the original contract (*anima pacti orignarii*) involves an obligation on the part of the constituting authority to the *kind of government* suited to the idea of the original contract. Accordingly, even if this cannot be done all at once, it is under obligation to change the kind of government gradually and continually so that it harmonizes *in its effect* with the only constitution that accords with right, that of a pure republic, in such a way that the old (empirical) statutory form, which served merely to bring about the submission of the people, are replaced by the original rational form, the only form which makes *freedom* the principle and indeed the condition for any exercise of *coercion*, as is required by a rightful constitution of a state in the strict sense of the word.[38]

Therefore, without a condition of stability and lawfulness, no matter how small a change it is from the state of nature, a movement toward the ideal of popular sovereignty is impossible. In this regard, the first necessity for the establishment of a just society is to leave the state of nature, for there is no possibility of a civil condition while in a constant state of war. From this basis, Kant maintains that there is a continued need to reform political order toward the metaphysical ideal of justice and public right.[39] As Antonio Franceschet claims, "Kant's view is that once the sovereign creates a mere lawful civil union out of anarchy, it alone will have the force and legislative legitimacy to progressively re-create itself and to produce a society based increasingly on the just principles of the original contract."[40]

We can draw two implications from Kant's position on domestic justice in relation to his cosmopolitan theory. First, the primacy of domestic law in Kant's overall global vision illustrates that Kant does not advocate the removal of states, as some realists and Hegelians have suggested. In fact, the basis for any continued move toward cosmopolitan principles is maintained and propagated through republican state reform and a dedication to approximate the metaphysical condition of public right, both internally (domestic positive law) and eventually externally (self-imposed dedication to international and cosmopolitan law). In this regard, the state's legal apparatus and republican government, as understood as a form of popular sovereignty, is given considerable priority in providing the foundations for a continued movement toward cosmopolitan justice. As Jeremy Waldron has recently expressed, for Kant "the state is a morally significant entity by virtue of the tasks it takes on, the spirit in which it addresses them, and the resources it brings to those tasks."[41] In this regard, a fairly robust and effective system of domestic law, which strives to approximate a legitimate condition of public right, is a necessary component to "make the moral difference that Kant thinks the state is capable of making."[42] Second, there is a consistency between the metaphysical ideal of popular sovereignty and the categorical imperative. This is due to the fact that Kant's republicanism is aligned with reason to promote universal law, which is based on creating those "conditions under which the choice of one can be united with the choice of another in accordance with a universal law of freedom."[43] In this case, what is needed is "a constitution allowing the greatest possible human freedom in accordance with laws which ensure that the freedom of each can coexist with the freedom of all the other."[44] As we will see below, a federation of free states that is premised on the first definitive article creates a foundation for a broader cosmopolitan order. Although the federation does not have any coercive power like that of a state, it does convey a legitimate condition of public right and establishes the normative principles for which the federation embodies and propagates.

## B.  International Law, Federation and International Justice

In *The Idea for a Universal History with a Cosmopolitan Purpose*, Kant writes that "the problem of establishing a perfect civil constitution is subordinate to the problem of a law governed external relationship with other states, and cannot be solved unless the latter is also solved."[45] Kant substantiates this claim through empirical qualifications and the historical reality that domestic freedom is not secured through the Westphalia model. Kant contends that this is due to the fact that states cannot enjoy their own freedom if they are constantly under threat from external forces. As

Kant submits, "civil freedom can no longer be so easily infringed without disadvantage to all trades and industries, and especially to commerce, in the event of which the state's power in its external relations will also decline."[46] Although this statement was meant to discourage states from military aggression and to highlight the counterproductive costs involved in expansionist policies, it was also meant to relate the fact that states have become increasingly interconnected and that warfare destabilizes the freedom of everyone. In addition, under the Treaty of Westphalia, international right was not seen in context of a rightful condition for mutual coexistence, but was often interpreted as an extended right for sovereignties to go to war. What reason dictates, according to Kant, is the establishment of a fully juridical condition of public right, where states obligate themselves to universal principles of law and mutually agreed principles of public right.

The second definitive article of *Perpetual Peace* addresses the establishment of international public right by prescribing that "The right of Nations shall be Based on a Federation of Free States."[47] Pace many realist critiques of Kant's international theory, the federation is not analogous to a coercive world state, but is meant as "a voluntary, progressively expanding association of free and independent states, whose defining purpose was merely to bring a permanent end to war."[48] Since states are in a continuous warlike condition under the Westphalia model, either preparing for war or engaged in one, Kant suggests that the federation would differ from traditional peace treaties. As Kant writes, the agreement to the *foedus pacificum* "would differ from a peace treaty (*pactum pacis*) in that the latter terminates *one* war, whereas the former would seek to end *all* wars for good."[49] In this regard, the federation is to be understood as the constitutional foundation that enshrines the normative regulative principles to which all consenting members obligate themselves.

Therefore, the federation relies on a voluntary dedication by each member state to observe the law established by the federation and to uphold their obligation to the principles of international right. In this sense, the federation has no centralized authority, but relies on self-policing by each individual state. By consenting to the formalities of the contract, states are in fact obligating themselves to the conditions of membership and to the encouragement of others to follow suit by maintaining the benefits associated with a pacific alliance. There are three normative principles that the federal constitution is meant to capture in regard to the commitments needed for state membership and for the establishment of public right. The first is a commitment to fulfill contractual agreements established between cooperating states in good faith. The second is based on a sense of internal freedom and a commitment not to intrude in the internal constitutions of cooperating states. The third dictates that wars should be limited to immediate threats to the federation and should always be constrained in such a way that the possibility of a future peace is not rendered impossible.

One practical question that immediately arises is to what degree this model would allow for international institutions or for the establishment of organizations designed to adjudicate the various complications that would undoubtedly occur within the federation. As we know from the previous chapter, Kant did not necessarily mean that the federation had an actual written constitution. Moreover, Kant did not provide guidelines for how states would organize various institutional aspects of the federation. This is because Kant's argument focuses specifically on the normative foundations that reason dictates as necessary for the establishment of a lawful condition of public right between all members of a shared earth. However, we can imagine that if the normative foundations of the federation were not codified and objectified in unambiguous terms, then misinterpretations and confusions would arise. Similarly, cooperating members would want verifiable proof of mutual consent and some institutional body would have to be entrusted to maintain such records. Additionally, Kant believed that international commerce and the interconnectedness of trade would grow exponentially under the *foedus pacificum* and it is reasonable to assume that current complications in international trade would also apply to the federation of free states. As can be imagined, transnational institutions and cooperative schemes would be needed to circumvent possible tensions between states and to adjudicate circumstances involving various conflicting claims to international right.

Despite the vagueness regarding the extent of cooperative schemes within the federation and Kant's lack of practical institutional design, movement towards a more cooperative multilateral and multisectoral network within the federation is possible. This is because there is no incongruity between the establishment of a lawful constitution and the establishment of procedures for the adjudication of disputes between cooperating states.[50] What Kant expressly prohibits is the establishment of a centralized authority. However, there is no inconsistency with procedural schemes between cooperative members as long as those federal procedures are in the first instance voluntary and do not authorize a centralized government with the power to coerce by force. Therefore, this provision does not exclude multilateral and multisectoral institutions designed to coordinate issues of public health, environment, mutual security, trade, migration and other international concerns. In addition, a system of arbitration could be established within the federation without the need for a world sovereign to mediate disputes. Through mutual deliberation agreements and a commitment to universal principles of right, it is fathomable that a fairly sophisticated network of multilateral bodies could regulate matters of cohabitation without the need for an overarching global sovereign. In this regard, the federation would not need to rely on *hard positivism* (i.e. a world government), but is based on a legal system of *soft positivism*, compliance rewards, communal pressure, legal arbitration, and possible threats of membership exclusion.

Nevertheless, it is true that the degree to which these multilateral institutions had any practical effect would depend on a commitment by states to police themselves and to uphold agreements decided through multilateral arbitration. In contrast to Kant's optimism about the rationality of republican cooperation, scholars who support the establishment of a world state advise that self-policing is not reliable enough to maintain rule compliance between federated states and that stronger institutional methods of enforcement are required. However, this critique is not altogether indicative of how states actually cooperate. Although institutional organizations under Kant's model do lack the power to enforce compliance, it does not necessarily mean that states would automatically fail to comply in opposition to established laws (especially if they were co-legislators of these laws). As Thomas Franck has illustrated, states often regulate themselves in relation to international covenants, especially if those international pacts are believed to be legitimate and representative of their overall interests. As Franck demonstrates, "there are obligations owed by states which they widely recognize as concomitants of community membership and which are accurate predictors of actual state behavior."[51] Franck elaborates by suggesting that, "in mature voluntarist communities . . . the capacity of members to obligate does not derive only from the specific consent of the members but as a concomitant of the status of membership."[52] In this regard, there is a strong pull for states to comply and uphold international commitments not only because they morally bind themselves through consent, but also because their membership status is derived from communal compliance and recognition.

In many respects Franck's conclusion regarding voluntarist communities captures the sense of normative obligation involved in the Kantian federation I have outlined. Thomas Donaldson reaches a similar conclusion when he writes that "Kant hoped to modify existing practice to allow a somewhat more centralized order and thus reduce the uncertainty of international rules while preserving the basic sovereignty of individual states."[53] Under the Kantian federation as outlined above, states play a primary role in reforming international ethics toward the demands of practical reason and the establishment of a universal law that is consistent with the idea of a united general will and the categorical imperative. This normative commitment is maintained on two fronts. First, only republican states that uphold Kantian principles of domestic justice can be considered sovereign in the true sense and this sovereignty is by design obligated to universal principles of public right.[54] Second, the ideal of a federation of free states is what like-minded states must seek to approximate and therefore should obligate themselves to universal principles that are consistent with reforming the existing order toward the metaphysical ideal. However, there is a third level necessary for a true condition of public right. For it is not until Kant introduces his most radical element of cosmopolitan law that a more profound sense of a global civil condition is produced.

### C. Cosmopolitan Law, Cosmopolitan Right and Global Justice

Without a doubt, the most novel aspect of Kant's international theory is located in the third definitive article of *Perpetual Peace* and the provision that "Cosmopolitan Right shall be limited to Conditions of Universal Hospitality."[55] Despite the fact that both the third definitive article and Kant's discussion of cosmopolitan law in the *Metaphysics of Morals* represent his most radical shift away from natural law, it also remained the least-developed aspect of his tripartite of law. Although Kant claimed that the maxims of "cosmopolitan right are easy to formulate and assess on account of its analogy with international right,"[56] the extrapolation of cosmopolitan jurisprudence has not been as straightforward and easy as Kant had assumed. This is because there remains considerable debate surrounding the logical extent that cosmopolitan law is to have on creating universal obligations in relation to the idea of an equal earth in common (this debate will be further discussed in the next section). Where widespread agreement seems to exist is that cosmopolitan law was meant to expand the scope of public right beyond a strict state-centered focus to one that encompassed all members of the earth. As Charles Covell suggests, cosmopolitan law "was the body of public international law . . . constituting the juridical framework for the intercourse of men and states, considered in their status as bearers of the attributes of citizenship in an ideal universal state that extended to embrace all mankind."[57] What remains a source of disagreement, however, is the extent to which Kant's universal citizenship should establish egalitarian principles of justice and to what magnitude this justice creates obligations between various communities of the world.

Some scholars have suggested that Kant's cosmopolitan law is synonymous with contemporary discussions of universal human rights and that cosmopolitan law demands a minimal threshold for which individual freedoms cannot be violated.[58] Others have dismissed the capacious readings of cosmopolitan law and have suggested that it is nothing more than a supplement to contemporary understandings of international trade law, merely stipulating how states should treat visiting foreign-nationals engaged in international commerce.[59] Adding to the confusion, some cosmopolitans have claimed that Kant's cosmopolitan law is an attempt to create additional institutions for the expression of individual autonomy under the growing interdependence of globalization.[60] Although various interpretations abound and many Kantians remain agnostic in respect to the aforementioned interpretations, it is broadly accepted that Kant sought to create a level of cosmopolitan law that would obligate both states and individuals to the hospitable treatment of all human beings regardless of their citizenship or national origin. As was discussed in Chapter 2, this conclusion is clear because Kant proclaims this much when he wrote: "hospitality means the right of a stranger not to be treated with hostility when he arrives on someone else's territory."[61] Although Kant maintains that individuals can be turned away, especially if they act in a lawless manner, he also stipulates that this can only be done if it is "done without causing his death."[62] Kant distinguishes hospitality as a form of right versus merely a type of philanthropy by arguing that anyone could "claim a *right to resort*, for all men are entitled to present themselves in the society of others by virtue of their right to communal possession of the earth's surface."[63] Kant goes on to ground this principle in his cosmopolitan teleology by suggesting that "no-one originally has any greater right than anyone else to occupy any particular portion of the earth" and "we are here concerned not with philanthropy, but with right."[64] Although states are not obligated to grant all visitors communal membership, for Kant believes this involves a further contractual agreement between individuals, Kant does impose the provision that states cannot act inhospitably toward foreign visitors.

Nevertheless, textual evidence makes it clear that Kant does not limit the extent of the third definitive article to the condition of internal federated hospitality. This is because Kant believes that hospitality is necessary in order to create "those conditions which make it possible for [individuals] to attempt to enter into relations with the native inhabitants. In this way, continents distant from each other can enter into peaceful mutual relations which may eventually be regulated by public laws, thus bringing the human race nearer and nearer to a cosmopolitan constitution."[65] Although this might seem limited in scope, this aspect of cosmopolitan law is in fact considerably more robust than it appears. This is because the clause not only dictates how states must treat all human beings, but also demands that civilized relationships be established between any communities that have contact with one another. One such example is in relation to colonial expansionism and the requirement that states cannot engage in "inhospitable conduct" in their discovery of new lands. As Kant strictly proclaims:

> If the settlement is made so far from where that people resides that there is no encroachment on anyone's use of land, the right to settle is not open to doubt. But if these peoples are shepherds or hunters (like the Hottentots, the Tungusi, or most of the American Indian nations) who depend for their sustenance on great open regions, this settlement may not take place by force but only by contract, and indeed by a contract that does not take advantage of the ignorance of those inhabitants with respect to ceding their lands.[66]

The potency of the third definitive article is that it moves beyond the internal affairs of federated members to stipulate practical standards of hospitality that all states must maintain in relation to all global communities, especially non-state communities affected by colonial/market expansion. In this regard, the third article makes three dramatic claims that directly diminish the role of state sovereignty. First, cosmopolitan law demands the hospitable treatment of all humans by all states regardless of nationality and locality. In consideration of this, states can no longer dictate the treatment of foreign-nationals based on self-interest, but must prevent hostilities that might violate an individual's legal claim to hospitable treatment. Second, this legal condition for hospitable treatment is to be grounded as an actual legal right that would be enshrined in the pacific constitution and act as a condition for federated membership. As several international lawyers have suggested, the formal codification of cosmopolitan right is reminiscent of contemporary discussions of universal human rights and it could be argued that there is a strong degree of connection between the two.[67] Third, any dealings with communities outside the federation must conform to the principles of cosmopolitan law and to peaceful mutual relations that will allow the potentiality for a future civil condition. In light of this, states cannot hold inconsistent internal/external relations, but must treat all non-member communities with a sense of equally valid consideration as long as those communities do not directly threaten the existence of the pacific federation.

In this regard, Kant's cosmopolitan law provides the judicious atmosphere necessary to regulate global interactions in line with reason and the establishment of a civil condition of global public right. By inscribing the requirements of cosmopolitan right into global public law, Kant seeks to eradicate various enticements to war and to create a lawful order where the violations of rights are no longer a sanctioned action under the prerogative of absolute state sovereignty, but are considered violations of international legal covenants. In the words of Kant, "the idea of a cosmopolitan right is therefore not fantastic and overstrained; it is a necessary complement to the unwritten code of political and international right, transforming it into a universal right of humanity . . . [and] only under this condition can we flatter ourselves that we are continually advancing toward a perpetual peace."[68]

## III. The Scope of Federation in a Cosmopolitan Order

Before examining the Kantian vision of cosmopolitanism outlined thus far in relation to contemporary international relations theory, it is important to further discuss whether or not Kant's cosmopolitanism should be understood as advocating a world federation of free states or as actually espousing the establishment of a centralized cosmopolitan republic. This predication is important to clarify since there remains considerable disagreement in contemporary political theory regarding Kant's ultimate global order. As was mentioned earlier, scholars from various disciplines have offered highly contested interpretations of Kant's cosmopolitan vision. Generally, the debate surrounds perceived inconsistencies in what scholars have labeled Kant's ideal-theory for a universal cosmopolitan purpose and Kant's non-ideal treatment of international relations. There are roughly three schools of thought within the debate.[69]

The first position suggests that Kant actually envisioned a world republic or a universal society and sought to create a community of individuals independent from states. This conclusion is reached either through interpretations that seek to rectify contradictions in Kant's cosmopolitan teleology or by those who suggest that Kant's moral and political philosophy can only be made consistent through a world republic reading. As Hedley Bull has written, Kantian "imperatives enjoin not coexistence and cooperation among states but rather the overthrow of the system of states and its replacement by a cosmopolitan society."[70] Some Kantian scholars have also endorsed a similar interpretation, maintaining that Kantian ideal-theory requires individuals to live under common civil laws of a cosmopolitan republic and that the idea of a federation was merely Kant's second-best ideal.[71] In addition, Hegelians are particularly cautious of Kant's cosmopolitan intentions, suggesting Kant's desire to overthrow self-determination and the right to self-protection afforded to autonomous communities by the Hobbesian paradigm. Although direct textual evidence often suggests the opposite conclusion, many Hegelian and realist scholars insist that Kant had hegemonic aspirations for a universal world state.[72]

An alternative to this interpretation is that Kant dismissed a world republic as dangerous to freedom and had considerable concerns about its potential for unbridled despotism. This interpretation is based on the fact that Kant explicitly argued for a global federation while attacking the idea of a world republic.[73] Attempting to make Kant's federation defendable, those who favor this reading cite substantive textual evidence in support of a federation of free states and delineate this from Kant's adamant stance against a world republic. As Kant himself proclaimed, "such a [world] state is in turn even more dangerous to freedom, for it may lead to fearful despotism . . . distrust must force men to form an order which is not a cosmopolitan commonwealth under a single ruler, but a lawful federation under a commonly accepted international right."[74] Kant clarifies this stance further when he adds, "this federation does not aim to acquire any power like that of a state, but merely to preserve and secure the freedom of each state in itself, along with that of the other confederated states."[75] Proponents of this view also propose that the first definitive article of *Perpetual Peace*, that the civil constitution of every state shall be republican, provides for continuity in the transition from Kant's moral philosophy to his political theory, since every state within the federation is obligated to be "representative and to respect human rights" without the presence of any overarching global authority.[76]

Nevertheless, there is a third position that provides somewhat of a link between the two aforementioned arguments. This interpretation stipulates that Kant did indeed favor a federation for practical and empirical reasons, but also believed that something more than the federation was needed to fulfill the ultimate cosmopolitan ideal. The explanation behind this argument is that Kant saw a global federation as an evolutionary stage in a more pragmatic move toward something resembling a world republic.[77] However, unlike the world republic interpretation mentioned above, this position does not assume that Kant necessarily advocated a world republic, but was only optimistic about a future movement toward a broader cosmopolitan political order.[78] The most persuasive aspect of this interpretation is that it is able to maintain Kant's firm stance that any movement toward transnational or global institutions would be voluntary and unforced. Although this position does not immediately rule out the possibility of a future world republic, as Matthias Lutz-Bachmann has argued,[79] it still accommodates the textual fact that a world republic was not Kant's immediate choice and that he had considerable reservations about the creation of a world republic.

A reconciliation of these three positions might be possible if we are willing to understand Kant's cosmopolitan theory as having serious concerns about the formation of a world republic, while also understanding that given the right conditions, the establishment of voluntary transnational cosmopolitan institutions is not ruled out. However, as was mentioned in Section II, the conditions necessary to consider this political order would have to be consistent with Kant's principles of external freedom and public right. For it is clear that the establishment of these institutions could only be justified on Kantian grounds if there were also guarantees that individual freedoms would not be threatened by a possible despotic world order. This conclusion is reasonable based simply on the fact that Kant's political theory is preoccupied with the freedom of the moral agent.[80] Therefore, the distinction that is being suggested by the third interpretation is an important one, but one that leads immediately back to considering the world federation interpretation over a world republic reading. For it seems that Kant was only optimistic about a future order with more institutional complexity than his initial federation of states, but was also unwilling to assign an overarching governmental structure as the best means to fulfill the cosmopolitan ideal. As was pointed out earlier, this position does not rule out the possibility of future cosmopolitan institutions, but it does stipulate that any movement toward transnational institutions must be completely voluntary and strongly anchored against the possibility of global despotism. If we are willing to consider this interpretation as plausible, then it also seems reasonable to assume that a system of checks and balances would be necessary to regulate these global institutions and that individual member states would maintain some right to defend themselves against possible tyranny.[81] In this regard, whatever form of global governance that is to evolve from the federation would still maintain the original underpinnings of the federal system and would provide for state succession when the original constitutional procedures were violated. Kant himself demands this much when he writes that the federation "must be an alliance which can be terminated at any time, so that it must be renewed periodically."[82]

Although the reconciliation above represents a plausible bridge between many ambiguities in Kant, it is nevertheless unnecessary to reach an immediate conclusion in order to provide a reconstruction of Kantian cosmopolitanism. What is necessary is that a federation of free states is understood as an important step in Kant's cosmopolitanism. It is also important to understand that Kant made certain not to pretend to understand the complexities of any practical cosmopolitan order. As Kant suggests, a cosmopolitan federation will be the result of international norm building and a recognized need for mutual coexistence that "will gradually spread further and further."[83] In this light, Kant's cosmopolitanism has no particular predictive institutional complexion because a global order will be the result of millions of variables, for which no design could foresee or account. In addition, considering Kant's belief in the progression of human enlightenment, a future form of political organization could still be invented and there is no reason to assume that Kant believed that a world republic had to be the only design that could effectively regulate a future cosmopolitan order.

Moreover, there is no theoretical reason why a federation model necessarily contradicts cosmopolitan justice and morality as some claim. Many contemporary cosmopolitans acknowledge that moral cosmopolitanism could be perfectly compatible in principle with a Kantian federation and its corresponding opposition to a world state. As Brian Barry and Charles Beitz indicate, "it may be that the best way to realize the ideals of moral cosmopolitanism lies in organizing humanity in a society of states that retain their separate statehood while subjecting themselves to the requirements of international covenants or some universal principles."[84] Therefore, whether or not Kant subconsciously sought a future world republic or required the continued maintenance of a federation of free states is immaterial. This is because it is clear that a federation of free states was his starting point and that any movement from this cosmopolitan foundation would have to be consistent with Kant's moral principles of external freedom, voluntary co-legislation and public right. It is from this basic premise that a further exploration of Kant's cosmopolitanism will be advanced in relation to the role of states and to contemporary understandings of state sovereignty.

## IV. KANT'S COSMOPOLITANISM AND ITS RELATIONSHIP TO CONTEMPORARY INTERNATIONAL RELATIONS THEORY

There are considerable implications stemming from Kant's cosmopolitanism in relation to the role of states in contemporary international relations theory. As mentioned throughout this chapter, there has been substantial confusion regarding how states figure into Kant's cosmopolitan vision. On the one hand, international relations theorists like Hedley Bull and Martin Wright have concluded that Kantianism seeks to replace the state system with the establishment of a cosmopolitan republic. On the other hand, there is also a belief by some cosmopolitans that Kant's international order is too minimalist to instigate any real global reform and that his theory of sovereignty surrenders his cosmopolitan principles to the absolute authority of states.[85]

However, these critiques do not capture the complexity involved in Kant's cosmopolitan federation. The confusion arises from the fact that Kant is both unwilling to endorse a world republic while also reluctant to accept the possibility that absolute sovereignty can support a cosmopolitan condition of public right. As we have seen throughout this chapter, Kant did not agree with those who advocated the inauguration of a world state. In fact, Kant sustained a very consistent critique of world government and clearly sought to provide an alternative to both the Westphalian and world state archetypes. Although there are indications that Kant hoped for a continued movement toward a broader cosmopolitan order, this order was to be propagated through internal state reform and a consensual movement toward multilateral cooperation. Nevertheless, despite the fact that Kant's federation is predicated on the willingness of states to obligate themselves to formal principles of public right, the conditions to which states must commit are not as minimalist and weak as some critics suggest. This is because the members of a Kantian federation already preserve domestic justice and a dedication to universal principles of right. As Teson rightly points out, "only an alliance defined by the definitive articles is morally justified" and membership is tightly restricted to states that are committed to uphold these universal principles.[86] In this sense, sovereignty is conditional within the Kantian federation. It is conditioned on the normative principles of popular sovereignty, conditions of public right, equal justice, external freedom and universal law.

Therefore, the concept of state sovereignty is both transformed and weakened in three significant ways by Kant's legal tripartite. First, Kant's sovereignty differs from traditional Hobbesian definitions that emphasize absolute claims to bounded territory and established power bases. Under the proposed Kantian model, the definition of sovereignty is premised on the ideal of popular sovereignty and domestic justice. Second, the condition of enjoying external freedom as a sovereign, and therefore of being truly able to exercise sovereign freedom, is contingent on the rule of law and the establishment of a global condition of public right. This demands commitment to universal principles that are sometimes beyond the prerogative of immediate state self-interest. Within the Kantian model outlined, it is only through federal membership that a legitimate claim to right can be maintained and instituted. Therefore, membership demands conformity to universal principles that directly reduce claims of absolute sovereignty and suppress international policies based on self-interest alone. Third, cosmopolitan law in effect supersedes state sovereignty in that it demands compliance to universal principles of human worth regardless of citizenship or national origin. States no longer have final authority concerning how to treat individuals internally or externally. Under the proposed Kantian model, a state cannot violate individual rights internally because the first article requires popular sovereignty and a condition of domestic justice. States are also unable to violate individual rights externally or to harm foreigners (visitors or visited) because the second and third articles prohibit any interference with another constitution and disallow the ill treatment of any visiting or visited person.

In this regard, my Kantian model moves beyond the conception of a *modus vivendi* because it establishes a normative society based on the general acceptance of common legal principles and on the creation of interest-trumping norms. Whereas a *modus vivendi* is based entirely on power relationships and therefore limits cooperation to the realm of self-interest alone, a Kantian federation is based on a universal normative order

111

where principles of public right supersede alterations based on self-interest. Nevertheless, this is not to say that self-interest is not a motivating factor in maintaining the Kantian federation. Kant clearly suggests that it is in the self-interest of states to organize themselves into a lawful condition of public right. The difference is that the Kantian federation seeks to establish a society whose members accept to be governed in the pursuit of their self-interest by the priority of common norms. From this acceptance, federated members reject the principle that modifications are possible without those modifications first being validated by universal considerations.

As a result, the Kantian model outlined in this chapter compliments and bolsters many international relations thinkers that have drawn influence from Kant's political theory in their discussions of international society. Andrew Hurrell and Andrew Linklater have both attempted to provide a consistent and relevant treatment of Kantian universal ethics within the study of international relations.[87] Nevertheless, both these treatments have started from a premise of Kant's federation and have only loosely justified why this position should or could be adopted. Taking this into account, the model provided in this chapter fits soundly with Linklater's claim that Kant's international relations theory sought to implement an "ethical community in which the ends of rational beings are harmonized in accordance with rational principles imposed upon themselves."[88] Nevertheless, the Kantian model that is advocated within this book is considerably more robust than that usually argued by most liberal internationalists and members of the English School. This is because Kant seeks to move beyond a basic society of states to also include stronger principles of cosmopolitan law and a sense of human interconnection, where individuals in fact treat each other *as if they were* mutual citizens of the world.[89] As explained in previous chapters, Kant's cosmopolitan legal theory moves beyond the establishment of a purely "international" order, in that it calls for significant changes to be made to the current system of international law, so that a global legal system can help to foster cosmopolitan principles of individualism, equality and universality.

In relation to other contemporary theories of international relations, the Kantian model sustains differences from the minimalist theory suggested by John Rawls in *The Law of Peoples*.[90] This is because, unlike Rawls, Kant is unwilling to accept a hierarchical ranking of societies and the various degrees to which these societies secure justice.[91] In this respect, the federation creates a universal ethical order because it is clear that the first definitive article of *Perpetual Peace* mandates the formal existence of popular sovereignty and a minimal sense of domestic justice based on Kant's *Metaphysics of Morals*. Since federal membership is formalized exclusively on representative government and a dedication to approximating the requirements of public right, many of Rawls' "decent" societies would fail to meet these Kantian requirements and would be disallowed membership. However, this rejection does not mean that some level of cooperation could not be maintained between members and non-members. This is because Kant explicitly claims that relations between societies are unavoidable and that they must be maintained in such a way that the potentiality of a future civil condition is possible. In this regard, as outlined in the previous chapter, the members of the federation should extend the reach of cosmopolitan norms to non-members and encourage conformity, but they cannot accept these societies as being sovereign representatives and must assure that they are not in fact providing assistance to despotic regimes. In addition, members of the Kantian federation must reject states that maintain violations to cosmopolitan right and who directly threaten the universal principles established by the pacific alliance. Despite the fact that Rawls borrows the term a *law of peoples* from Kant, his theory does not provide a significant law of peoples like Kant's cosmopolitanism because it is too relativistic in its willingness to abdicate certain universal human protections in exchange for the supremacy of localized systems of order.[92]

Nevertheless, there are two contemporary cosmopolitan positions that both resonate and encapsulate many of the normative elements involved with the Kantian federation as it has been outlined so far. The first position comes from what Jürgen Habermas has labeled "The Kantian Project" and advances the idea of a global order based on various "stages and degrees of constitutionalization," where the continual establishment of robust international law can bring states closer and closer to a cosmopolitan order.[93] Unlike those who favor the establishment of a world republic, Habermas argues that various empirical trends in international law still favor the idea that a more robust form of cosmopolitan law can be established from current legal regimes.[94] In this regard, Habermas fully rejects the need for a world state and the establishment of a world authority with coercive ability. According to Habermas, it is theoretically possible to have a world society based on federalist notions of divided sovereignty, multilevel governance and through the establishment of a political constitution that constrains power versus constructing political authority.[95] As Habermas suggests, "a political constitution primarily geared to setting limits to

113

power founds a 'rule of law' that can normatively shape existing power relations, regardless of their democratic origins, and direct the exercise of political power into legal channels."[96] By doing so, states create legal and extra-legal norms that become increasingly "self-referential," "constructive" and "part of a circular learning process."[97]

In many ways Habermas' conception of *constitutionalization* captures the essence of the Kantian model that has been outlined. This is because Habermas rejects the need for a world state, while understanding that a robust cosmopolitan legal order could be established through an iterative process of law creation that seeks to restrict global power. However, it is important to note that the model presented by Habermas differs somewhat from the Kantian vision outlined in this book. First, it is unclear whether Habermas would endorse or reject the idea of a written cosmopolitan constitution as an anchoring legal element within the constitutionalization process, as was advocated in Chapter 2. Although he would agree with my position that constitutions are not limited to establishing political authority, and can be used as a method to objectify normative commitments, his concept of constitutionalization seems to mirror something closer to Kant's broadened constitutionalism. This is because Habermas suggests that constitutionalism represents the totality of various laws that interlock and mutually reinforce each other to create a legal order. In this regard, Habermas' conception of constitutionalization does not explore the idea of a formal constitution per se, but focuses on a system of laws that could underpin and reinforce the Kantian project. Although there is no theoretical reason why a cosmopolitan constitution could not form a significant part of Habermas' project as a complement to constitutionalization, Habermas himself does not examine this possibility and it therefore highlights a difference between our projects. Secondly, in contrast to my interpretation, Habermas believes that Kant "to the very end . . . advocated the idea of a world republic, even though he proposed the 'surrogate' of a league of nations as a first stage toward realizing such a commonwealth of nations."[98] Consequently, Habermas suggests that Kant was too "hasty" in favoring a world state position and that Kant was wrong to suggest that the federation could only act as a surrogate in light of practical considerations.[99] Although Habermas believes that "republican states can remain subjects of a world constitution without a world government," he believes that Kant does not clearly realize this possibility. However, as has been suggested in this chapter, there is an alternative reading available to bridge this perceived divide, and the world state interpretation of Kant is not as obvious and consistent as Habermas and others often assume. In addition, the reading presented by Habermas suggests that Kant could not have changed his mind later in life and that Kant's concern about transitions from theory to practice are somehow overly "flawed." This is a particularly troublesome position for Habermas to maintain, considering his claim that the relationship between theory and practice is vital if we are to understand the "idealizing presuppositions of everyday practices."[100] Considering Kant's many discussions about theory and practice, it seems rather dogmatic to suggest that Kant could not have continually rethought his political philosophy in light of practical circumstances, especially with an eye toward moving theory to practice. Furthermore, despite Habermas' focus on an iterative process of constitutionalization, it would seem that he fails to fully appreciate Kant's reiterative system of moving toward a cosmopolitan condition. As discussed in the last section, we can understand that Kant saw the federal model as only the first iteration toward a cosmopolitan constitution, while leaving the final complexion of this order open to future deliberation and public reason. What Kant provides are the normative conditions necessary for this cosmopolitan enthusiasm to naturally progress without conflict. Whether this would finally culminate in something like a world republic, or remain a minimalist federation of independent states, the idea is that this result would be seen as legitimated by public reason, since it would be in line with Kant's basic guarantees of international and cosmopolitan right as outlined in the last section.

Nevertheless, this still leaves us with the consideration as to how collective decision making can legitimately take place both within and beyond the borders of the federation. It is in relation to this concern that a second cosmopolitan theory seems to share various normative elements with the Kantian vision suggested thus far. This theory is generally known as *cosmopolitan democracy* and advocates the position that cosmopolitan principles of human worth, as well as democratic procedures for autonomous co-legislation, should be institutionalized into a more robust system of global governance. This theory corresponds well with the Kantian model that has been outlined because, unlike some arguments for establishing a world state in order to guarantee a robust form of democratic citizenship,[101] most forms of cosmopolitan democracy promote a system of multilateral and transnational global governance that still leaves room for states to determine significant aspects of domestic policy.[102] The cosmopolitan democracy model therefore endorses the Kantian shift away from the idea of coercive global institutions to a system of democratic institutions based on consent and a dedication to self-regulating normative principles. However, unlike the vacuum of Kant's institutional design, the cosmopolitan democracy model suggests that states should commit themselves to additional democratic principles in order to create global institutions that can tackle problems of global cohabitation. Although this does not mean that states necessarily give up their independence, it does suggest that states would have to bind themselves to additional procedures of global interdependence and to the final outcomes of a mutually agreed governance process. As David Held writes, "by inscribing a set of democratic rights into a constitution, a political community commits itself both to safeguarding individuals in certain ways and to protecting the community as a democratic association; for these rights are the rules and procedures which cannot, without inconsistency and contradiction, be eliminated: they are the self-binding conditions of democracy."[103]

Prima facie, an additional commitment to democratic procedures does not seem to necessarily conflict with the normative foundations involved with a Kantian federation. In fact, it illustrates one possible move toward a broader cosmopolitan order that might be provided without also establishing a centralized world government. One important feature about the relationship between cosmopolitan democracy and Kant's cosmopolitanism is the crucial element of consent and self-binding obligation. If a global federation is to function based on institutionalized commitments to a multilateral or multisectoral system of global governance, these institutions will need to contain important protective principles that all participating states believe as self-regulating. In this sense, states would have to see themselves as participating with others in grounding the authority of those moral rules and that these rules increase an equal condition of co-legislation and public right. However, the most important similarity between cosmopolitan democracy and Kantian cosmopolitanism is the stress that both theories place on the need to establish universal principles of justice beyond immediate state self-interest. In the case of this chapter, the focus has not been on what international law has provided historically based on realist assumptions, but on what law should provide globally in relation to the normative foundations necessary to create a condition of cosmopolitan law. The assumption has therefore been a Kantian one in direct contrast to the realist position, that mutual cohabitation and external freedom is not possible without a normative ethical system of public right and universal law.

## V. CONCLUSION

The focus of this chapter has been to provide some clarification in respect to the role of states and state sovereignty within Kant's cosmopolitanism. By examining the various ambiguities involved in the formation of a Kantian federation, it has been argued that Kant did not seek to create a world state as several international relations theorists suggest. In fact, the direct opposite has been indicated and it has been shown that states actually play a significant role in any future move toward a cosmopolitan order. In addition, it has also been argued that despite Kant's unwillingness to support the possibility of a coercive world government, his theory still manages to provide a minimal foundation for a coherent normative order based on universal principles and the concomitance to those principles by like-minded states.

Although Kant provides a fairly consistent outline for a possible cosmopolitan federation, there still remain significant ambiguities that future scholarship must redevelop, reconstruct and work through. At least three major areas of reconstruction and development are needed in order to provide a truly comprehensive and tenable account of Kantian federation. The areas that Kantian cosmopolitan vision must seek to rectify are based on questions surrounding the institutional complexion of the federation, its scheme of distributive justice, its relationship with various cultural perspectives, and with how a transition from theory to practice might be sustained. In other words, Kantian cosmopolitans need to provide additional provisions for how the federation will function institutionally; how it deals with burdened states; the relationship it maintains between itself and repressive or rogue states/cultures; and how it will rectify problems associated with global inequality. It is essential that further theories are developed for these concerns before Kantian cosmopolitanism can have a universally convincing moral claim to reform the existing global system. It is for this reason that the next chapter attempts to understand the relationship between cultural diversity and Kant's cosmopolitanism, while the final two chapters attempt to extrapolate some normative principles for a Kantian system of global distributive justice and various links between Kantian theory and actual world practice.

## NOTES

1. An interpretation of this kind can be attributed to Hedley Bull, *The Anarchical Society* (London: Macmillan, 1977).

2. For the origin of this argument see, G. W. F. Hegel, *The Philosophy of Right*, S. W. Dyde (trans.) (New York: Prometheus Books, 1996), especially Part III.

3. For a radical interpretation of the world republic argument, see Sidney Axinn, "Kant on World Government," in G. Funke & T. Seebohm (eds), *Proceedings of the Sixth International Kantian Congress*, vol. 2 (Washington, DC: University Press of America, 1989), pp. 243–51. For an interpretation suggesting a world federation, see Fernando Teson, "Kantian International Liberalism," in D. Maple & T. Nardin (eds), *International Society: Diverse Ethical Perspectives* (Princeton: Princeton University Press, 1998).

4. For an interesting discussion of the ambiguity involved in Kant's concept of sovereignty see Antonio Franceschet, *Kant and Liberal Internationalism: Sovereignty, Justice and Global Reform* (New York: Palgrave, 2002).

5. One interpretation of this kind can be found in F. H. Hinsley, *Power and the Pursuit of Peace* (Cambridge: Cambridge University Press, 1963).

6. Immanuel Kant, "On the Common Saying: This May be True in Theory, But it Does not Apply in Practice," in Hans Reiss (ed.), H. B Nisbet (trans.) *Kant's Political Writings* (Cambridge: Cambridge University Press, 1970), p. 92. [8:312]

7. In 1794, many international lawyers referred to the Treaty of Westphalia and the Treaty of Utrecht in order to justify the dividing of Poland by larger states. Kalevi J. Holsti, *Peace and War: Armed Conflicts and International Order 1648-1989* (Cambridge: Cambridge University Press, 1992). Kant was highly critical of these justifications.

8. Kant, "Perpetual Peace: A Philosophical Sketch," in Hans Reiss (ed.), H. B. Nisbet (trans.), *Kant's Political Writings* (Cambridge: Cambridge University Press, 1970), p. 103. [8:355]

9. This is a complicated aspect of Kant's political theory. Unfortunately, the subject is too complex for a general summary and I cannot deal with it here. However, for a good discussion of this aspect of Kantian philosophy, see Georg Cavallar, *Kant and the Theory and Practice of International Right* (Cardiff: University of Wales Press, 1999), especially Chapters. 3, 4, 5 and 6. Also see Brian Orend, *War and International Justice: A Kantian Perspective* (Waterloo: Wilfrid Laurier University Press, 2001).

10. Christian Wolff, *The Laws of Nations Treated According to a Scientific Method*, H. Drake (trans.) (Oxford: Clarendon Press, 1934).

11. Kant, "On the Common Saying: This may be True in Theory, But it Does not Apply in Practice," in Hans Reiss (ed.), H. B. Nisbet (trans.), *Kant's Political Writings* (Cambridge: Cambridge University Press, 1970), p. 90. [8:310–11]

12. Kant, "Perpetual Peace," p. 96. [8:346]

13. Unlike the "sorry comforters," Kant defends the peaceful intent of Saint-Pierre and Rousseau. See Kant, "Perpetual Peace," p. 104. [8: 355–56]. Kant also defends Saint-Pierre and Rousseau in "Idea for a Universal History with a Cosmopolitan Purpose," in Hans. Reiss (ed.), H. B. Nisbet (trans.), *Kant's Political Writings* (Cambridge: Cambridge University Press, 1970), pp. 47–8. [8:24]

14. There is considerable disagreement about how far Rousseau was willing to give a federation any coercive power. For a distinctive anti-federalist interpretation, see David Fidler, "Desperately Clinging to Grotian and Kantian Sheep: Rousseau's Attempt to Escape from the State of War," in I. Clarks & I. Neumann (eds), *Classical Theories of International Relations* (Basingstoke: Macmillan Press, 1996). For a more pro-global institution interpretation, see Grace Roosevelt, *Reading Rousseau in the Nuclear Age* (Philadelphia: Temple University Press, 1990).

15. According to Rousseau, "well constituted" states are generally republican in nature, but always representative of the general will.

16. Kant, "Perpetual Peace," pg. 99. [8:349]

17. This Kantian assumption is yet another area for considerable contention between scholars. Many have attempted to exonerate Kant by proving this as an empirical fact. However, there are several scholars who maintain that democracies are only less likely to fight one another at best and that Kant's assumption is empirically incorrect. Needless to say, this debate is beyond the scope of this chapter. For the first view, see John Oneal and Bruce Russett, "The Kantian Peace: The Pacific Benefits of Democracy, Interdependence, and International Organizations, 1885–1992," *World Politics*, 52 (1999). For an overview of this theory in general and some critiques, see R. J. Rummel, "Democracies ARE Less Warlike Than Other Regimes," *European Journal of International Relations*, vol. 1 (4) (1999), pp. 429–56. Also see Bruce Russett, *Grasping the Democratic Peace* (Princeton: Princeton University Press, 1993) and Michael Doyle, "Kant, Liberal Legacies, and Foreign Affairs," *Philosophy and Public Affairs*, 12 (3) (1983), pp. 204–35 and 12 (4) (1983), pp. 323–53. For two more contemporary discussions on this subject, see Michael Doyle, "Kant and Liberal Internationalism," in P. Kleingeld (ed.), *Toward Perpetual Peace and Other Writings on Politics, Peace and History* (New Haven: Yale University Press, 2006) and Otfried Hoffe, *Kant's Cosmopolitan Theory of Law and Peace* (Cambridge: Cambridge University Press, 2006), pp. 177–84.

18. Kant's explanation for this conclusion rests on the idea that "the consent of the citizen is required to decide whether or not war is to be declared, [and that] it is very natural that they will have great hesitation embarking on so dangerous an enterprise." Kant, "Perpetual Peace," p. 100. [8:352]

19. Immanuel Kant, *The Metaphysics of Morals*, M. Gregor (ed. & trans.) (Cambridge: Cambridge University Press, 1996), p. 24. [6:230]

20. Kant, "Perpetual Peace," pp. 107–8. [8:360]

21. Thomas Pogge, "Kant's Theory of Justice," *Kant-Studien*, 79 (1988).

22. Mary Gregor, "Kant's Approach to Constitutionalism," in A. Rosenbaum (ed.), *Constitutionalism: The Philosophical Dimension* (New York: Greenwood Press, 1988), p. 71.

23. Kant, *The Metaphysics of Morals*, p. 41. [6:246]

24. Kant, "Perpetual Peace," p. 99. [8:349]

25. Kant's justification for this argument can be found in *The Metaphysics of Morals*, pp. 89–95. [6:311–18]

26. Kant, "Perpetual Peace," p. 101. [8:352]

27. Ibid., p. 99. [8:349–50]

28. Kant, *The Metaphysics of Morals*, pp. 90–91. [6:313–14]

29. The exchange of liberal democracy and Kantian republicanism is common. For a good discussion regarding the various views on this subject, see Franceschet, *Kant and Liberal Internationalism*, especially Chapter. 4.

30. Cavallar, *Kant and the Theory and Practice of International Right*, p. 57.

31. Kant, "Perpetual Peace," p. 101. [8:350]

32. Kant, *The Metaphysics of Morals*, loc. cit. [6:313–14]

33. The idea of a "united general will" is open to several conflicting interpretations and it is beyond the scope of this chapter to flush out the various distinctions. For an

interesting discussion of the major interpretations and the adding of an additional view, see Katrin Flikschuh, *Kant and Modern Political Philosophy* (Cambridge: Cambridge University Press, 2000), Chapter. 5. Also see Mary Gregor, *The Laws of Freedom* (Oxford: Blackwell Press, 1963).

34. Kant, "Perpetual Peace," p. 118, footnote. [8:374]
35. Kant, *The Metaphysics of Morals*, p. 95. [6:319]
36. Kant, "The Idea for a Universal History with a Cosmopolitan Purpose," p. 46. [8:23]
37. Franceschet, *Kant and Liberal Internationalism*.
38. Kant, *The Metaphysics of Morals*, p. 112. [6:340]
39. Ibid.
40. Franceschet, *Kant and Liberal Internationalism*, p. 50.
41. Jeremy Waldron, "Kant's Theory of the State," in P. Kleingeld (ed.), *Toward Perpetual Peace and Other Writings on Politics, Peace and History* (New Haven: Yale University Press, 2006), p. 187.
42. Ibid., p. 183.
43. Kant, *The Metaphysics of Morals*, p. 24. [6:230]
44. Immanuel Kant, Appendix, "Transcendental Logic II, Dialectic, I, Ideas in General," in J. M. D. Meiklejohn (trans.), *The Critique of Pure Reason* (New York: The Colonial Press, 1900). [3:247]
45. Kant, "The Idea for a Universal History with a Cosmopolitan Purpose," p. 47. [8:24]
46. Ibid., pg. 50. [8:27–8]
47. Kant, "Perpetual Peace," p. 102. [8:354]
48. Charles Covell, *Kant and the Law of Peace: A Study in the Philosophy of International Law and International Relations* (New York: Palgrave, 1998), p. 124.
49. Kant, "Perpetual Peace," p. 104. [8:356]
50. Covell, *Kant and the Law of Peace*, p. 138.
51. Thomas M. Franck, *The Power of Legitimacy Among Nations* (Oxford: Oxford University Press, 1990), p. 192.
52. Ibid., p. 193.
53. Thomas Donaldson, "Kant's Global Rationalism," in D. Maple & T. Nardin (eds), *Traditions of International Ethics* (Cambridge: Cambridge University Press, 1992), p. 148.
54. A contemporary variation that explores this foundation as the basis of a future system of international law can be found in Allan Buchanan, *Justice, Legitimacy, and Self-Determination: Moral Foundations for International Law* (Oxford: Oxford University Press, 2004).
55. Kant, "Perpetual Peace," p. 105. [8:357]
56. Ibid, p. 128. [8:384]
57. Covell, *Kant and the Law of Peace*, pp. 141–2.
58. This interpretation is a popular one. For various discussions regarding this connection, see Derek Heater, *World Citizenship* (London: Continuum, 2002) and Sharon Anderson-Gold, *Cosmopolitanism and Human Rights* (Cardiff: University of Wales Press, 2001).
59. Hinsley, *Power and the Pursuit of Peace*.
60. For a general overview of this argument, see D. Archibugi & D. Held (eds),

*Cosmopolitan Democracy: An Agenda for a New World Order* (Cambridge: Polity Press, 1995).

61. Kant, "Perpetual Peace," p. 105. [8:357-8]
62. Ibid., p. 105-6. [8:358]
63. Ibid.
64. Ibid., p. 105. [8:357]
65. Ibid., p. 106. [8:358]
66. Kant, *The Metaphysics of Morals*, p. 122. [6:353]
67. Fernando Teson, *A Philosophy of International Law* (Boulder, CO: Westview Press, 1998).
68. Kant, "Perpetual Peace," p. 108. [8:360]
69. For brevity, I have classified many interpretations into three general categories. However, each interpretation maintains distinct and unique arguments which this chapter cannot explore at length.
70. Bull, *The Anarchical Society*, p. 25.
71. Pierre Laberge, "Kant on Justice and the Law of Nations," in D. Maple & T. Nardin (eds), *International Society: Diverse Ethical Perspectives* (New Jersey: Princeton University Press, 1998), pp. 82–102. Jürgen Habermas also believes that Kant proposed his federation as a "surrogate" to a more theoretically preferred world state, but suggests that Kant's reasoning is flawed and that this "surrogate" version is actually a preferable choice when applied in contemporary context. This will be explored further in the next section. See Jürgen Habermas, *The Divided West*, Ciaran Cronin (ed. & trans.) (Cambridge: Polity Press, 2006), p. 126.
72. Martin Wight, "An Anatomy of International Thought," *Review of International Studies* 13 (1987), p. 226. An expansion of this interpretation of Kantian cosmopolitanism can also be found in M. Wight, *International Theory: The Three Traditions*, G. Wight & A. Roberts (eds) (Leicester: Leicester University Press, 1991).
73. It should be mentioned that Kant originally advocated a world republic in his writings prior to 1793. However, Kant abandoned this position for a model based on a federation of free states and remained committed to this model in all his political writings after 1793.
74. Kant, "On the Common Saying: This may be True in Theory, but does not Apply in Practice," p. 90. [8:310-311]
75. Kant, "Perpetual Peace," p. 104. [8:356]
76. Teson, "Kant's International Liberalism," p. 105.
77. Cavallar, *Kant and the Theory and Practice of International Right*.
78. For an extrapolation of what a new form of Kantian cosmopolitan governance might look like, see Daniele Archibugi, "Models of International Organization in Perpetual Peace Projects," *Review of International Studies*, 18 (1992), pp. 295–317.
79. Matthias Lutz-Bachmann, "Kant's Ideal of Peace and the Philosophical Conceptions of a World Republic," in J. Bohman & M. Lutz-Bachmann (eds), *Perpetual Peace: Essays on Kant's Cosmopolitan Ideal* (Cambridge: The MIT Press, 1997), pp. 59–77.
80. Donaldson, "Kant's Global Rationalism," pp. 136–57. Also see Gregor, "Kant's Approach to Constitutionalism," pp. 67–87.
81. Kant maintained that "rightful states" had an obligation to protect themselves from external aggression and that this right was inalienable. See Kant, *The Metaphysics of Morals*, pp. 116–120. [6:346–6:351]

82. Ibid., pg. 115. [6:345]. These principles illustrate that peaceful coexistence is the paramount concern of the alliance and that any federation must be contractual and ratified continually by member states in order to reiterate mutual agreements and secure obligation.

83. Kant, "Perpetual Peace," pg. 104. [8:356]

84. Brian Barry, "International Society from a Cosmopolitan Perspective," in D. Maple & T. Nardin (eds), *International Society* (New Jersey: Princeton University Press, 1998), pg. 144. For a similar statement from Beitz, see Charles Beitz, *Political Theory and International Relations* (New Jersey: Princeton University Press, 1979), p. 124.

85. Raffaele Marchetti, *Global Democracy For and Against: Ethical Theory, Institutional Design and Social Struggles* (Oxford: Routledge, 2008).

86. Teson, "Kantian International Liberalism," p. 104.

87. Andrew Hurrell, "Kant and the Kantian Paradigm in International Relations," *Review of International Studies*, 16 (3) (1990), pp. 183–205. Andrew Linklater, *Men and Citizens in the Theory of International Relations* (Basingstoke: Macmillan, 1990).

88. Linklater, *Men and Citizens in the Theory of International Relations*, pg. 103.

89. I outline the difference between Liberal, English School and cosmopolitan models of international legal theory more thoroughly in Garrett Wallace Brown, "Moving Cosmopolitan Legal Theory to Legal Practice: Models of Cosmopolitan Law," *Legal Studies*, vol. 28, no. 3 (2008).

90. As outlined in John Rawls, *The Laws of People* (Cambridge, MA: Harvard University Press, 1999).

91. For a more detailed contrast and comparison between Rawls and Kant, see Patrick Hayden, *John Rawls Toward a Just World Order* (Cardiff: University of Wales Press, 2002), especially Chapter. 4.

92. For a critique that Rawls maintains a relativistic conception of human rights, see Hayden, *John Rawls Toward a Just World Order*.

93. Jürgen Habermas, *Between Naturalism and Religion*, Ciaran Cronin (ed. & trans.) (Cambridge: Polity Press, 2008), p. 318.

94. Habermas, *The Divided West*, p. 147–78.

95. Habermas, *Between Naturalism and Religion*, p. 318.

96. Ibid., p. 316.

97. Ibid., p. 321.

98. Ibid., p. 314.

99. Habermas outlines three reasons why he thinks Kant may have done so in *Between Naturalism and Religion*, pp. 314–18.

100. Ibid., pg. 334.

101. Raffaele Marchetti, *Global Democracy For and Against*.

102. Daniele Archibugi, *The Global Commonwealth of Citizens: Toward Cosmopolitan Democracy* (New Jersey: Princeton University Press, 2008).

103. David Held, *Democracy and the Global Order* (Cambridge: Polity Press, 1995), pg. 200.

# CHAPTER 4

# Cultural Difference and Kant's Cosmopolitan Law

"Human reason is a dye spread more or less equally through all the opinions and all the manners of us humans, which are infinite in matter and infinite in diversity."
– Michel de Montaigne[1]

## INTRODUCTION

One usually does not characterize an anthropological quotation by Michel de Montaigne as having much in comparison with Kantian cosmopolitanism. Scholars of both Montaigne and Kant would suggest that the cultural pluralism of Montaigne's theory directly conflicts with the legal cosmopolitanism of Kant. However, this assumption not only neglects some similarities between Montaigne and Kant, but also exemplifies the general confusion regarding what Kant's cosmopolitan law is meant to achieve. In comparison to Kant, Montaigne suggests that human reason is a characteristic found universally in all forms of social morality. In relation to Montaigne, Kant maintains the empirical reality that human diversity exists, but that the bounded surface of the earth forces us into consistent interaction and therefore creates a philosophical need for practical reason in the formation of universal ethical principles and cosmopolitan law.[2] Where Kant and Montaigne differ is not in regard to the fact that human reason is the basis for all morality or with the fact that diversity exists, but in regard to whether human reason can ever reconcile our various differences under some form of cosmopolitan law. For Montaigne, the diversity of opinion is infinite, suggesting that universal cosmopolitan principles cannot capture all the complexities of various cultural perspectives. In contrast, Kant argues that the scope for social diversity is finite and inherently interconnected, bound by the spherical shape of the earth. As Kant suggests, "since the earth is a globe, [humans] cannot disperse over an infinite area, but must necessarily tolerate one another's company."[3] Since the surface of the globe is finite, "the peoples of the world have entered in various degrees into a universal community, and it has developed to the point where a violation of rights in one part of the world is felt everywhere."[4]

What is interesting about Montaigne, is that he accepts the universalized notion of human reason as the underpinning for social morality, but maintains that this capacity in and of itself creates infinite and irreconcilable divisions. Montaigne seems to be suggesting that since human reason is infinite in ability, it is therefore also infinite in creating antithetical and incommensurable differences. In contrast, Kant maintains that human reason is a universal mechanism that can provide the means to bridge particular cultural divisions in a confined global community. Although Kant recognizes the difficulty of materializing a cosmopolitan ethic, he was enthusiastic about the potential of practical reason to resolve problems that are confined by empirical considerations of spherical cohabitation. As Kant proclaims, "no one can or ought to decide what the highest degree may be at which mankind may have to stop progressing, and hence how wide a gap may still of necessity remain between the idea and its execution . . . for this depends on freedom [of reason], which can transcend any limit we care to impose."[5] In this regard, both Kant and Montaigne believe the creative possibilities of human reason to be endless, but disagree whether this infinite human capability can ever reconcile our various moral differences.

The aim of using this quotation at the start is not to directly compare and contrast Montaigne's theory with the cosmopolitanism of Kant. The quote was used to give a snapshot of the tensions that are usually believed to exist between cultural pluralists and cultural relativists on the one hand, and Kantian-based cosmopolitanism on the other. Although historical divisions between versions of cosmopolitanism and these theories exist, I believe these tensions have been overestimated in relation to a Kantian form of cosmopolitanism. Critics of Kant's cosmopolitanism have articulated a much more demanding and imperialistic vision of cosmopolitanism than Kant seems to have prescribed. Contrary to these views, Kant does not advocate the removal of communal ties or the replacement of culture with an ethical rationality beyond human reach. As has been suggested in the previous chapters, Kant's cosmopolitanism seeks to create a minimal global standard for cosmopolitan law that not only protects individual human worth, but also creates the minimal normative principles necessary to make the peaceful coexistence of individuals, associations, cultures and states in a pluralistic global society possible.

The purpose of this chapter is to examine a cosmopolitan understanding of culture and to determine whether contemporary claims from culture necessarily inhibit a Kantian vision for cosmopolitan law. By providing an alternative view of culture, and by responding to cultural critics of cosmopolitanism, this chapter will defend a place for Kant's cosmopolitan law within contemporary debates about cultural diversity. In the broadest sense, the cosmopolitan position I defend in this chapter consists of two related parts. The first part seeks to reevaluate the significance of traditional formulations of cultural identification and broaden the scope of human interconnectedness. What I mean by this is that the first focus of any form of cosmopolitanism, and the first section of this chapter, is to reevaluate the philosophical merit traditionally attached to cultural community. In doing so, this chapter will examine the significance of cultural identification, whether culture must be considered as a protected entity, and where the boundaries of cultural identification end, if these boundaries end anywhere at all. The second focus of this chapter is to provide an alternative perspective on cultural communities in discussions of global diversity and to assess whether cultural relativism and cultural pluralism necessarily undermine Kant's cosmopolitan theory.

To understand how the idea of culture fits into the type of Kantian cosmopolitanism outlined so far in this book, this chapter is divided into five sections. In the first section, a brief summary of the critiques made against cosmopolitanism by cultural relativists and cultural pluralists is given. The second section then moves from these critiques to a discussion of the difficulty involved in delineating cultural boundaries and locating an accurate epistemology of culture. Section III provides a Kantian-based alternative to contemporary claims of culture by providing an alternative cosmopolitan epistemology of culture. The fourth section contains two parts. First, a response will be given to the relativist argument that humans are constituted by their community and therefore cannot live valuable lives without immersion in a culture of meaning and purpose. The second part will further examine the claims of cultural relativism by focusing on whether a lack of universal morality necessarily makes cosmopolitan law an impossible theory. Section V moves beyond cultural relativism by discussing the role of pluralism in Kant's cosmopolitanism, arguing that the Kantian model actually derives rational motivation and justification from a notion of plural antagonism. The chapter concludes by presenting three main propositions involved in my recapitulation of Kantian cultural cosmopolitanism and how this relates to cultural diversity. In that section, I outline what this cosmopolitan perspective entails and recap how cosmopolitanism might adequately provide an alternative to contemporary claims from culture. Throughout this chapter, my argument is that Kant's cosmopolitanism is not only theoretically relevant in contemporary debates regarding cultural diversity, but that many cosmopolitan critiques from culture only offer practical considerations of coordination and do not necessarily render the cosmopolitan perspective incoherent or impossible.

## I. CLAIMS FROM CULTURE: CULTURAL RELATIVISM AND CULTURAL PLURALISM

Similar to the theory of Montaigne, cultural relativists and pluralists generally posit three general attacks against a Kantian vision for cosmopolitan ethics. These critiques are meant to theoretically undermine cosmopolitanism and illustrate the unattractiveness of the normative conclusions maintained by Kant. First, many relativists criticize Kant for ignoring the moral significance of communal belonging. These critics argue that Kant's cosmopolitanism is grossly unrealistic in its psychological assumptions of the perfectibility of human reason to create universal ethical understanding outside, and sometimes in direct contrast to, particular cultural norms and practices. The underlining premise of this critique is that individuals *need* to belong (and indeed already belong) to immediate communities of meaning and purpose, without which, individuals suffer an existential void of nothingness that fosters psychological and sociological instability. In this regard, cosmopolitanism is often accused of demanding a "psychological revolution" away from communal embeddedness, thus destroying various social allegiances and the order of human meaning provided by those obligations.[6]

The second criticism suggests that Kant's cosmopolitanism is too demanding a form of utopianism that replaces a plurality of meaningful world values with aspirations for a universal ideal. This argument, which is generally made by cultural pluralists, suggests that the avocation of cosmopolitanism fails to take into account the complexities of a world where a plurality of values exists. As some theorists argue, these pluralities of stabilizing cultural and ethical perspective are greatly jeopardized by the "nightmarish hegemony of cosmopolitanism"[7] that seeks to override the meaningful plurality of differing communities. Within this argument is the underlining principle of cultural pluralism, that conflicting conceptions of the good are a real aspect of humanity, and should be accounted for in political schemes which threaten this diversity and the corresponding right to various forms of self-determination.

The third criticism comes from conventionalist cultural relativism and is an extension of the aforementioned critique. Cultural relativists often maintain that Kant's cosmopolitanism seeks to replace a plurality of values in the world with a moral universalism that both diminishes the richness of human diversity, but also has the aspiration to create a universal world state.[8] Similarly, postcolonial critiques of Kant have often argued that his cosmopolitanism is culturally imperialistic, demanding a level of assimilation into a European vision of world order.[9] As Ronald Beiner has described the anti-cosmopolitan position, "scratch a cosmopolitan and you'll find an imperialist just below the surface."[10] Although Martin Wight's concerns are with the cosmopolitan ramifications of destabilizing international power balance, whereas James Tully is more concerned with Western imperialism, they nevertheless both illustrate various sentiments indicative of relativism. For Wight, Tully and cultural relativists argue that there are no universally valid moral principles and that morality must be understood as being in some meaningful sense relative to particular cultures. In this regard, Kant's cosmopolitanism is seen as a destabilizing force that ignores the moral conventions of particular cultures and the relative moral validity derived from being immersed in those cultural communities.

As with Wight, all three cosmopolitan critiques hold that humans are not perfectly reasonable beings, that they have various competing conceptions of the good, that this diversity cannot/should not be forced into a hegemonic universal ethic, and that by attempting to underscore the moral significance of local communities, cosmopolitans are in fact attempting to create an imperialistic utopia. However, for these criticisms to derail cosmopolitanism and render it incoherent, they must show that their arguments are not accounted for by cosmopolitan theory. In order to make the kind of cosmopolitanism advocated in this book an unattractive theory, communitarians must prove that individuals can only derive a meaningful existence from one particular culture and that this relationship is so profound that culture retains an intrinsic worth that cosmopolitanism necessarily threatens. In addition, cultural relativists must show that there is no possibility for cross-cultural ethics and that cultures are themselves so morally isolated that cosmopolitan law is impossible. Finally, in order for cultural concerns to truly render a Kantian vision of cosmopolitanism as unfeasible, pluralists must show that a plurality of goods in the world actually limits the possibility of cosmopolitan law. If appeals from culture are successful in proving these points, then cosmopolitanism is indeed in jeopardy. Nevertheless, as this chapter will illustrate, all three critiques fail to convince and indeed in some ways strengthen Kant's argument for cosmopolitan law.

## II.   SOME CONFUSION REGARDING CULTURAL COMMUNITIES AND IDENTITY

Before discussing the role of culture in Kant's cosmopolitanism, it is necessary to highlight a central and immediate problem that all discussions of culture face. The problem is in discovering what a cultural community is and how we should understand the value of culture in political theory. One of the principle concerns of a cosmopolitan approach is the way in which this question is answered. In many respects, it seems that there is little agreement or accepted approach to the idea of communal identity and culture. However, despite this lack of common definition and understanding, many theories of multiculturalism, communitarianism, cultural pluralism, nationalism, realism, cultural relativism, individualism, liberalism and cosmopolitanism discuss community and culture as if they are self-evident entities.[11] Contemporary political and international relations theory is rife with claims for cultural self-determination and with normative prescriptions premised on the assumption of clearly delineated cultural identities. As Seyla Benhabib has suggested, "culture has become a ubiquitous synonym for identity, an identity marker and differentiator."[12] Benhabib has termed this oversimplified epistemology as a *reductionist sociology of culture* and suggests that many contemporary discussions of culture are based on three faulty assumptions about cultural entities: (1) that cultures are clearly delineable wholes; (2) that all individuals have some kind of culture and a description of that culture is possible; and that (3) subgroup variants pose no important problems in the formation of cultural identities.

128

It is an underlining theme within this chapter that the complexities between culture and identity is a difficult, if not impossible, relationship to understand and is not as self-evident as has been traditionally assumed. In addition, there are serious implications in assuming a reductionist sociology of culture. As Terence Turner maintains, we "risk essentializing the idea of culture as the property of an ethnic group or race; it risks reifying cultures as separate entities by overemphasizing their boundedness and distinctiveness; it risks overemphasizing the internal homogeneity of cultures in terms that potentially legitimize repressive demands for communal conformity; and by treating cultures as badges of group identity, it tends to fetishize them in ways that put them beyond the reach of critical analysis."[13] Even if there were an ability to recognize the existence of distinct cultural entities through scientific observation, as some scholars maintain,[14] what is there to suggest that we would also be able to understand their epistemological complexities over time? As even the more communitarian-minded Michael Waltzer suggests, cultural communities are in constant change and flux, making a consistent knowledge of those groups difficult.[15] In this regard, the first concern for cosmopolitanism is with understanding exactly what is meant when theorists appeal to culture and whether or not these appeals are consistent enough to restrict the limits of normative ethics in relation to cosmopolitan law.

So how has culture been historically defined? Classical definitions suggest that cultural communities represent and embody some form of identifiable group cohesion which is manifested through various combinations of common language,[16] a desire for a common homeland,[17] ethnoracial similarities,[18] communal ethics,[19] common rituals,[20] nationality,[21] collective memories, ethnic similarities,[22] common religion,[23] shared history and/or shared mission.[24] Many anthropologists understand culture as something interpreted through group practice that can be positively identified through group rites, myths and rituals of *belonging*.[25] Some multiculturalists have attempted to define cultural community as something intuitively perceived in historical context, where cultural communities are groups that can be understood as exhibiting *shared lives*.[26] Others, understanding the difficulties of definition, have suggested a more flexible classification for cultural community that is based on the notion of group *recognition*, where social groups derive their identity not through internal aspects alone, but from their relationships with external groups who acknowledge the existence of that group.[27]

129

Nevertheless, these distinctions of cultural community are still problematic in that they immediately appeal to further internal aspects that are often both essentially contestable and subject to problems of infinite regress. What seem to be the consistent aspects found within these definitions of cultural community are the condition that individuals within a group believe that they are in fact members of that community and that these individuals are somehow distinguishable as belonging to that particular culture. In this case, two elements are common between the definitions of cultural community: (1) That people identify with one another as members of their respective group and believe they share common values of mutual interchange; (2) and that this sense of kinship can be identified externally, creating forms of recognition between delineated groups. In the broadest sense, a cultural community is usually defined as a group of individuals who identify with and derive epistemological meaning from similar values. What makes the community an identifiable culture is that other groups can recognize that these individuals maintain some aspects of meaningful mutual interchange and feelings of belonging.

However, as was alluded to earlier, understanding what a cultural community is and the normative weight political theory should assign to these social groups is difficult, since communal values and personal identifications are in a state of constant change and flux. In addition, every community, even intolerant communities who force strict obedience, have subgroup complexities which make the determination of a cultural community's make-up difficult to externally understand, if not impossible. This problem is further compounded by the fact that communal identification is fluid and often contains indefinite configurations. It is reasonable to assume that cultural communities have complex levels of hierarchical values and that various members can identify with cultural aspects that span a large distribution of beliefs and obligations.

The foregoing points suggest that when focusing on the role of culture in political theory, it would be an error to base normative prescriptions on what Benhabib has described as a reductionist sociology of culture. As an alternative, a cosmopolitan approach based on Kant's political and critical philosophy allows for four very different assumptions about culture. These premises will have considerable theoretical implications for the understanding of culture and the place for culture in political theory. It is in the next section that I will outline these four Kantian-based premises in relation to the reductionist sociology of culture.

## III. KANT'S PRAGMATIC ANTHROPOLOGY AND THE COSMOPOLITAN ALTERNATIVE TO THE REDUCTIONIST SOCIOLOGY OF CULTURE

As was outlined earlier, a reductionist sociology of culture is based on three assumptions: that cultures are delineable wholes; that all individuals belong to some kind of culture and that a description of that culture is possible; and that subgroup variants pose no important problems in the formation of cultural identities. In contrast to viewing culture in this manner, a cosmopolitan approach based on Kant's political and critical philosophy might posit four alternative premises.

The first premise of Kant's pragmatic anthropology is to suggest that cultures are already cosmopolitan. That is, cultures are indeterminate amalgamations of various influences that consist of a multiplicity of allegiances, ideas, beliefs and values. In this sense, a culture cannot be assumed as a single bounded entity, but must be viewed as a fluid organism that is constantly swayed by converging tides of internal and external narratives. The boundary of culture is not whole, but blurred and interlocked with multifarious cultural connections.[28] Although cultural communities display practices of kinship and signification, the identification relationships between participants consist of both self-affirming and opposing narratives.[29] Many of these narratives originate from external sources or through adaptations of traditional ideals. History itself seems to suggest as much, since cultures have evolved with, and adapted to, various internal and external influences and traditions. It seems rather absurd to suggest that cultures have not historically developed from various external sources or that they maintain a consistently anchored and unified identity.

In relation to the second reductionist assumption that all individuals have some kind of culture and that a description of that culture is possible, the cosmopolitan position becomes much more complicated. A cosmopolitan could agree that everyone belongs to at least *one* culture, but would disagree that everyone maintains only a single unified cultural identity. In this sense, all humans are born into one culture or another (by chance) and therefore have been influenced by at least one cultural source. However, the cosmopolitan does not accept that everyone is confined to a single identity, but that humans actually maintain complex identification relationships with various and sometimes conflicting cultural sources. This is not to say that an individual cannot identify or believe to identify with a dominant cultural source. What is being suggested is the rarity of finding singular cultural influences and that most humans maintain complex identification relationships.[30] It is not uncommon to hear someone describe themselves as being many things, such as a Democratic Sunni Iraqi, an Island Marsh Iraqi Arab or as an African American Christian Conservative. Within each of these signifiers we find multifaceted cultural connections and identities, none of which can be easily reduced to represent a unified whole.[31]

Complete knowledge of a cultural community is impossible in the sense that we cannot empirically know what a cultural community is, only that as a totality, various individuals are thought as coordinated together to form a whole. Since individuals are made up of a plethora of cultural influences, a description of a cultural community can only be understood with the application of metaphysical categories. However, in order to suggest such metaphysical categories of community, we also have to assume the existence of certain a priori principles for categorical organization. As Kant maintains within the *Critique of Pure Reason*, community should be thought of as "a whole divided into its parts, and since no one of them can be contained under the other, they are thought as coordinated with, not subordinated to, each other, and so determining each other, not in one direction only, as in a series, but reciprocally, as in an aggregate."[32] In this sense, cultural identity is not understood as prior to and representative of all, but is thought of as a possible category of coordinated interests between mutually exclusive parts. These reciprocal relationships can only make sense if the individual is seen as the locus of cultural meaning in relation to a universal whole. In contrast to the reductionist sociology of culture, Kant makes a distinction between the terms *communio* (exclusive sharing of time and space protected from the outside) and *commercium* (associations deriving from dynamic exchanges and respect between individuals), favoring the use of the second in his metaphysical understanding of cultural community.[33]

The cosmopolitan and multifarious make-up of culture forces a reconsideration of cultural identity away from exclusive and unified *communal identities* to notions of individual *identification relationships*. This has considerable implications for the reductionist assumption regarding internal variants and subgroup complexities. Since subgroup complexities and their exchanges with various cultural elements play a critical role in how cultural communities form, they also create difficult hurdles for claims of cultural solidarity. In the Kantian case, we can only assume the category of cultural identity if we also assume coordinated influences and reciprocal identities that are confirmed and recognized by participating members. In this regard, the category of cultural identity becomes transcendentally significant through principles of participation and individual representation. If the principles of mutual coordination and coexistence are not understood as categorically a priori, then the concept of a unified cultural community is incoherent and is replaced by notions of determinism and tyranny. In order to form the perception of a "thorough-going community" we cannot design an object of possible perception, but must ground the notion of cultural identity on metaphysical principles of "mutual interaction and coordination" to which empirical factors must relate.[34]

Nevertheless, many appeals from culture wish to avoid the inherent individualism involved in taking a Kantian approach to cultural community. Some argue that culture constitutes self-identification and is therefore somehow an entity prior to subjective identification that "has to be worth fostering, not as contingent instruments, but for themselves."[35] If these types of cultural claims are to be taken seriously in political theory, then we must ask important questions regarding the role of culture in the formation of universal ethics and make decisions as to what value we should therefore place on normative appeals made from cultural communities. It is in the next section that my Kantian-based cosmopolitan alternative will be applied in response to two arguments made from culture. First, a brief response will be given to the argument that humans are constituted by their community and therefore cannot live valuable lives without immersion in an immediate cultural community of meaning and purpose. Second, a response will be given to the relativist argument that morality can only be understood in relation to particular cultures and that the idea of universal cosmopolitan law is both culturally destructive and practically impossible.

## IV. Cultural Relativism and the Critique of Kantian Universalism

In the last section, a cosmopolitan alternative to the reductionist sociology of culture was given. From that discussion it was suggested that: (1) Cultures have blurred boundaries with indeterminate narratives and influences; (2) Although individuals have at least one cultural source, they are not necessarily restricted to a single cultural influence and generally identify with a multiplicity of different values; (3) Knowledge of a cultural identity is impossible without metaphysical categories based on a priori assumptions of mutual coordination; and (4) Internal subgroup complexities must be understood in relation to these a priori principles before a claim of cultural identity can be coherent. However, this epistemology of culture is in direct contrast to many contemporary arguments that stress the importance of bounded cultures. Cultural relativists, for example, maintain that moral principles are only valid relative to particular bounded cultural entities. From this premise, cultural relativists make two claims. The first claim is generally called the *dependency thesis*, which specifies that all moral values are constituted from cultural immersion and enculturative conditioning. The second claim is often referred to as the *diversity thesis* and argues that morality varies from culture to culture, so that there are no moral principles that can be accepted universally.

### A.   The Cosmopolitan Response to the Dependency Thesis

The dependency thesis maintains that cultural communities are the source of our social nature and constitute our moral beliefs about what makes a good life possible. These virtues are derived and transmitted through cultural immersion and have profound influence on the reciprocal relationships formed between human beings. Many relativists argue that cosmopolitanism fails to capture the value derived from a cultural community.[36] They have criticized the inherent individualism of cosmopolitanism because it neglects "the causal process of *enculturative conditioning*" and therefore fails to account for the fact that cultural communities act as exclusive sources of moral virtue and social understanding.[37]

There are two troubling normative implications that follow from the relativist demand that all sources of morality are constituted by causal processes of enculturative conditioning. First, the dependency thesis is a literal application of a reductionist sociology of culture, insofar as it holds that morality is dependent on the fact that individuals are immersed in a single bounded culture without which they are unable to establish meaningful moral lives. As was stated earlier, the claim that cultures are bounded entities is not representative of how most cosmopolitans understand cultural communities. According to the Kantian epistemology outlined above, cultures maintain complex and blurred boundaries with indeterminate narratives and influences. If we hold this position as plausible, then it would be an error to understand individuals as constituted solely by a single cultural source. In order to account for cultural complexities we must understand individuals as having multifarious identification relationships where various moral commitments are derived. The claim that individuals must have a single culture in order to form moral lives places tremendous normative purpose on maintaining homogeneous ethical beliefs regardless of the ethical principles involved.

Moreover, a cosmopolitan position is not suggesting that individuals do not derive moral value from their cultural community or that humans should abandon communal obligations.[38] This statement would be false since most cosmopolitan theories recognize that individuals need access to cultural material in order to form conceptions of the good life. Where cosmopolitanism differs greatly from cultural relativists is in the fact that cosmopolitans believe there is nothing to suggest that membership in a single cultural community is required in order to form a meaningful life. As Jeremy Waldron has argued, cultural material can be found through various cultural sources and these multiple sources can both influence and support perfectly rewarding lives. Although cultural immersion in a single culture may be what people are circumstantially provided, the claim that immersion is necessary for meaningful existence is by empirical measurement questionable. As Waldron states, "the cosmopolitan strategy is not to deny the role of culture in the constitution of human life, but to question the assumption that the social world divides neatly into particular distinct cultures, one to every community, and the assumption that what everyone needs is just one of these entities – a single, coherent culture – to give shape and meaning to his life."[39] What the cosmopolitan perspective suggests is that although each individual has an equal ability for a social existence, they also have an equal capacity to be an active co-legislator and translator of multifarious cultural values and there is no theoretical reason why the need for one automatically rules out the other.

The second normative concern with the dependency thesis is that causal conditioning does not seem to be based on any rational human process, but seems to be a purely determined and conditioned response to cultural embeddedness. By holding a singular view of moral conditioning, cultural relativists seem to dismiss human reason as a possible source of moral identification and therefore devalue any imperatives people might develop for holding certain universal morals as true. What is troubling with this account is the level of reductionism that relativists assign to their understanding of culture. For cultural relativists seem to be basing their normative arguments on strict determinism, maintaining that the reasons for holding certain moral beliefs are not predicated on any rational criteria, but are simply determined by bounded cultural circumstances.

135

However, this conception of morality is not entirely convincing, for it seems that cultural norms are often maintained and facilitated in context of rational thought and human reasoning. It would seem that if there are norms and practices that matter to us, then those practices contain some form of rational justification. Although one culture might justify their norms differently than another culture, it does not mean that the process of human reasoning in moral justification is absent. In this regard, *enculturative conditioning* can only be part of the story, for humans and communal groups take their norms and practices seriously precisely because those norms are embedded in a structure of reason and reasoning.[40]

So why do cultural relativists place so much normative weight on the idea of a bounded cultural morality? What seems to be the primary concern with the relativist critique of cosmopolitanism, and Kant's cosmopolitanism in particular, is the moral focus that cosmopolitanism places on individual moral reason versus cultural community. Since all cosmopolitan theories advocate equal moral significance to human beings universally, devaluing certain aspects of particularism as a source of moral significance, relativism can be seen as a defense of communal identification derived from cultural immersion. Generally, relativistic attacks contain an existential fear, of an "unencumbered self,"[41] where individuals live without a sense of immediate community and meaningful purpose. In this regard, many claims from culture are based on a fear that cosmopolitanism promotes the idea of individuals as isolated rational atoms that are disconnected from social bonds or from other meaningful obligations.[42] Where the crucial divide between cosmopolitanism and relativism exists is that relativism assigns the role of "enculturative conditioning" to be the source of moral importance versus allowing for the creation of moral obligations derived from abstract universal principles of reason. Therefore, cultural relativism represents a prominent opposition to cosmopolitan ethics, for they directly advocate reductionist schemes of bounded community versus the more individualist-based constructions of universal ethics found within cosmopolitanism.

In their insistence for bounded cultural communities, cultural relativists are clearly claiming that cultural communities are encapsulated entities that should be protected from cosmopolitan ethics. Behind this suggestion is an implication that any devaluing of cultural supremacy results in radical normative shifts that reduce immediate communities of meaning and purpose. However, this approach is awkward in relation to the Kantian form of cosmopolitanism outlined in this book, because it seems to be suggesting that universal principles will in effect make particular cultures less meaningful or reduce feelings of belonging. Although we can accept that some cultures are more or less equipped to accommodate the necessary changes associated with cosmopolitan ethics, this does not necessarily mean that universal principles are inherently anti-communal or will ultimately cause a whole culture to disintegrate.

This suggests that there is confusion by cultural relativists regarding what a Kantian cosmopolitan approach might entail in regard to culture. The Kantian cosmopolitanism that I am suggesting does not claim that culture is not valuable in the formation of individual morality, but is arguing that cultural morality also has a contingent value based on the reasoned beliefs of its members. Although scholars discuss things called cultural communities, it seems that it can only be at an abstract and generalized level because we cannot define them without alluding to the fact that the people within the cultural community identify themselves as members or derive meaningful life purpose through some form of cultural participation. In this case, cultural communities should not be discussed in terms of inalienable worth based on a concept of enculturative conditioning, but must be explored in relation to the value derived by the participants of that cultural community. In this case, there is human reason behind cultural identification and this rational process should not be dismissed simply because reductionists claim cultural integrity as more important for meaningful existence than the reason behind human existence in the first place. For it seems absurd to consider a bounded cultural entity as intrinsically good regardless of any good relayed to its members.

## B.   A Cosmopolitan Response to the Diversity Thesis and the Possibility of Cosmopolitan Law

There are two claims made from the *diversity thesis*. The first claim is anthropologically descriptive and asserts that there are no universally objective morals. What follows from this claim is that judgements between cultures cannot be substantially made since there is no objective measurement in which to make an appeal. The second claim is a prescriptive claim that since we cannot make cross-cultural comparisons cultures should therefore be considered to have equal value as entities in themselves. In this regard, cultures are to be respected as equally valuable entities and cannot/should not be subject to external judgements by other cultural entities.[43]

What is troubling about the second claim is that the normative argument for equality of culture is a universal claim in opposition to its own descriptive premise. If we are unable to make judgements because each culture is relative only onto itself, then how can cultural relativists make the normative assertion that cultures are to be held equally valuable in relation to one another? Surely this qualifies as a universal standard of measurement. If the descriptive claim is correct, then the implication is that the prescriptive claim made by cultural relativists lacks merit. In this regard, there is an inherent conflict between its descriptive, prescriptive and anti-universal claims.

Moreover, the descriptive component of the diversity thesis and its assertion that cosmopolitanism fails because of a lack of universal morality is not without its own inherent confusion. The fact that there is no universal moral code does not mean that there cannot be equally recognized morals. In addition, the entire cosmopolitan project exists exactly for the reason that there is a lack of universal ethics in the world. In this regard, cosmopolitans accept the notion that there is not a universal morality as a matter of fact, but reject the idea that universally recognized ethics is necessarily impossible to construct. For my Kantian vision of cosmopolitanism to be impossible, the cultural relativist would have to prove this impossibility, otherwise cosmopolitan ethics only has practical coordination problems and not problems that are necessarily theoretical roadblocks.

Furthermore, a relativist perspective that cultural communities are bounded entities that need to be protected from external influence and judgement seems to contradict the reality of cultural transiency.[44] The fact that cultural relativists complain that Kantian cosmopolitan principles, in effect, reduce the bonds of cultural groups is nevertheless not truly representative of how groups evolve, interconnect, share traditions and assimilate into other cultures. As Jeremy Waldron suggests, "people have always lived in a kaleidoscope of culture, moving freely amongst the products of innumerable cultural traditions."[45] Charles Westin agrees with this when he argues that, "cultures are not rigid monoliths given once and for all, but are receptive and responsive ways of constructing meaning, continuously battered by requirements to change and develop, and by counterforces stressing ideals of purism, opposing newfangled expressions and interpretations."[46]

History itself shows this vision of culture to be correct, for massive cross-cultural pollination has taken place throughout the chronology of human existence. As Chandran Kukathas states, "the fact that in the history of interaction people have been able to understand each other sufficiently to trade, immigrate, and intermarry suggests a substantial commonality amongst peoples."[47] As was suggested before, the main tenet of my Kantian approach is the belief that cultural communities are largely already cosmopolitan. What was meant by this suggestion is that cultural communities have historically evolved alongside other groups, thus assimilating, emulating and infusing with the various ethical perspectives of their neighbors. As history has shown, groups often borrow, steal and copy the more successful aspects of other cultural communities. Furthermore, cultural communities often fuse with one another, to the point that distinctions are no longer visible or believed, thus creating new cultural formations.

One cosmopolitan concern is that individuals often identify with their cultural and communal obligations. Therefore, its task is to assess whether this cultural identification prohibits the acceptance of any form of cosmopolitan law. As Waldron has suggested of a Kantian position, "we are always likely to find ourselves alongside others who we disagree with" and it is this reality that supports the cosmopolitan philosophy that some sort of mechanisms for peaceful coexistence should be considered.[48] In addition, humans have lived "side by side, clustered together in circumstances where they simply have to deal with one another, wherever the initial disparity between their views of justice, morality and right."[49] Although historically cultural communities have engaged in conflicts that end in bloody and violent war, they have also figured out ways to coexist next to, and tolerate, various associations and communities. It is from the reality of an ability for mutual cohabitation that cultures can in fact share common goals of security and right, and that they can agree to, fuse, change, evolve and coordinate ethical principles. It is on this ideal of agreed coexistence based on cosmopolitan law that both Kantian and non-Kantian cosmopolitans peg their hopes for the emergence of a normative ethical cosmopolitan order.

Thus, the Kantian cosmopolitan position advocated in this book is not suggesting that local obligations should be universally abandoned or that a universal morality exists. What this position is suggesting is that existing cultural communities are not to be considered as bounded entities containing the pure source of human morality. The point of cosmopolitanism as a whole is that human beings are living in a world of human beings and only incidentally are members of community organizations.

Furthermore, those organizations are simply creations of many different factors that have historically evolved from indeterminate amalgamations. Given the possibility for cultural normative shifts, it is not impossible to imagine various levels of subjective obligation and identification, one of which could be cosmopolitan law. As has been suggested by Kant, just because a theory has a degree of difficulty does not mean that it cannot be achieved, but simply that there will be complications involved in the effort to achieve it.[50]

## V. COEXIST VERSUS COHERE: KANT'S COSMOPOLITANISM AND CULTURAL PLURALISM

A common critique of Kant's cosmopolitanism is that the world consists of a plurality of incommensurable cultural goods and that these antithetical perspectives restrict the idea of universal ethics. Cultural pluralism suggests that since a plurality of viewpoints exists, various cultural communities will lack the motivation to accept cosmopolitan principles. The question cultural pluralists often ask cosmopolitans is: why would a cultural community give up their notion of the good life for some imported perspective? In addition, if some viewpoints are in drastic opposition, then how could a bridge be forged between these incommensurable differences?

A Kantian response is to accept the cultural pluralist premise, but deny the conclusion. In other words, the very fact that various conceptions of the good exist, does not mean that minimal ethical foundations cannot be formed. In contrast, Kant believed that the motivation behind the creation of cosmopolitan law was because there is a necessity to adjudicate disagreement between cohabitants of a spherically bounded world. In this sense, pluralism provides the rational motivation behind the creation of cosmopolitan law. Brian Barry summed up this notion when he wrote, "the very fact of irresolvable disagreement over the nature of the good life, once we get beyond the basics, is itself a premise in the argument for liberal institutions. For, in the face of these disagreements, what we need is a fair way of adjudicating between conflicting demands that they give rise to."[51]

If we conceive of Kant's cosmopolitan law as concerned with the rightful existence of various cultures, then cosmopolitanism is not a revolutionary threat to various communities, but serves as an attempt to facilitate coexistence. Although communitarians are correct in their claims that a cosmopolitan order will, in some psychological sense, result in a normative mental shift, this does not necessarily mean that this normative change has to be destructively revolutionary and sudden.[52] The goal of Kantian cosmopolitanism should not be advocated as a method of radical universalism at the cost of plurality. How Kantian cosmopolitanism should be understood is as an attempt to come to terms with the plurality of various societies in some sort of minimally recognized framework of cosmopolitan law.[53] In other words, we should not view Kantian cosmopolitanism as utopian imperialism, but as a conception for seeking peaceful global coexistence through the utilization of jurisprudence and constitutional coordination. This coordination should be understood as being the result of a genuine consensus and understanding for hospitable coexistence, and not understood as philosophical imperialism aimed to subvert natural order by demanding violent psychological shifts.

However, those who make appeals for the respect of a plurality of cultures are still extremely skeptical of any form of cosmopolitanism. For many, the cosmopolitan project is not about coexistence, but about moral cohesion, that is, about moving human beings toward a universal and hegemonic ethic that denies plural differences and various forms of life. Nevertheless, ascribing this view to Kant is mistaken. It is not how Kant believed humans actually existed or how we naturally evolve. As will be shown below, Kant's justification for cosmopolitan law was not only to adjudicate disagreement, but to provide an environment where disagreements could continue the evolution of humanity without the murderous effects witnessed throughout history.

The best expression of Kant's pluralism is discovered in what would initially seem an unlikely work. In the *Idea for a Universal History with a Cosmopolitan Purpose*, Kant outlines several propositions relating to human nature and how we might understand a unified human purpose. Within this essay, Kant maintains that human evolution is not situated in the reason of one human being or the collective reason of a single society, but is only reasonably understood as having purpose when derived from the entire human species. As Kant claims, "accordingly, every individual man would have to live for a vast length of time if he were to make complete use of all his natural capacities; or if nature has fixed only a short term for each man's life, then it will require a long, perhaps incalculable series of generations, each passing on its enlightenment to the next, before the germs implanted by nature in our species can be developed to that degree which corresponds to nature's original intention."[54] For Kant, culture was not the product of one individual, or a series of individuals, but was produced by mankind as a whole. If a diversity of culture is to have a historical purpose for humanity, it must be thought of as also having a universal purpose for humanity. However, for this idea of universal purpose to be rendered practically coherent, political circumstances ought to be organized according to universally valid laws which mirror the ideal.

In some regards, Kant's idea of a cosmopolitan purpose can be related to John Stuart Mill's concept of *experiments in living*. In both cases, a minimal framework of law is meant to provide an environment where competing perspectives could be reasoned through and tested socially. The importance for this exchange of ideas was that it continued the evolutionary progression of humanity. Like Kant, Mill believed that disagreement was the necessary spark plug for human enlightenment and for the promotion of the species. It is through an open forum of debate that humankind could partake in various experiments in living, constantly reforming and reevaluating better ways of living. As suggested by Kant, "nature should thus be thanked for fostering social incompatibility . . . Without [this], all man's excellent natural capacities would never be roused to develop."[55] Nevertheless, like Kant, Mill understood that disagreement left alone and unchecked would lead to violent restrictions of reason and liberty, thus threatening the major mechanism from which all conclusions of living are derived. For both Kant and Mill, the lawless limiting of reason also limited the ability to exchange our experiments and ultimately hampers the possibility for progress. As Kant himself maintains, "this purpose can be fulfilled only in a society which has not only the greatest freedom, and therefore a continual antagonism among its members, but also the most precise specification and preservation of the limits of this freedom in order that it can coexist with the freedom of others."[56] Kant's cosmopolitan purpose is in this sense an educational process in both our private and social lives that seeks to limit prejudices which might prevent the discovery of better methods for furthering the human experiment.[57]

Therefore, the pluralist assumption that Kant seeks to create a single utopian culture is not what Kant seems to be suggesting. What Kant advocates is a minimal legal framework that allows for a plurality of various forms of life to coexist. As was highlighted in Chapter 1, cosmopolitan law was sought not only for Kant's perpetual peace project, but to create an intellectual environment from which humanity could continue to evolve and adapt. Kant's metaphysical ideal of history cannot alone command the universal respect of others, but merely illustrates that if external freedom is to be understood as having a human purpose, it should only be understood in accordance with universal principles of public right. In this case, what is needed is "a constitution allowing the greatest possible human freedom in accordance with laws which ensure that the freedom of each can coexist with the freedom of all the other."[58]

## VI. CONCLUSION: KANTIAN COSMOPOLITANISM AND DIVERSITY

The chapter began with a discussion contrasting Kant's cosmopolitanism and Montaigne's cultural relativism. In that discussion, I suggested that Kant and Montaigne both believed the creative possibilities of human reason to be endless, however disagreed whether this infinite human capability could ever reconcile our various moral differences. The disagreement between Montaigne and Kant pertains, not to the idea that human reason acted as the basis for cultural morality, but to the degree to which the infinitive scope of human reason has to create antithetical and incommensurable cultural differences. The purpose of this chapter has been to argue that the cosmopolitan epistemology of culture is a viable alternative in contemporary concerns for cultural diversity. Although the chapter did not offer a complete analysis of the relationship between culture and Kant's cosmopolitanism, it hopefully demonstrated that cultural relativism and cultural pluralism do not provide inherent restrictions on the possibility of cosmopolitan law.

By trying to defend Kantian cosmopolitan law I have recommended some grounding for an alternative approach to culture in global theory. The cosmopolitan approach that I have suggested consists of three theoretical propositions for continued discussions within culture, cosmopolitan law and political theory.

First, cultural communities are already cosmopolitan. What this means, is that cultural communities are fluid amalgamations of various cultural influences and obligations. Cultures are therefore not the bounded entities that many claims from culture assume. They are categorical shapes that are in a constant process of creation and reformation. In this regard: (1) Cultures have blurred boundaries with indeterminate narratives and influences; (2) Although individuals have at least one cultural source, they are not necessarily restricted to a single cultural influence and generally identify with a multiplicity of different values; (3) Knowledge of a cultural identity is impossible without metaphysical categories based on a priori assumptions of mutual coordination; (4) Internal subgroup complexities must be understood in relation to these a priori principles before a claim of cultural identity can be coherent.

Second, although humans share a need for cultural material in order to form meaningful moral lives, they also identify with a multiplicity of cultural influences and can derive perfectly rewarding lives from multifarious cultural sources.[59] As Waldron has suggested, people maintain and are able to adapt to "a variety, a multiplicity of different and perhaps disparate communal allegiances."[60] What this suggests is that the relativist thesis that humans must be immersed in a single culture of meaning and purpose in order to live rewarding moral lives is empirically suspect. It seems reasonable to assume that both individuals and communities adapt to new influences and that members often maintain multilevel obligations and identification relationships. Furthermore, the fact that humans maintain multifarious cultural identities supports the notion that cosmopolitan law is not an idealistic impossibility, but a theoretically plausible alternative. Although it is true that we often inherit norms from our social environment, it is also true that these traditions are constantly in a state of metamorphosis between external and internal cultural influences. Given the possibility for multifarious cultural identities, it is not impossible to imagine various levels of subjective obligation and identification, one of which could be cosmopolitan law.

Third, cultural pluralism and Kant's cosmopolitanism are not necessarily incompatible. Cosmopolitan law does not deny the existence of a plurality of possible conflicting cultural goods, but suggests that these conflicting goods should be organized under a cosmopolitan framework that allows for adjudication through minimal ethical principles. The fact that a plurality of communal interests exists, supports the claim that cosmopolitan law is a viable alternative to adjudicate global disagreements. It seems that contemporary political philosophy is wrestling with the problem of diversity and coexistence in an increasingly interdependent and globalized world. From this a Kantian-based form of cosmopolitanism strives to answer the question of how a diverse world can coexist freely and peacefully. In this regard, cosmopolitan law is not a denial of cultural diversity and pluralism, but an offered solution. For Kant, the solution is to provide human beings with a global environment that supports the coexistence of various cultural identities under an umbrella of cosmopolitan law, which may eventually lead us to a more robust sense of universal citizenship, without the strict demand for homogeneous and bounded cultural entities.

# NOTES

1. Michel De Montaigne, "On Common; and Never Easily Changing a Traditional Law," M.A. Screech (ed.), *The Complete Essays* (London: Penguin Classics, 1993).
2. Immanuel Kant, "Perpetual Peace," in Hans Reiss (ed.), H. B. Nisbet (trans.), *Kant's Political Writings* (Cambridge: Cambridge University Press, 1970), p. 106. [8:358]
3. Ibid.
4. Ibid., p. 107–8. [8:360]
5. Immanuel Kant, "Appendix: Transcendental Logic II, Dialectic, I, Ideas in General," *The Critique of Pure Reason*, J. M. D. Meiklejohn (trans.) (New York: Colonial Press, 1900). [3:247]
6. Ronald Beiner, "Nationalism, Internationalism, and the Nairn-Hobsbawn Debate," *Archives for European Sociology* XL, 1 (1999), p. 178.
7. Martin Wight, "An Anatomy of International Thought," *Review of International Studies*, 13 (1987).
8. Ibid.
9. James Tully, *Strange Multiplicity* (Cambridge: Cambridge University Press, 1995). Also see James Tully, "The Kantian Idea of Europe: Critical and Cosmopolitan Perspectives," in A. Pagden (ed.), *The Idea of Europe* (Cambridge: Cambridge University Press, 2002).
10. Beiner, pg. 178.
11. This is certainly true with communitarian theorists, but is also evident within liberal movements, particularly with John Rawls and Will Kymlicka, who base their theories of justice on the assumption that communities are closed and bounded. As Yael Tamir suggests, "most liberals are liberal nationalists." The implication I am trying to suggest is that most modern theories utilize arguments from community or culture without analyzing what these "things" actually are. It is in this section that I attempt to understand these "things" better. For more on Tamir's critique, see Yael Tamir, *Liberal Nationalism* (Princeton: Princeton University Press, 1993). See page 139 for above comment. For a more extensive discussion regarding the assumption of cultural entities, see R. Grillo, *Pluralism and the Politics of Difference: State, Culture and Ethnicity in Comparative Perspective* (Oxford: Clarendon Press, 1998).
12. Seyla Benhabib, *The Claims of Culture: Equality and Diversity in the Global Era* (Princeton: Princeton University Press, 2002), p. 2.
13. Terence Turner, "Anthropology and Multiculturalism: What is Anthropology and What Multiculturalists should be Mindful of?" *Cultural Anthropology*, vol. 8, no. 4 (1993), p. 413.
14. Samuel Huntington, *The Clash of Civilizations and the Remaking of the World Order* (New York: Simon and Schuster, 1996).
15. Michael Waltzer, "Pluralism: A Political Perspective," in Will Kymlicka (ed.), *The Rights of Minority Cultures* (Oxford: Oxford University Press, 1995), p. 139.
16. Charles Taylor, *Philosophical Arguments* (Cambridge: Harvard University Press, 1995). For a classic discussion, see Jean-François Lyotard, *The Postmodern Condition: A Report of Human Knowledge*, G. Bennington (trans.) (Minneapolis: University of Minneapolis Press, 1984).
17. David Miller, *On Nationality* (Oxford: Oxford University Press, 1995).
18. Will Kymlicka, *Politics in the Vernacular: Nationalism, Multiculturalism and Citizenship* (Oxford: Oxford University Press, 2001).

19. For a relativist discussion of ethics and culture, see Emile Durkheim, *Ethics and the Sociology of Morals*, T. Hall (trans.) (Buffalo: Prometheus Books, 1993).

20. For a classic anthropological analysis of cultural kinship, see Claude Lévi-Strauss, *Elementary Structures of Kinship* (Boston: Beacon Press, 1967).

21. Ernest Gellner, *Nations and Nationalism* (Oxford: Blackwell, 1983), especially the introduction.

22. Anthony D. Smith, *The Ethnic Origins of Nations* (Oxford: Blackwell, 1986).

23. Scott Thomas, *The Global Resurgence of Religion and the Transformation of International Relations* (New York: Palgrave, 2005).

24. Although some cultures might contain all of the aforementioned qualities, all of the definitions I have examined suggest that cultures must contain at least one or more of the aspects outlined above. However, there is considerable disagreement between various scholars and each generally occupies their own niche as to what aspects of culture are of critical importance. However, the plethora of views does suggest one fact, that whatever culture is, it is many things and that it is not easily understood.

25. John Monaghan & Peter Just, *Social and Cultural Anthropology* (Oxford: Oxford University Press, 2000).

26. For an example of this view of cultural definition, see Bhiku Parekh, *Rethinking Multiculturalism* (Basingstoke: Palgrave, 2000).

27. For a contemporary example of this type of preference for "groups" versus culture, see Iris Marion Young, *Justice and the Politics of Difference* (Princeton: Princeton University Press, 1990).

28. Immanuel Kant, *Anthropology from a Pragmatic Point of View*, V. Dowdell (trans.), H. Rudnick (ed.) (Carbondale: Southern Illinois University Press, 1978), especially Part 2, Section E. [7:321–333]

29. Immanuel Kant, *Critique of Judgement*, J. Meredith (trans.) (Oxford: Oxford University Press, 1973), Section. 83. [5:429–34]

30. Kwame Anthony Appiah, *Cosmopolitanism: Ethics in a World of Strangers* (New York: Norton, 2006).

31. The fact that individuals maintain multifaceted cultural connections can be witnessed by the increased use of "cosmopolitan ethnographies" and "multi-site" research in contemporary anthropology.

32. Kant, *The Critique of Pure Reason* [(A)3:112]

33. *Communio* is the Latin word for "fortification" and was used by Johann Gottfried Herder in describing the exclusivity of communal identity and language. *Commercium* on the other hand is the Latin word for communal identity formed through respectful communication and exchange. Kant had great concern with Herder's isolationist and "determined" understanding of community. In fact, Kant rarely used Herder's favorite word *Gemeinschaft* (community), preferring the word *Gesellschaft* (society) in his discussions of moral communities. For the Latin translations, see *The Oxford Latin Dictionary: Collectors Edition* (Norwalk: The Easton Press, 1993). For a discussion on the tension between Herder and Kant, see F. M. Bernard (ed.), *Herder on Social and Political Culture* (Cambridge: Cambridge University Press, 1969).

34. Kant, *Critique of Pure Reason*, [(B)4:211–12]

35. Charles Taylor, *Philosophical Arguments*, p. 137.

36. Ibid., p. 127.

37. Melville Herskovits, *Cultural Relativism: Perspectives in Cultural Pluralism*, F. Herskovits (ed.) (New York: Random House, 1972).
38. Appiah, *Cosmopolitanism: Ethics in a World of Strangers*, pp. 115–35.
39. Jeremy Waldron, "Minority Cultures and the Cosmopolitan Alternative," in Will Kymlicka (ed.), *The Rights of Minority Cultures* (Oxford: Oxford University Press, 1995), p. 105.
40. Jeremy Waldron, "What is Cosmopolitan?," *The Journal of Political Philosophy*, vol. 8, no. 2 (2000), p. 239.
41. Michael Sandel, *Liberalism and the Limits of Justice* (Cambridge: Cambridge University Press, 1982).
42. The argument that cosmopolitanism, and liberalism in particular, "atomizes" the individual is best expressed by Charles Taylor, "Atomism," in S. Avineri and A. de-Shalit, *Communitarianism and Individualism* (Oxford: Oxford University Press, 1992).
43. Herskovits, *Cultural Relativism: Perspectives in Cultural Pluralism*.
44. Appiah, *Cosmopolitanism: Ethics in a World of Strangers*, pp. 30–1.
45. Jeremy Waldron, "Minority Cultures and the Cosmopolitan Alternative," *University of Michigan Journal of Law Reform*, 25 (1992), p. 782.
46. Charles Westin, "Temporal and Spatial Aspects of Multiculturality", in R. Baubock & J. Rundell (eds), *Blurred Boundaries: Migration, Ethnicity, Citizenship* (Aldershot: Ashgate, 1998), p. 61.
47. Chandran Kukathas, *The Liberal Archipelago: A Theory of Diversity and Freedom* (Oxford: Oxford University Press, 2003), p. 66.
48. Waldron, "What is Cosmopolitan?," pp. 240–1.
49. Ibid, p. 241.
50. Immanuel Kant, "On the Common Saying: This May be True in Theory but it Does not Apply in Practice," in Hans Reiss (ed.), H. B. Nisbet (trans.), *Kant's Political Writings* (Cambridge: Cambridge University Press, 1970), p. 92. [8:313]
51. Brian Barry, *Culture and Equality* (Cambridge, MA: Harvard University Press, 2001), p. 263.
52. History provides vivid examples of "revolutionary" changes in ethical belief that did not result in massive upheaval and destruction of social and ethical structures. The peaceful "revolutions" in the former Eastern European states are an excellent example of normative shifts in ethical thought that did not weaken social cohesion, but in fact strengthened communal obligation and normative order. For a good discussion of the non-violent normative shift in Eastern Europe, see Jan Pakulski, "East European Revolutions and Legitimacy Crisis," in J. Frentzel-Zagorska (ed.), *From One Party State to Democracy* (Amsterdam: Rodopi, 1993), p. 67–87.
53. Sankar Muthu, *Enlightenment Against Empire* (Princeton: Princeton University Press, 2003).
54. Immanuel Kant, "Idea for a Universal History with a Cosmopolitan Purpose," in Hans Reiss (ed.), H. B. Nisbet (trans.), *Kant's Political Writings* (Cambridge: Cambridge University Press, 1970), p. 42. [8:19]
55. Ibid., p. 45. [8:21]
56. Ibid. [8:23]
57. Immanuel Kant, "An Answer to the Question 'What is Enlightenment?'," in Hans Reiss (ed.), H. B. Nisbet (trans.), *Kant's Political Writings* (Cambridge: Cambridge University Press, 1970), p. 55. [8:36]

58. Kant, *Critique of Pure Reason*. [3:247]
59. John W. Cook, *Morality and Cultural Differences* (Oxford: Oxford University Press, 1999), p. 156.
60. Waldron, "Minority Cultures and the Cosmopolitan Alternative," in Will Kymlicka (ed.), *The Rights of Minority Cultures* (Oxford: Oxford Universtiy Press, 1995), p. 110.

# Chapter 5

# Distributive Justice and the Capability for Effective Autonomy

"Modern constitutions owe their existence to a conception found in modern natural law according to which citizens come together voluntarily to form a legal community of free and equal consociates." – Jürgen Habermas

## Introduction

Contained in the quote above is a principle inherent to the contractarian tradition, whereby constitutions numerate the rights individuals must grant one another if they want to socially cooperate under an order of universal positive law. In this regard, the modern constitution becomes the instantiation of cooperative moral law. The modern constitution translates moral law to positive law, which is meant to both reflect the beliefs of individual participants, but also to secure these individual freedoms by a commitment to equal and universal obligation. However, implicitly lurking within the quote is a conception of universal justice. In other words, these rights are mutually granted to individuals on some formulated understanding of social cooperation and this understanding rests on a conception of justice. Furthermore, in order to formulate how benefits and burdens are to be fairly allocated in connection to a conception of social cooperation we would also need to understand which normative principles this distribution is ultimately concerned to protect. The question would have to be asked by any participating member; who should have rights, who should have duties, and who owes what to whom? It would seem that John Rawls located this contractarian concern correctly when he suggested that, "the first virtue of a scheme of social cooperation is a mutually agreed conception of justice."[1]

149

The purpose of this chapter is to examine Kant's principle of justice and to develop some primary normative principles of distributive justice necessary for a cosmopolitan constitution. In other words, my goal is to discover, outline and argue for normative principles of distributive justice that would be consistent with Kant's discussion of justice and his general outline for a cosmopolitan constitution. Nevertheless, it should be stated from the start that I will by no means provide all the normative substance of Kantian distributive justice. This chapter is only an attempt to understand some of the primary elements implicit in Kant's discussion of justice and relate them to a consistent construction of cosmopolitan distributive justice. Through an examination of Kant's justice and an extrapolation of his theory, this chapter will argue that Kantian autonomy demands robust normative principles of distributive justice and that these principles should be moral considerations for human capabilities within a formulation of a Kantian-based cosmopolitan constitution.

The chapter is comprised of four sections, each dedicated to examining the distributive principles required by a possible scheme of Kantian cosmopolitan justice. The first section will explore Kant's principles of justice and attempt to relate Kant's concern with freedom to normative principles of distribution. In the second section, the concept of Kant's social welfare and distributive justice will be analyzed in order to show a strong relationship between Kant's notion of freedom, human autonomy and social justice. The third section will compare the concept of effective autonomy to Martha Nussbaum's capabilities approach, arguing that her capabilities approach provides the basic normative requirements necessary for Kantian autonomy. In the fourth section, an association is made between Kant's discussion of justice and his cosmopolitan theory, outlining how his normative principles for human autonomy could translate into a concern for global justice.

## I. NORMATIVE PRINCIPLES OF KANT'S DISTRIBUTIVE JUSTICE

What is Kant's concept of justice? It would seem that any attempt to understand Kant's cosmopolitanism in relation to schemes of distributive justice would have to begin by resolving this question first. Furthermore, since Kant does not fully develop a theory of distributive justice, it would make sense to examine any construction of Kantian social distribution in light of his overall theory of justice. By understanding the primary normative concern within Kant's works, it will help guide the further extrapolation of a Kantian conception of distributive justice. This section examines four areas of Kant's principles of justice: A. Kant's conception of freedom and justice; B. Kant's civil justice; C. Some implications of civil justice for distributive schemes; D. The idea of effective autonomy and the normative concern of distributive justice. By exploring these four subjects, I wish to make the argument that Kantian justice requires normative principles of distributive justice which focus on the individual ability to effectively translate self-law into a hypothetical *kingdom of ends*.[2] In order to provide an environment for effective autonomy, it will be argued that Kant's theory of justice demands a fairly robust distributive scheme. It will be in Section III that a further outline of these normative principles in comparison with contemporary discussions involving capability theory will be provided.

### A.   Freedom and Justice

The concept of freedom is the pivotal concern in Kant's philosophy of justice. As we have seen in Chapter 1, freedom of the *will* becomes a necessary condition for continued social freedom, for individuals can only self-legislate moral law if they are unrestricted by external constraints. In which case, the overall concept of Kant's freedom maintains two related aspects: *negative freedom*, or the capacity to act independently of external restraint; and *positive freedom*, the "property of the will to be a law onto itself."[3] It is through the aspect of positive freedom that individuals subject themselves voluntarily to moral law by legislating it for themselves. The capability to self-legislate is the power to be morally autonomous and is what Kant maintains as the ultimate source of human dignity.

Nevertheless, there is a further distinction within Kant's conception of freedom that should be discussed if we are to understand what Kantian justice requires. The distinction is between what Kant called *internal* and *external* freedom. The concept of internal freedom directly relates to an individual's psychological/physiological ability to have an independent *free will* and, in return, autonomously create self-motivating law. Internal freedom is purely cognitive and is Kant's response to both Michel De Montaigne's social determinism and David Hume's psychological empiricism. Correspondingly, external freedom is concerned with self-legislation in relation to an individual's social context and the ability to co-legislate in a kingdom of ends. In regard to external freedom, it contains a concern for both negative and positive freedom, for negative freedom is meant as an absence of external "lawless" coercion,[4] while positive freedom is concerned with how the autonomous *will* can be translated to the co-legislated *general united will*. In the Kantian model of justice, negative freedom is a necessary condition of positive freedom, because individuals can only set the moral law for themselves if they are free from "lawless" restrictions.

As a result, internal freedom is related primarily to Kant's ethical discussions (autonomous self-law), whereas external freedom is the main focus of Kant's theory of justice (equal autonomy within a kingdom of ends).[5] It is through Kant's discussions of external freedom, based on the assumption of internal freedom, that he claims a necessity to secure public right and "the restriction of each individual's freedom so that it harmonizes with the freedom of everyone else."[6] As has been discussed in previous chapters, Kant's wider conception of justice is related directly to the principle of public right, where "the sum total of those conditions within the will of one person can be reconciled with the will of another in accordance with a universal law of freedom."[7]

So what is Kant's conception of justice? From the short discussion above, we can understand Kantian justice as an attempt to facilitate a civil society where autonomous agents can socially coexist in accordance with universal freedom, which is for Kant, the property of co-legislation and the voluntary subjugation to moral laws legislated by themselves. Kant himself sets out to answer the question of justice when he proclaims, "what else, then, can freedom of the will be but autonomy, i.e. the property that the will has of being a law unto itself."[8] Therefore, for Kant, justice is "a systematic union of different rational beings through common laws"[9] which have been determined as universally valid through autonomous reflection (internal freedom) and cooperative co-legislation (external freedom).

The implications of Kant's theory of justice are considerable and a few clarifications might aid in the further development of distributive principles. First, the concept of internal and external freedom is an individualist construct. This is obvious in the fact that Kant's concern is not with how social morality determines human morality per se, but with how social morality is to be legitimated or invented through autonomous reflection and social co-legislation. Second, the concept of right is an egalitarian principle, since it affirms the equal restriction of everyone's external freedom in order to promote more equal external freedom. Since autonomy is the ultimate source of human dignity, Kant maintains that freedom must be equally respected, and as a result, equally guaranteed for everyone under a condition of public right. Third, the concept of justice is universal, since it demands the universal restriction of freedom in order to maximize an equal freedom of everyone, in all places and at all times. Fourth, Kant's theory of justice is an a priori ideal for determining a condition of public right and is meant to provide the normative grounding to which all external laws are to be legislated. In this regard, Kantian justice is meant to provide the a priori categorical standard that all external legislation is to be held accountable. Fifth, the main function of civil authority is to maintain the rule of law, protect the rights of its subjects and to legislate civil laws in accordance with the principle of justice. All of these principles and definitions express essentially the same thought, "that justice is a condition in which each individual's external freedom is restricted so as to make it consistent with the freedom of all others in the framework of a common law or system of laws."[10]

Nevertheless, Kantian justice takes on further dimensions in relation to external freedom. Kant's discussion of justice is divided into two subdivisions, *civil justice* and *criminal justice*. Both divisions relate directly with external freedom in that they address the relationship between autonomous individuals and social cooperation. However, for the purposes of this chapter, it is the realm of civil justice where exploration of distributive justice is meaningful.

## B.   Civil Justice and Kant's Distributive Vagueness

Civil justice is itself a complex assortment of concepts, but can be reduced to three forms, *protective, commutative* and *distributive*. Protective justice relates directly to negative freedom and the cooperative role of securing equal protection under equal rights. Commutative and distributive justice are concerned more with aspects of positive freedom, or with securing a person's freedom to do certain things within a social environment. All forms relate directly to Kant's broader use of justice, namely, how to distinguish rightful external freedom from the "lawless" freedom found within the state of nature.[11] With this in mind, both protective and commutative justice are regarded as private rights (rights held by individuals that can be secured through one-on-one relations), whereas distributive justice is what Kant believes to be public right (right held by individuals only under civil conditions). The distinction between private and public right is defined by the possibility of universal external freedom. This is because protective and commutative justice can be found (albeit in extremely limited form) within the state of nature, whereas distributive justice can only be possible within a civil condition. For Kant, the only way to guarantee all three forms of justice is within a civil condition of justice, although limited forms of protective and commutative schemes are possible in the state of nature.

Although Kant arranges the three forms of justice in complicated fashion, the first two concepts are easily understood. Protective justice is the idea of equal security under equal rights and "the restriction of each individual's freedom so that it harmonizes with the freedom of everyone else."[12] In this regard, protective justice is concerned directly with equal protection from physical harm or from other acts of "lawless" coercion. Kant believed that individuals could form limited protective schemes in the state of nature, but that only within a civil society could negative freedom (absence of violent coercion and "lawless" threat) and therefore the possibility for external freedom, be ultimately secured for everyone.

Commutative justice is directly related to Kant's concept of external freedom, where individuals can relate their autonomous self-law to "binding" social obligations. Kant maintained that within the state of nature, individuals could form limited schemes of cooperative interchange, where basic contracts could be secured between one individual and another (or small groups), and where some obligations could therefore be considered as morally binding. Nevertheless, Kant maintains that without universal cooperation and equal enforcement from all members, schemes of commutative justice in the state of nature will quickly disintegrate back to warlike anarchy. It is therefore only in a universal scheme of civil justice that external freedom can be secured for everyone.

Kant's vision of distributive justice is not as clearly defined as the other concepts of civil justice. Distributive justice is certainly concerned with external freedom and the obligatory relationships between individuals within a scheme of social cooperation. However, the discussion of this public right is limited. When we unpack all the discussions of distributive justice within Kant's text, we find that distributive justice relates to the distribution of rights, but is ultimately referred back to the a priori ideal of justice without many practical examples or detailed analysis. The concept seems to be directly concerned with social cooperation and the civil state's role in both assigning rights, but also in adjudicating conflicts between individual rights. This suggests that when rights conflict, distributive justice is the area of political legislation aimed at resolving these conflicts. These conflicts are to be resolved by legislating laws that reflect the principle of justice and therefore secure "the restriction of each individual's freedom so that it harmonizes with the freedom of everyone else."[13] According to Kant, distributive justice is the realm where public rights are maintained in accordance with the principle of justice and a broader application of the categorical imperative. Distributive justice, in this sense, is meant as an expansion of the categorical imperative, for it is broadened to a more universal concept of public right, namely: "act in such a way that you treat humanity, whether in your own person or in the person of another, always as at the same time as an end, and never as a means."[14] Unfortunately, what Kant means by this in relation to a scheme of distributive justice remains unclear, for he fails to explain how benefits (ends) and burdens (means) of distributive justice are to be socially assigned.

## C.  *Kant's Civil Justice and some Implications for Distributive Justice*

The primary focus of justice for Kant is securing external freedom and autonomy. As we have seen, this freedom consists of both an internal freedom (*free will*) and an external freedom (co-legislation and autonomy in social context). Distributive justice, or how Kant's social cooperative scheme fairly distributes rights, is the exclusive concern of external freedom and the relationship between co-legislation and justice. One consideration for distributive justice is the assigning of negative rights from "lawless" coercion. These negative rights are for Kant to be distributed evenly, so that everyone's external freedom harmonizes with the external freedom of everyone else. In this sense, negative rights from violence, coercion, fraud, theft and general acts against individual property are equally assigned and therefore demand equal obligation from all cooperating members. Kant is very clear about this when he states that the use of state coercion is to prevent interference with liberty.[15]

However, the assignment of social rights of distributive justice becomes more complicated in relation to Kant's positive duties, or in regard to a public claim for the assistance of others. Nevertheless, if Kant's ultimate normative concerns are external freedom and autonomous co-legislation in the kingdom of ends, then there seems to be an argument to be made for a fairly robust concept of positive distributive justice. If equal autonomy is the ultimate protective value for Kantian justice, then we must also assume that the effective use of one's autonomy requires a certain civil environment beyond the realm of respecting only negative freedom. Autonomy as protected by only negative duties to non-interference raises the question; what good is being autonomous in self-direction, if an individual has no resources in which to survive? Even if we assume that one has access to subsistence level resources, we can further ask what good is individual autonomy if people have an unequal ability to co-legislate for reasons outside their control? How can those without sufficient life opportunities in Kant's society effectively translate their autonomous reflections to a hypothetical kingdom of ends? Kant certainly maintained that a legitimate and just order is one that derives its legislation from the reasoning of a hypothetical general united will. In order for the expression of this co-legislated will to be possible, it would seem logical to assume that certain political organizations would be critical in fostering the effectiveness of one's autonomous expression.

The immediate problem with Kant's discussion of distributive justice, in regard to positive freedom, is that he does not sufficiently explain how to secure an effective use of one's autonomy in social context. Although having negative rights to autonomous expression is an important step for continued civil co-legislation, having this negative right is useless if one does not have the means to exercise it. In this case, individual autonomy is a hollow procession, for it's very existence is not only based on process-ing the ability to think autonomously (internal freedom), but also on processing a reasonable ability to act upon one's own self-reflection in co-legislation (external freedom).[16] What results from Kant's theory of justice is that we have a priori external restraints and requirements, but no cohe-sive distributive outline for guaranteeing the effective use of one's external freedom and autonomy. More coherent principles of distributive justice are needed to move Kant from a priori demands for freedom within a kingdom of ends, to the effective use of autonomy in social co-legislation.

## D.   The Idea of Effective Autonomy

It is at this point that I wish to introduce the idea of effective autonomy. The concept of effective autonomy directly relates to Kant's concern for human autonomy and the distributive principles needed for the develop-ment of external freedom (co-legislation). The relationship I have in mind is the following: *effective autonomy is the ability to reasonably achieve the intended or desired result of one's conscience and self-legislation in a social context (co-legislation, external freedom and the kingdom of ends).* The effective condition of one's autonomy is considerably influenced by what I call an *aspect capacity,* or the interrelationship between an individual's social environment and the development of their co-legislative capabilities. The concept of *aspect capacity is the ability to formulate, hold and act upon an individual's social conscience based on external elements (aspects or facets for external freedom) affecting the development of one's co-legislative capabilities.* In this regard, effective autonomy is meant as an a priori ideal of autonomy and the social capability to pursue self-determined ends, while aspect capacity relates to whether social conditions exist that promote the effective ability of this autonomous capability.

It might be best to further introduce the concept of effective autonomy and aspect capacity by use of analogy. In microbiology, specifically in genetic research, the development of genotypes is often affected by the regulation of proteins from other genetic strands or dominant genes within a specific genetic pool. If certain genes have genetic malformalities, genes further down the double-helix lose valuable proteins and thus fail to develop to their genetically determined capacity. The area between their determined capacity and the actual level of development could be labeled as what I am calling aspect capacity. Since the gene is unable to develop to its full capacity, due to a failure from external nutrition, the gene suffers from a reduction in its aspect capacity (the restrictions placed upon the capacity of a gene by external factors outside the capabilities of the gene).

The concept of effective autonomy is analogous to the development of the gene. On the assumption that internal freedom is possible, as Kant assumes, external forces beyond one's total control shape the development of one's external freedom and ability to co-legislate. If the civil state reduces the possibility for autonomous development, then the individual's aspect capacity is reduced and the effectiveness of one's autonomy is retarded and lacks external freedom. Nevertheless, if the civil state provides an environment that allows for the development of one's autonomy, and individuals are actually able to participate in co-legislated ends, then that individual's aspect capacity is increased along with the effectiveness of their autonomous external freedom.

If we assume that all human beings have certain capabilities for autonomous judgement and a corresponding ability to act upon them (given an environment that in some way supports this ability), then the area between their capacity and their actual development can be called an aspect capacity. The aspect capacity, in this regard, is the area where an agent's personal ability for autonomous action is either retarded or promoted in its development by external aspects. One social scenario could be that individuals can reason, judge and can wish to act upon their autonomous thoughts, but are unable to, since political, environmental and economic factors adversely affect one's effective autonomy by limiting one's aspect capacity. However, if the political, environmental and economic elements increase the capability to reasonably achieve the intended result of autonomous self-legislation, then we could say that the individual enjoys more effective autonomy and that the civil environment increases one's aspect capacity.

The goal of Kant's justice, it seems to me, is to equally legitimate the restricting external elements on one's aspect capacity (negative freedom) while providing a social position in which everyone's autonomous capabilities develop and function (positive freedom) towards a kingdom of ends. In the Kantian model of justice, negative freedom is a necessary condition of positive freedom, because individuals can only set the moral law for themselves if they are free from "lawless" restrictions. Nevertheless, the realization of external freedom requires both the reducing of inequalities created by "lawless" freedom and also the reducing of arbitrary civil inequalities, so that each individual is an effective agent in co-legislation and the kingdom of ends. For Kant, the ultimate source of human dignity is the ability to be morally autonomous and to obligate oneself to co-legislated morals within civil society, based on universal principles of public right.

Besides the problem one might have with Kant's assumption that internal freedom (free will) is possible, my definition of effective autonomy immediately raises another critical point of clarification. A clarification is needed for what I mean by "reasonably achieve." To clarify what the limitation of this means, it needs to be connected to the principle of justice, since effective autonomy is directly related to external freedom. As we know, justice requires that the will of one person can be reconciled with the will of another in accordance with a universal law of freedom. The universal law of freedom suggests the categorical imperative, which mandates that all moral actions should be considered in light of whether they can be made universal. The "reasonably achieve" clause of my definition suggests the same, that co-legislation must conform to the categorical imperative in order to eliminate moral legislation that cannot be reconciled with the will of others and therefore violates justice.[17]

So what are the implications of effective autonomy for Kant's distributive justice? I believe the implications are that a Kantian theory of justice ultimately demands a reasonable effectiveness of one's autonomy and the ability to co-legislate in a hypothetical kingdom of ends. In order to secure the effectiveness of individual autonomy, it seems necessary to provide a civil environment that in some sense promotes the development of external freedom equally. In order to further provide for this environment, normative duties for distributive justice must be incorporated into the civil constitution. Furthermore, these normative principles of distributive justice are primarily concerned with the ability for effective autonomy and increased aspect capacity by all participating members. In other words, under a Kantian conception of justice, the civil authority has to distribute rights so that both basic needs and the development of individual autonomy are secured under a perpetual condition of public right. It will be my argument in Section III, that this idea of effective autonomy can be best understood in relation to Martha Nussbaum's *capabilities approach*.

## II.   KANT'S SOCIAL WELFARE AND DISTRIBUTIVE JUSTICE

However, before we discuss the relationship between effective autonomy and capability theory, it is important to understand exactly how Kant discussed social welfare policy and governmental duties to protect external freedom. This will enable us to further expand his theory of justice into more concrete normative principles of distributive justice. Once we further understand that effective autonomy demands a certain amount of social welfare and a normative commitment to distributive justice, a brief examination of a Kantian argument for global justice can be undertaken. In addition, it will be from this discussion of effective autonomy and Kant's social welfare that a strong case for distributive justice can be made in comparison with capability theory.

There is a problem, however, with uncovering Kant's relationship between the satisfaction of human development, social welfare legislation and the role of authoritative power. In many instances, Kant seems to make contradicting claims concerning social welfare. On the one hand, Kant claims the political order should be nothing more than a minimalist watchman state. Many Kantian scholars profess that Kant envisioned only a negative duty of the state to protect the polity from outside threats, to

159

protect individual liberty, enforce contracts and to prevent fraud. Related to this minimalist conception, social welfare legislation is interpreted as an abuse of political power outside the legitimate scope of state duty. Only in cases of extreme upheaval or economic chaos can a government legitimately take positive social action to secure the stability of the state, in an attempt to avoid a return to the Hobbesian state of nature.

Conversely, textual evidence also provides compelling evidence that Kant envisioned a fairly robust system of social welfare. In some circumstances, Kant proclaimed a duty to provide welfare, where government has a moral duty to ensure the "human needs" of its citizens. In order to make sense of this contradiction, it is important to discuss both the minimalist and the more robust interpretations of Kant's social welfare theory and to attempt to generate a coherent understanding. From this exercise, it can be shown that Kant maintained that there was a necessary and strong relationship between welfare and the protection of external freedom under a condition of public right. A relationship that ultimately demands a more robust system of distributive justice than has typically been assumed. A system of distributive justice that supports the sort of effective autonomy and conditions for external freedom that is profoundly important to Kant's ideal kingdom of ends.

## A.   *The Minimalist Interpretation of Kant's Social Welfare*

Kantian scholars who endorse the minimalist interpretation point to three major areas of Kant's thought. The first argument is that Kant had a profound fear of governmental paternalism. Kant repeatedly proclaimed that state legislation directed toward fostering the happiness of citizens effectively treats autonomous individuals as "immature children who cannot distinguish what is truly useful or harmful to themselves."[18] According to Kant, legislation based on governmental ends produces the "greatest conceivable despotism" and removes the individual's *right* to pursue their own end. In his strongest statement against governmental promotion of social welfare and a state conception of happiness, Kant claims that this sort of "paternal government [demands] . . . how one ought to be happy . . . leaving subjects with no rights whatsoever."[19]

The second argument for the minimalist state is to be found in Kant's conception of public right. Kant claims that "external right . . . the mutual external relationships of human beings . . . has nothing to do with the end which all men have by nature (i.e. the aim of achieving happiness)

160

or with the recognized means of attaining that end."[20] All right requires is a concept of justice that demands "the restriction of each individual's freedom so that it harmonizes with the freedom of everyone else."[21] Minimalists argue that this statement, in addition to Kant's vague discussion of distributive justice, supports the notion that individuals only have negative duties to respect the freedom of others, and therefore do not have a duty to provide for their needs. It has been argued from this textual evidence and many other similar passages found throughout the works of Kant, that social welfare can not be based on Kant's conception of public right.[22]

The final argument for the minimalist interpretation derives from the aforementioned discussion but focuses on Kant's corresponding argument for autonomous choice. As Kant outlines in *The Doctrine of Right*, the only justified use of state coercion is to prevent the mutual interference of each other's freedom so that "the choice of one can be united with the choice of another in accordance with a universal law of freedom."[23] Many scholars who use Kantian philosophy as an argument for the minimalist state claim that this negative interpretation of right can be the only acceptable justification for state coercion.[24] It is therefore asserted that no state policy to improve the lives of others is acceptable without consent. The application of social welfare policy without direct consent is coercion and in violation of the first principle of right. Furthermore, Kant's taxonomy of duties seems to forbid the state to compel anyone to adopt an end. Since an end is a goal formulated from an individual's autonomous reflection and choice, the state cannot force an end to assist others. The *duties of virtue* are the consensual adoption of ends and are exclusive of the *duties of right*, which only demand the omission of external violations of liberty.[25]

As textual evidence shows, the argument against a social welfare interpretation of Kant is not a weak one. Throughout the works of Kant, readers will find textual evidence to support many of the aforementioned minimalist claims. As a result, the only social welfare legislation believed by minimalist interpretations as valid is a system of social welfare promoted when the civil state is threatened by collapse. In other words, minimalists agree that Kant maintained a governmental duty for the survival of the civil state and that state survival can override the negative freedoms protected within the *Doctrine of Right*. However, overriding negative freedom is only legitimate under special circumstances where the existence of the state is threatened. Bruce Aune perhaps provides the best articulation of what the minimalists accept as the only form of appropriate welfare legislation when he states that "it is therefore justifiable . . . when and only when it is necessary for the continued existence of civil society."[26] In this regard, the minimalist argument can therefore be summarized as containing two main attacks. First, that the state cannot force the acceptance of an end and therefore cannot promote social welfare. Secondly, governmental duties regarding social welfare are not imperative and are therefore secondary to the ultimate imperative of negative freedom. Only in the case of extreme decline or protracted security concerns can the government compel welfare legislation for the continued existence of the civil state.

### B.  Kant's Principle of Publicity and the Argument for Distributive Justice

Before the minimalists can assume the validity of their interpretation, it is important to reconsider why Kant thought that the existence of civil society was necessary for both internal and external freedom. The reason civil order is significant is that it acts as the mechanism to protect and foster individual autonomy and a system of public right. It is the concern with individual autonomy and the right to equally express this autonomy socially (external freedom), that the existence of the civil state becomes so critical. If the civil state is ill, then the possibility for meaningful external freedom is also ill, and there exists the possibility that the cooperative order will collapse. This collapse, according to Kant, is more destructive than any legislation aimed at rebuilding the health of the state, and in essence, at securing the individual autonomy that provides co-legislation and the extended formulation of a possible united general will.[27] Kant understands that equal autonomy is only effective when bound within a civil order and therefore allows social welfare legislation in cases where the relationship between autonomy (internal freedom) and universal co-legislation (external freedom) is threatened. Nevertheless, Kant takes this further:

> The general will of the people has united itself into a society which is to maintain itself perpetually; and for this end it has submitted itself to the internal authority of the state in order to maintain those members of the society who are unable to maintain themselves. For reasons of the state the government is therefore authorized to constrain the wealthy to provide the means of sustenance to those who are unable to provide for even their most necessary natural needs . . . on this obligation the state now bases its right to contribute what is theirs to maintaining their fellow citizens.[28]

Kant goes on to argue:

> This can be done either by imposing a tax on property or the commerce of citizens, or by establishing funds and using the interest from them, not for the needs of the state (for it is rich), but for the needs of the people. It will do this by way of coercion (since we are speaking here only of the right of the state against the people), by public taxation, not merely by voluntary contributions . . . to support organizations providing for the poor, founding [institutions] . . . widows homes, schools, hospitals, and the like.[29]

It would seem from this passage that several important implications concerning social welfare legislation could be made. First, the governmental duty for human welfare is a united commitment reflecting the will of citizens in a hypothetical kingdom of ends. Second, autonomous individuals create civil society and the governmental apparatus for a critical purpose, namely the preservation of civil society and, in essence, the continued possibility for external freedom and public right. From this comes the third and most important implication, namely that basic human needs must be provided for by the government in order to fulfill the duties of the state apparatus (enforcing maxims directed by autonomous reflection and acceptance) and for the assumption of a hypothetical united general will to be a legitimate expression of co-legislation.

From the discussion above, it would seem that there exists a tension within Kant between the governmental duty to provide social welfare and the argument suggested by minimalist interpretations. Although no absolute discovery can be made as to Kant's original intention, we can attempt to make coherent sense of his social welfare theory in general. It is in attempts to clarify and reconcile Kant's theory that I will discuss Kant's social welfare argument as it has been interpreted by Allen Rosen and Otfried Hoffe. This will be done in order to illustrate that a general priority is given to the position of effective autonomy in civil order. Through this discussion it will be argued that the ultimate protection of external freedom demands a system of distributive justice and that this system does not contradict, and in fact compliments, Kant's overall concern of justice.[30]

In *Perpetual Peace*, Kant outlines the welfare duties of government and the deliberation process necessary for legislation to remain consistent with external freedom and public right. Kant discusses a negative and a positive corresponding political duty that work in tandem to create the *principle of publicity*. The negative "political" duty relates directly to identifying maxims that morally violate the principle of public right and are

163

thus inappropriate for domestic law, international law and cosmopolitan law. The positive duty of government is to identify maxims that are both consistent and complementary with the interest of public right. The principle of publicity asserts that maxims that do not fail the test of application and in fact promote public right are required to be made public and are therefore "reconciled with both right and politics."[31]

Accordingly, Kant maintains that maxims that satisfy the rule, "conform to the universal aim of the public (which is happiness)."[32] Furthermore, this is not a violation of governmental duty, as minimalists claim, since it is "the particular task of politics" to facilitate the principle of publicity.[33]

Unfortunately, Kant does not expand on the principle of publicity and proclaims that he must "postpone the further elaboration and discussion of this principle until another occasion."[34] However, unlike the claims made by minimalists who suggest that Kant is simply contradictory or was senile at the time,[35] his discussion of the principle of publicity fits nicely with what Rosen labels Kant's *principle of humanity*.[36] For example, Rosen suggests that "the principle of publicity amounts to the rule that maxims are fit to serve as public laws if their adoption as laws would promote the happiness of all citizens."[37] It would seem that this is a generally beneficial interpretation, for the principle of publicity can reconcile the concerns championed by the minimalists. As Rosen maintains, a lexical ordering is in place; rights and benevolence are authentic moral obligations, where the duty to respect individual rights trumps the duty of benevolence, but only when they come into conflict with justice.[38] It is the duty of government to test distributive policies and thus further the "particular aim of politics."[39] In other words, the duty of government is the process of politics and finding a suitable equilibrium between social benevolence and a general conception of equal public right. Since the united general will is meant to legitimize benevolent principles, the government is not forcing an end, but overseeing the fact that these principles meet co-legislated demands of universal public reason.

In order to further extrapolate a universal duty of social welfare policy and devise a maxim of distributive justice, Rosen has applied the Kantian method of indirect proof by method of *reductio ad absurdum*. Since all rational individuals *will* that their needs are met, and since there are no guarantees that the satisfaction of needs can be achieved without the assistance of others, the rational person would *will* that the help of others would be equally available should he find himself in need of it. When coupled with the *principle of publicity*, the government becomes the appropriate expression of maxims derived by a general united will, and since the general united will is the collective expression of autonomous actors, if this maxim meets the co-legislated demands of public right, then a social welfare policy could be legitimately instituted.[40]

Nevertheless, Hoffe suggests that it is "not necessary to fall back on the duty of virtue" as Allen does when he invokes Kant's principle of humanity.[41] This is because Hoffe believes that Kant's discussion for a welfare state can be understood through an analysis of the *Doctrine of Right* alone, by focusing on what he calls the "argument from perpetual stability."[42] As Hoffe states, Kant is clear that "the general will of the people has united itself into a society which is to maintain itself perpetually" and that under Kant's moral law a "welfare state that is indispensable to the rule of law is morally imperative."[43] Under this reading, any condition that threatens the perpetual stability of the state "must be combated" in order for the civil apparatus to guarantee a continued condition of public right and external freedom.[44] As Hoffe suggests, Kant stipulates that government "takes on the responsibility that emerges from the duty of people, since the people subject themselves to the executive power only under the proviso ('for this end') that they are preserved 'perpetually'."[45] In this regard, "the government must take on the task of subsistence that the members of the society originally guaranteed each other, since, as an executive power, the government influences the scope of action by society."[46] This, according to Hoffe, does not mean that the system is exclusively geared toward maintaining external freedom, although this is certainly the point of maintaining a perpetual condition of public right, but that it is also meant to compensate for the loss of power originally held by individuals prior to submitting to a civil union.

However, the two positions are not incompatible, since Rosen also seeks to understand how a provision of welfare in a condition of perpetual stability could be situated in the original constitution. Rosen tackles this question in a slightly different way than Hoffe, but with a similar conclusion, by thinking hypothetically about Kant's rational contract, suggesting that "no people could rationally agree to a constitution that failed to contain a provision guaranteeing (at least) the basic needs of all citizens. Constitutionally guaranteed rights to a minimal level of well-being are thus, on Kantian principles, part of the structure of any just and rational civil society."[47] In comparison with Hoffe, Rosen bases this interpretation on Kant's understanding of why states must exist and their ultimate invention for the protection of civil society. Allowing Rosen's conclusion to speak for itself, "survival is a primary purpose of political society, it is natural to suppose that rational participants in a social contract would give recognition to this fact by incorporating into the constitution of their state a duty on the part of governments to provide for their basic needs."[48] It is the importance of achieving some greater equality of autonomy through cooperation and the long-term security of civil society that participants in constructing the original contract would rationally accept welfare principles. We find that Kant confirms Rosen's conclusion when he states that "[Individuals] have acquired an obligation to the commonwealth, since they owe their existence to an act of submitting to its protection and care, which they need in order to live; on this obligation the state now bases its right to contribute what is theirs to maintaining their fellow citizens."[49]

However, there remains an important question. If Rosen and Hoffe are correct in arguing that a condition of public right requires a formulation of social cooperation that supports a system of distributive justice (and that this system is based on an effective form of public reason), then we still need to know what normative principles of distributive justice underpin this condition. It is in response to this question that Kant fails to provide an acceptable distributive theory moving from a priori principles of public right to distributive cooperation. Although Kant's discussion of a priori principles of moral imperative and the corresponding taxonomy of duties underline the importance of effective autonomy, perpetual stability and the need for some form of distributive justice, Kant himself does not provide elaboration beyond the fact that an individual's basic needs must be met. Kant's pronouncement that he must "postpone the elaboration and discussion of this principle until another occasion"[50] best expresses the reason why Kant's theory of publicity and distributive justice is not well developed. Nevertheless, it is from understanding Kant's concern with external freedom and how basic human needs must be met to allow for the effective use of one's autonomy under a perpetual scheme of public right that we understand why Kantian justice could demand a substantial form of distributive justice. The remainder of this chapter will examine the relationship between effective autonomy and capability theory. It is through the following discussion that a comparison between effective autonomy and Martha Nussbaum's capability theory is given. From this discussion I argue that her outline of human capabilities best expresses the primary normative principles necessary to create an environment of increased aspect capacity and effective autonomy as argued in Section II.

## III.   EFFECTIVE AUTONOMY AND CAPABILITIES FOR FREEDOM

The last two sections attempted to examine and outline the normative concerns implicit in Kant's distributive justice, namely, the effectiveness of external freedom in the kingdom of ends. It has been my suggestion that in order to provide an environment conducive to Kantian freedom, the civil constitution would have to implement distributive principles that could act as normative considerations for the promotion of effective autonomy and external freedom. In this section, I compare effective autonomy with Martha Nussbaum's capability theory[51] and suggest that a capabilities focus best provides the additional normative principles necessary for a scheme of Kantian distributive justice and for the promotion of effective autonomy (external freedom) under a condition of perpetual stability.

Nussbaum states, "the aim of the project [capability theory] as a whole is to provide the philosophical underpinning for an account of basic constitutional principles that should be implemented by the governments of all nations, as a bare minimum of what respect for human dignity requires." With this in mind, Nussbaum suggests that this basic social minimum would be best served by focusing on human capabilities, or as Nussbaum proclaims, "what people are actually able to do and to be – in a way informed by the intuitive idea of a life that is worthy of the dignity of the human being." By this, Nussbaum suggests that her list of capabilities acts as the normative principles in determining *a threshold level of capability*, under which "human functioning is not available to citizens." The normative social goal is to provide an environment that brings individuals above the threshold.[52]

Before I continue to outline what these capabilities are and why they might act as constitutional normative principles, I wish to examine Nussbaum's stated aim in relation to the Kantian project I have been sketching. Although I am justifying human dignity through a Kantian argument (external freedom and autonomy), whereas Nussbaum is not,[53] it would seem that both Nussbaum and I share an interest in providing normative elements to secure constitutional principles of distributive justice and human freedom. In this sense, Nussbaum's capabilities act within the area I have been calling aspect capacity, with her *threshold level* being an indicator of where autonomy is no longer considered effective. It should also be noted that Nussbaum's capabilities are complementary to Kant's public right, for her capabilities "should be pursued for each and every person, treating each as an end and none as a mere tool for the ends of others."[54] In order to facilitate this idea, she states them as *the principle of each person's capability*, based on *a principle of each person as end*. Nussbaum grounds these principles in Kantian fashion, albeit not directly, by suggesting that both concepts are justified by the possibility of an overlapping consensus, where individual conceptions of the good can be reconciled under a normative conception of universal justice.[55] In this regard, Nussbaum sounds rather Kantian in that her system of justice requires "the sum total of those conditions within the choice of one person can be reconciled with the choice of another in accordance with a universal law of freedom."[56]

The universal human capabilities, which, according to Nussbaum, should underwrite a distributive scheme of social cooperation, can be paraphrased as follows:

1. Life. The ability to live to the natural end of one's life, and not to live at a reduced state where life is not worth living.
2. Bodily health. The ability to live in good health; including nourishment and adequate housing.
3. Bodily integrity. Freedom of movement and protection from bodily harm.
4. Senses, imagination and thought. The ability to use one's reason in a truly human way, including access to adequate education in all subjects, freedom of expression and having the ability to enjoy pleasurable experiences. "Being able to search for the ultimate meaning of life in one's own way."
5. Emotions. The ability to form emotional attachments, not having "one's emotional development blighted by overwhelming fear and anxiety."
6. Practical Reason. "Being able to form a conception of the good and to engage in critical reflection about the planning of one's life."
7. Affiliation. The ability to live with others, to form conceptions of justice and friendship. "Having the social bases of respect and non-humiliation," being treated as an end.
8. Other beings. The ability to live with the world of nature and to have concern for future generations.
9. Play. The ability to enjoy "recreational activities."
10. Control of one's environment in both political and material terms. "Being able to participate effectively in political choices that govern one's life; having the right to political participation." The ability to hold goods and property for the advancement of real opportunities.[57]

Nussbaum's argument is that the attainment of these capabilities is possible for everyone and that it is generally an individual's political, social and economic environment that determines whether these capabilities are developed. Furthermore, Nussbaum claims that these are not separate components, for the development of one capability usually relies on the functioning of the other. Therefore, in order to provide an environment that develops these capabilities, it should be done with all of them equally in mind and with universal application. As Nussbaum suggests, "human beings are creatures such that, provided with the right educational and material support, they can become fully capable of all these human functions."[58]

The Kantian concepts of internal and external freedom can be directly related to Nussbaum's argument for human capabilities. For Kant, the ability to be autonomous has internal aspects, namely the freedom from "alien causes," and external aspects, or the combined (internal and external) ability that allows for autonomous translation in the kingdom of ends. Based on the assumption of internal freedom, Kant's conception of justice is concerned with the ability to be an autonomous member in a scheme of social cooperation. In order to provide for the effective autonomy of individuals, the social order must not only "promote the appropriate development of their internal powers, but also prepare the environment so that it is favorable for the exercise of practical reason and the other major functions."[59]

The capabilities enumerated above add specific considerations for principles of distributive justice. However, these principles in and of themselves do not constitute a complete theory of justice. In this regard, capabilities act as normative considerations within the formation of a cooperative order and its corresponding constitutional framework. The capabilities focus attention on human functioning and the elements of development that are necessary in order for individuals to formulate autonomous beliefs and to transfer them to co-legislation. Nevertheless, Nussbaum's list of capabilities should not be considered as complete, for many of her required capabilities might not fit the Kantian mold, or will need to be expanded to accommodate other Kantian constitutional requirements. What the list provides is some normative substance to a scheme of Kantian justice and how Kantian cosmopolitans might consider human autonomy in relation to global distributive justice.

Where capability theory still needs improvement is in the area of determining where the threshold level can be reasonably placed and what role questions of equality will play once individuals move beyond the threshold standard. I would suggest that both of these are critical concerns that should be advanced by those advocating the capability approach.

However, the most relevant critique of capability theory is that it does not provide any further assistance as to where to place the threshold level. Thomas Pogge, for example, claims that the capability approach cannot deliver a more "plausible public criterion of social justice" than resource-based theories.[60] Furthermore, the capability approach does not seem to provide a minimum standard where capability development can be reasonably expected across cultural boundaries. Where capability theory has difficulty setting a threshold minimum, it also has difficulty providing a reasonable explanation why various cultures would accept any minimal standard based on Nussbaum's liberal notion of selfhood.[61]

One answer to the concern of threshold placement can be made by suggesting that the more institutional considerations, can and will, take place only within the process of cooperation and cannot be determined without participating insight. In addition, the question of threshold can at our present stage of world development be largely factored intuitively. By this I mean that we can usually determine when the development of an individual's capabilities are hampered by their political, social and economic environment. For example, it is not difficult to determine that someone does not have significant capability development when they are beaten daily, or sleep outside a storefront in a state of starvation. Furthermore, since the current world environment (not to mention a vast majority of states) hardly provides for the development of human capabilities, we can, with less reservation, understand Nussbaum's suggestion to defer questions of social minimums until some reasonable level of developmental improvement is upon us.

Nevertheless, Nussbaum's list of capabilities does invite criticisms as to whether it can be applied cross-culturally. Although Nussbaum denies having metaphysical assumptions, the major critique against cross-cultural application is based on the fact that her list of capabilities rests on a conception of autonomy and moral selfhood. Even though Nussbaum argues that the capability list only reflects inherent human qualities, her overall argument is nonetheless "based on the philosophical conviction that all people could flourish better as free and responsible moral agents."[62]

A Kantian version of capability theory, although guilty of some cross-cultural difficulty, must be based on the metaphysical assumption of human agency and therefore derive its normative principles from this understanding of selfhood. This is because Kant's conception of external freedom is based on the assumption of *free will* and therefore must be grounded on a conception of justice that reflects this notion of autonomy in order to remain consistent. These universal principles of autonomy are exactly the intended ideals for Kant's cosmopolitanism. The result of Kant's demand is that normative shifts will have to occur within certain cultures in order to realize this metaphysical ideal. Nevertheless, the goal for a universal order based on autonomy is not meant to restrict the freedom of choosing one's end, but to allow for one's chosen end to have social meaning. The basis for any ideal of universal freedom, even strict cultural relativism, has to have a normative grounding for what it considers as being "free." The Kantian outline that I have tried to make does not deny this metaphysical assumption, but attempts to facilitate the creation of a *kingdom of ends* where "the choice of one person can be reconciled with the choice of another in accordance with a universal law of freedom."[63] In guaranteeing that central human capabilities are accessible to all citizens, capability theory leaves room for individuals to decide for themselves how useful the capabilities are to further their ends. "In aiming to promote people's capabilities to different valuable human functioning what it ultimately strives at is to promote them as free and responsible moral agents who recognize themselves and others as capable human beings."[64]

Although the capability approach leaves considerable questions for a theory of justice unanswered, it does provide some useful normative guidelines for the universal promotion of human development. It is in terms of providing metaphysical constitutional requirements, namely, what effective autonomy might need in the way of distributive principles, that the theory can be useful for Kant's move toward a kingdom of ends. Metaphysics for Kant is the elaboration of a priori propositions approximated by constructed laws of reason. Kant accepts that a complete account of justice is impossible and therefore maintains that his principles are only meant to provide the foundations for future discussions regarding practical application. In the next section, I will briefly discuss why Kant's belief in autonomy extends to an overall concern for constitutional cosmopolitanism and global justice.

## IV. EFFECTIVE AUTONOMY AND COSMOPOLITAN CONCERNS FOR DISTRIBUTIVE JUSTICE

As it was discussed in Chapter 1, Kant outlines his argument for a cosmopolitan order in two ways. On the one hand, he makes his appeal on an empirical level, outlining the practical need for order through historical examination and through the examination of international tensions that plagued his time. On the other hand, he sets up normative a priori principles of jurisprudence, where practical reason dictates a *cosmopolitan right* to external freedom. Kant defines cosmopolitanism as "the matrix within which all the original capacities of the human race may develop . . . [by] attaining a civil society which can administer justice universally."[65] In a fusion of empirical experience with normative principles, Kant maintains that humans cannot avoid physical contact with one another and therefore must enter into a global constitution that secures mutual right and spheres of external freedom for everyone. Nevertheless, Kant does not tell us exactly how this international order will ultimately look, or provide details as to how global institutions and economic structures will function to protect mutual cosmopolitan right.

In regard to questions concerning international distributive justice, global justice, or what some contemporary cosmopolitan theorists call global economic justice,[66] Kant offers as little commentary as he does with regard to domestic economic justice. In the works of Kant, only direct appeals for the creation of cosmopolitan law to overcome the global state of nature are made. Like Kant's domestic view, the perceived Hobbesian international state of nature not only continually threatens international order, but also weakens the possibility of sustainable domestic order. In relation to international economic stability, Kant believed that "civil freedom can no longer be so easily infringed without disadvantage to all trades and industries, and especially to commerce, in the event of which the state's power in its external relations will also decline."[67] What is explicit in Kant's quote is an understanding that economic prosperity has a direct effect on both domestic and international order. Kant alludes that by weakening the global economy through self-motivation, states in fact weaken their own domestic political concerns by disadvantaging the polity's access to commerce. This implies that laws to maintain international order are in the state's best interest (for the ends of its people), because failure to adjudicate economic and political concerns eventually ends in empirically evidenced conflict and international economic decline.[68] Kant believed that to protect both a civil and economic order (perpetually), an international order must guarantee a cosmopolitan right to universal hospitality as a minimal basis for a continued move toward a more robust cosmopolitan condition. As mentioned in Chapters 1 and 2, hospitality can be seen as a minimal level of respect for an individual's external freedom and cosmopolitan right to fairly associate, trade, communicate and exchange ideas without conflict or mistreatment. As Kant suggests, "since the earth is a globe, [humans] cannot disperse over an infinite area, but must necessarily tolerate one another's company."[69] Since the surface of the globe is finite, "the peoples of the world have entered in various degrees into a universal community, and it has developed to the point where a violation of rights in one part of the world is felt everywhere."[70]

Although Kant maintains that cosmopolitan right is necessary for an individual's autonomy to flourish in regard to his need to engage in economic trade and to expand the possibility of instituting a cosmopolitan condition, he never broadens this argument by adequately outlining what positive distributive elements are necessary for this effective use of one's autonomy and how this can be pursued at the global level.[71] In addition, Kant never expands his discussions on social welfare and the implications of economic distributive justice to his cosmopolitan thought. The lack of discussion is simply due to the fact that Kant did not foresee the demand for complex international distribution systems that exist today. For Kant, the moral requirements of distributive justice are placed on political states. It is the duty of domestic institutions to promote a conception of justice mandated by the concept of a general united will and the principle of publicity. Kant was more concerned with the more contemporaneous and pressing matter of how the state could be one that represented the will of the people. Additionally, Kant seems to assume that if domestic states were republican and represented the will of the people, then the international economic order would also come to reflect an accepted conception of cosmopolitan right. Kant failed to elaborate because he believed that just states would be the product of enlightened cooperation and therefore promote a system of distributive justice that would eventually protect and promote the external freedom of individuals. In this regard, the best that Kant's cosmopolitanism can provide in terms of global distributive justice is a normative blueprint. A blueprint asking for "a constitution allowing the *greatest possible human freedom in accordance with laws which ensure that the freedom of each can coexist with the freedom of all the others* (not one designed to provide the greatest possible happiness, as this will in any case follow automatically)."[72] As Kant suggests, this is "a necessary idea which must be made the basis not only of the first outline of a political constitution but of all laws as well . . . even if the latter should never come about, the idea which sets up this maxim as an archetype, in order to bring the legal constitution of mankind nearer and nearer to its greatest possible perfection, still remains correct."[73]

Nevertheless, just because Kant fails to elaborate on a system of distributive justice, it does not also mean that we cannot abstract from this blueprint in order to locate various generalities within contemporary cosmopolitanism that are useful comparisons with the philosophy of Kant. In general, albeit with variations in detail, cosmopolitan theories share three major elements with Kant's position. First, cosmopolitanism maintains that the principle units of moral concern are individual human beings. Second, cosmopolitan theories share the element that this moral concern should be universally applied, meaning that "the status of ultimate concern attaches to every living human equally."[74] Third, cosmopolitanism requires generality in its application, proclaiming that humans are the ultimate moral concern for everyone, regardless of race, nationality, citizenship, social status and religious belief.

As Simon Caney has suggested, a theory of distributive justice must provide answers to two sets of questions. The first set attends to the scope of justice, namely, A) "what sorts of entities are included" and, B) who is responsible for distributing these goods. The second pair of questions is meant to determine A) "what should people have fair shares of" and, B) "what criterion of distributive justice should goods be distributed."[75] In response to the first set of questions, we can understand that Kant's cosmopolitanism is individualistic and thus places priority on distributing rights and goods to individuals. This is defensible by the fact that Kant's overall philosophy is preoccupied with the moral capacity of individuals to be self-legislators in a universal kingdom of ends. As is also present in Kant, the duty bearers are not only individuals themselves as possible legislating members in a hypothetical kingdom of ends, but also state entities who are charged with fulfilling the conditions of public right perpetually. In relation to the second pair of questions, it is clear that Kant does not use individual happiness as a unit to be distributed, but focuses instead on the ability of individual freedom so that it can harmonize with the freedom of all others. According to Kant, this requires an equal distribution of negative rights as well as the various positive opportunities needed to exercise one's autonomous will socially. As argued in Section I, I believe this would require various political and social conditions that allowed for one's effective autonomy to have deliberative access to a hypothetical kingdom of ends. In this regard, a Kantian scheme of global distributive justice requires that any individual who is a potential member of a universal kingdom of ends should be assigned basic rights and the goods necessary to allow one to be a participating member of universal public reason. In relation to global justice, if we are to understand all humans as potential members of a universal kingdom of ends, as did Kant, then the basic principles of distributive justice that are to apply at the domestic level would also be relevant at the level of a cosmopolitan constitution. Consequently, as was argued in the last section, the capability approach helps to provide the criterion for what combination of resources, rights, goods, services and institutional structures are needed to constitute human capabilities toward this condition. Although the capability approach does not provide a complete theory of distributive justice at the global level, it does provide additional normative criteria for our thoughts about how to constitute a more robust system of global justice.[76]

In addition, a Kantian concern for the possibility of effective autonomy in a universal kingdom of ends has direct relation to contemporary cosmopolitan arguments that have focused on global inequality and where the current global order drastically violates the three aforementioned cosmopolitan elements. One of the major arguments of contemporary cosmopolitanism is that if we hold the dignity of humans as the ultimate human value, then the current global system of unequal economic distribution is morally corrupt. The cosmopolitan suggests that what is necessary to correct this injustice is a coherent theory of international distributive justice, where human plight has moral priority in the distribution of wealth, rights, primary goods, welfare, resources, capabilities, moral obligations, happiness or some combination of these factors. This requires that negative rights, as well as positive obligations to others, would be respected. Thomas Pogge, for example, argues that the current global socio-economic order perpetuates an unjust structure where massive inequality, injustices and disrespect for human dignity have become institutionalised. Since this structure is perpetuated by human action and through the support of our membership in such an order, we are therefore morally responsible for the consequences of this order. In other words, if we take the respect for basic negative liberty seriously, then we have a "negative duty not to uphold injustice, nor to contribute to or profit from the unjust impoverishment of others."[77] What this requires, in similarity to Kant's principle of publicity, is a duty to alter unjust institutional arrangements so as to approximate a mutually consistent condition of public right and socio-economic distributive justice.

However, similar to criticisms about the universal scope of Kant's vision of cosmopolitan law, a specific critique of cosmopolitan global justice is that it puts liberal egalitarian agendas for socio-economic distributive justice above more relevant considerations regarding a plurality of global values and national responsibilities to maintain domestic social justice. Theorists such as David Miller have pointed out that "in a culturally plural world there is no reason to expect that different national communities would all decide to distribute matters in the same way, or even in similar ways."[78] As Miller suggests, the world is made up of communities whose "place in the world is conditioned by the particular national identities they share . . . [and feel] loyalties to those inside the lines, and value the special cultural features that they believe they share with their compatriots."[79] Others, such as Thomas Nagel, have further argued that "the idea of global justice without a world government is a chimera."[80] According to Nagel, global justice is unattainable without a world sovereign to organize such a task or to force positive compliance with various distribution schemes. Consequently, cosmopolitanism faces an attack on its underlined universalistic belief in universal egalitarianism, because it fails to consider the various ways in which societies conceive of justice and economic distribution. For a global actuality remains, that individuals do live in communities that they largely identify with and choose to obligate themselves, and that those societies can have radically divergent conceptions of what social justice requires.[81]

However, there is a critical distinction between practical application and normative principles of justice within contemporary cosmopolitan theory, a distinction that Kant also noted between theory and practice. The distinction is made between what Charles Beitz has defined as *moral cosmopolitanism* and *institutional cosmopolitanism*. What the distinction suggests is that moral cosmopolitanism "applies to the whole world the maxim that answers the questions about what we should do, or what institutions we should establish, based on an impartial consideration of the claims of each person who would be affected by our choices."[82] As Brian Barry has pointed out, "moral cosmopolitanism leaves open the final questions of the ideal constitution of international society."[83] Therefore, this distinction is related to, but separate from, institutional cosmopolitanism, which is focused on how to implement the normative considerations of its moral counterpart in some form of global governance. Although both are closely related and it is difficult to imagine institutional strategies without some normative grounding, it is an important distinction to be made, for it is critical to understand that "there is no automatic move from the ethical premises to any particular conclusion about the ideal world constitution."[84] In other words, moral cosmopolitanism is concerned with what *should* be done, while an institutional component is concerned with *how* the moral principles are to be structured in practice. There exists an overlap between them, but the moral theory is prior to implementation and acts as an ethical grounding for possible institutional schemes. In the case of Kant's cosmopolitanism, it is from a moral position that we have duties to each other in line with the categorical imperative and it is from this reasoning that all institutional designs should attempt to approximate. In this regard, the Kantian argument is a form of moral cosmopolitanism, based not only on our duties to fellow human beings, but also to guide our practical need to construct "a constitution allowing the *greatest possible human freedom in accordance with laws which ensure that the freedom of each can coexist with the freedom of all the others.*"[85]

Nevertheless, in light of pluralist and communitarian criticisms among others, some self-proclaimed Kantian-based theorists[86] have abandoned their earlier concerns for domestic justice for a more communitarian approach. For example, in the application of *justice as fairness* to the international level, John Rawls did not reach the same conclusion as many contemporary cosmopolitans. According to Rawls, "to some degree, the more general liberal ideas lack the three egalitarian features [globally applied] of the fair value of the political liberties, of fair equality of opportunity, and of the difference principle. These features are not needed for the construction of a reasonable law of peoples and by not assuming them our account has greater generality."[87] In so many words, like Miller, Rawls believes that the more egalitarian principles of justice conflict with various cultural perspectives and therefore would violate other liberal conceptions such as tolerance. Since various *decent* cultures have identifiable methods of justice, the liberal conception of tolerance forbids that we alter the richness of cultural pluralism by applying liberal egalitarian principles. In addition, Rawls believed that the efficiency of the *difference principle*, in the face of states that could not responsibly control themselves in relation to population and political stability, was greatly compromised and therefore should not apply globally.

It is difficult to relate Rawls' abandonment of the difference principle in *The Law of Peoples* to Kant's cosmopolitan theory. As I outlined earlier, Kant offers little discussion of international economics and certainly does not outline any significant model of international distributive justice. However, where I believe Rawls fails his self-proclaimed Kantian formulation of moral legislation is in relation to effective autonomy and the existence of global inequalities. It is clear that Kant believed the principle of publicity was designed to alter unjust policies in schemes [global and domestic] of social cooperation. As Kant claims, cosmopolitan morality demands a duty to reform existing injustices so "that they are corrected as soon as possible."[88] This scheme of public right, as I outlined earlier, contains political rights for negative freedom and positive duties to assure the effective use of one's autonomy. The effective use of autonomy is critical to Kantian enlightenment and the rational process of co-legislation in a hypothetical kingdom of ends. If we are to envision the international realm as another form of social cooperation, then these moral principles have validity on the cosmopolitan level.[89] Rawls fails Kant, in that Rawls removes the necessary element of justice and basic principles of mutual right on an international level, elements that are clearly violated within the current global order.[90]

It is in regard to effective autonomy that contemporary cosmopolitanism better mirrors Kant's cosmopolitan concern. Since the international economic environment supports a system of radical inequality and systematic poverty, this system in turn supports the eradication of external freedom and forces individuals to suffer without means to pursue ends, political voice or attractive life choices. On the global level, Kant's moral requirement is that systematic economic inequalities are to be pulled toward the three cosmopolitan normative principles. Furthermore, since Kant's autonomy demands that each individual must provide rational deliberation for the accepted justification of social ends, the cosmopolitan concern for a more equal economic and political scheme to assure co-legislation is morally defensible from a Kantian constitutional standpoint. Therefore, in the international realm as much as in the domestic, effective autonomy demands that minimal schemes of distributive justice, based on the idea of human capabilities within a hypothetical universal kingdom of ends, be incorporated within the normative principles of any cosmopolitan constitution.

## V. CONCLUSION

The primary concern in this chapter has been in regard to effective autonomy and the related distributive demands of Kantian justice. I have argued that the effective use of one's autonomy requires that human capabilities are to be constitutionally enhanced and that the capacity for effective autonomy is a critical moral concern for Kantian co-legislation within a universal kingdom of ends. In addition, I have suggested that it is not incoherent to assume that Kant's domestic principles of justice

178

are related to his cosmopolitan theory, since both versions are rooted on Kant's metaphysical belief that individuals are the ultimate unit of moral concern and that this concern is attached to everyone equally, under "a universal law of freedom."[91]

One major critique of Kant's cosmopolitanism pertains to the difficulties attendant on applying normative principles in practice. Contemporary cosmopolitans have suggested that there is "a great deal of room for disputes about global institutions"[92] and how moral principles should be applied. With this in mind, contemporary cosmopolitans have been particularly careful to separate moral positions from prescriptions for the institutional make-up of a cosmopolitan order. Kant also made certain to not pretend to understand the complexities of any practical cosmopolitan order. As Kant suggests, cosmopolitan justice will be the result of international norm building and of recognized a priori juridical principles that "will gradually build further and further."[93] In this light, cosmopolitanism has no particular predictive institutional complexion and will be a result of a slowly applied cosmopolitan enthusiasm. As has been suggested, Kant's theory only provides the metaphysical principles and it will be our experience and rational reflection that will eventually tell us how to enhance, apply, enforce and realize them. However, this will not be a simple process, or have a clearly defined application theory for every situation. Similarly, it would seem that extensive world poverty and the substantial destruction caused by tyrannical politics since Kant's time has not been enough to provide for Hume's "heroic medicine" and the idea that people eventually learn from their mistakes.[94]

Although the awareness of global inequality has grown and the attempt for global cooperation has continued to progress slowly, the results are still unacceptable, and it would be difficult to find a reasonable individual who could not share that conclusion in one form or another. Therefore, the immediate goal of cosmopolitanism is to reduce inequalities toward the a priori ideal of external freedom and justice. Where the capabilities of every human being have global stature as an ultimate unit of moral concern. To what extent cosmopolitan enthusiasm will evolve into application is uncertain, for it will be the result of millions of variables, for which no explanation could account. Nevertheless, there is considerable difference in stating that normative principles are impossible to apply and saying that their application is difficult. The fact that Kant's normative principles are difficult to apply does not imply that those principles cannot be applied in practice. Furthermore, the fact that a theory is particularly complicated in application does not mean that it is therefore not what we ought to do. The distinction is important and suggests the force behind the cosmopolitan enthusiasm discussed in the next chapter. As has been suggested by Georg Cavallar, cosmopolitan enthusiasm is not based on what human beings do now. It is based on what they rationally ought to do. In this regard, the enthusiasm is not rooted entirely in the empirical past, but directed toward the changeable future.[95]

## NOTES

1. John Rawls, *A Theory of Justice* (Cambridge, MA: Harvard University Press, 1971), pg. 5.
2. The kingdom of ends is a metaphysical ideal "of every rational being as one who must regard himself as legislating universal law by all will's maxims . . . [in] a systematic union of different rational beings through common laws . . . according to universal validity." Immanuel Kant, *Grounding for the Metaphysics of Morals*, J. Ellington (trans.) (Cambridge, MA: Hackett Publishing Company, 1981), p. 39.[4:433]
3. Ibid., p. 49. [4:446–7]
4. A distinction between lawful and lawless coercion should be made. For Kant, the principle of justice determines what is the legitimate lawful use of coercion and what is lawless coercion (Kant also calls lawless coercion "violence"). Since civil law is a matter of coercion, Kant believed any coercion that does not conform to the a priori ideal of justice is "lawless violence" and a direct violation of external freedom. Nevertheless, lawful coercion based on principles of justice, which is the subject of co-legislation of wills, is therefore what justice requires in order to maintain everyone's "rightful" external freedom.
5. Internal freedom is usually associated with Kant's critical philosophy as found in the three critiques, whereas external freedom is usually associated with Kant's political theory or with areas of transitional overlap from his critical concerns (free will) to his political (autonomy). As Kant, I assume that internal freedom (free will) is possible, focusing on external freedom for the rest of this chapter. It is also worth noting that internal and external freedom are synonymous with autonomy, for they both relate the formulation of ends in relation to external forces. In most cases, when I discuss external freedom I am also suggesting the possibility of autonomy and vice versa. For a more detailed discussion of Kant's use of autonomy, see Karl Ameriks, *Kant and the Fate of Autonomy* (Cambridge, Cambridge University Press, 2000), pp. 1–66.
6. Kant, Immanuel, "On the Common Saying: This May be True in Theory, But it Does not Apply in Practice," in Hans Reiss (ed.), H. B. Nisbet (trans.), *Kant's Political Writings* (Cambridge: Cambridge University Press, 1970), p. 73. [8:290]
7. Immanuel Kant, *The Metaphysics of Morals*, Mary Gregor (ed. & trans.) (Cambridge: Cambridge University Press, 1996), p. 24. [6:230]
8. Kant, *Grounding for the Metaphysics of Morals*, p. 49. [4:447]
9. Ibid. p. 39. [4:433]
10. Allen Rosen, *Kant's Theory of Justice* (Ithaca: Cornell University Press, 1993), p. 9.
11. As I suggested before, the Kantian definition of justice is a metaphysical a priori ideal

180

and is meant to provide the normative grounding to which all external laws are to be both legislated and considered as promoting greater external freedom. I discuss this process further in Section II.

12. Kant, "On the Common Saying: This May be True in Theory, But it Does not Apply in Practice," p. 73. [8:290]

13. Ibid.

14. Kant, *Grounding for the Metaphysics of Morals*, p. 36. [4:429]

15. Kant, *The Metaphysics of Morals*, pp. 23–6. [6:229–34]

16. My argument is that autonomy is only useful for Kant if one's autonomy is in fact effective within social co-legislation. This aspect of autonomy is different from the pure psychological ability to be autonomous, in that it focuses on the ability to reasonably act upon one's autonomous conclusions in social context.

17. My term "reasonably achieve" needs another obvious clarification, namely, how do you know when someone is effectively autonomous and has "achieved" the requirement of distributive justice? Although my response to this question is developed at greater length in my discussion of capability theory, I can try to provide a response here. Reaching the ideal of effective autonomy, intuitively speaking, requires adequate nourishment, education, health care, political and social access, and freedom of conscience to a level where any less would diminish the capacity to act autonomously within an agreed conception of justice. In the Kantian sense, autonomous actors would rationally agree to a social contract only if they subjectively believed their power to be co-legislators was effective and that their participation in the formation of the kingdom of ends was socially guaranteed. This, as I said earlier, would have to include both principles of distribution and principles of right. For a different Kantian approach with a similar conclusion, see Onora O'Neill, *Faces of Hunger: An Essay of Poverty, Development and Justice* (London: Allen & Unwin, 1986), Chapter. 7 & 8.

18. Kant, "On the Common Saying: This May be True in Theory, But it Does not Apply in Practice," p. 74. [8:290–1]

19. Ibid.

20. Ibid., p. 73. [8:289]

21. Ibid., p. 73. [8:290]

22. For an argument defending this minimal interpretation of Kantian justice, see Howard Williams, *Kant's Political Philosophy* (New York: St. Martin's Press, 1983), pp. 196–8.

23. Kant, *The Metaphysics of Morals*, p. 24. [6:230]

24. Robert Nozick claims that Kant's first principle of law and the corresponding duties of justice prohibit anyone from using someone as a means. Nozick proclaims that all external policies are coercive without expressed consent to being a participant in the end itself. Nevertheless, G. A. Cohen has correctly shown that Nozick has misinterpreted Kant, for Kant does not only proclaim that everyone is to be "never as a means," but that duty demands that we also treat others "always at the same time as an end." In other words, Cohen suggests that the Kantian model allows for individuals to use one another as a limited means, as long as they are also treated as an end. For these conflicting arguments, see Robert Nozick, *Anarchy, State, and Utopia* (New York: Basic Books, 1974), and G. A. Cohen, *Self-Ownership, Freedom and Equality* (Oxford: Oxford University Press, 1995). Quotes involved in this footnote are from Kant, *Grounding for the Metaphysics of Morals*, p. 36. [4:429]

25. This argument is best articulated by Mary Gregor, *Laws of Freedom: A Study of*

*Applying the Categorical Imperative in the Metaphysics of Morals* (New York: Barnes & Noble, 1963), pp. 35–6.

26. Bruce Aune, *Kant's Theory of Morals* (New Jersey: Princeton University Press, 1979), p. 157.
27. Jeremy Waldron, "Kant's Theory of the State," in P. Kleingeld (ed.), *Toward Perpetual Peace and Other Writings on Politics, Peace and History* (New Haven: Yale University Press, 2006).
28. Kant, *The Metaphysics of Morals*, p. 101. [6:326]
29. Ibid, pp. 100–1 [6:326]
30. A similar conclusion suggesting that social welfare and Kant's justice are compatible can be found in Alexander Kaufman, *Welfare in the Kantian State* (Oxford: Clarendon Press, 1999). However, his argument is based on an examination of Kant's teleological argument regarding "purposive agency" and how humans require economic and social equality in order to realize this purpose. A similarly argued conclusion based on agency and happiness has been furthered by Paul Guyer in *Kant on Freedom, Law and Happiness* (Cambridge: Cambridge University Press, 2000). In both cases, these arguments are complementary to my argument for effective autonomy in that they concern the ability of individuals to be an active agent in social context and the formulation of co-legislated social morality.
31. Kant, "Perpetual Peace: A Philosophical Sketch," in Hans Reiss (ed.), H. B. Nisbet (trans.), *Kant's Political Writings* (Cambridge: Cambridge University Press, 1970), p. 130. [8:386]
32. Ibid., p. 130. [8:386]
33. Ibid.
34. Ibid.
35. Both Aune and Williams suggest that the *principle of publicity* is simply inconsistent and underdeveloped, and should therefore be considered as irrelevant to Kant's general theory (p. 157, p. 196, respectively). However, I believe this stance to be dangerous for Kantian scholars, for it fails to allow for the possibility that Kant's theory evolved and grew. Although Kant was quite old, I believe this is more reason to suggest that his attempt to reconcile equality and autonomy was furthered by this principle.
36. The principle of humanity can be understood as Kant's claim that there is a "maxim of common interest, of beneficence toward those in need, [that it] is a universal duty of human beings, just because they are to be considered fellowmen, that is, rational beings with needs, united by nature in one dwelling place so that they can help one another." See Kant, *The Metaphysics of Morals*, p. 202. [6:453].
37. Rosen, *Kant's Theory of Justice*, p. 182–3.
38. Ibid., p. 183.
39. Kant, "Perpetual Peace," p. 130. [8:386]
40. Rosen, *Kant's Theory of Justice*, pp. 198–208.
41. Otfried Hoffe, *Kant's Cosmopolitan Theory of Law and Peace* (Cambridge: Cambridge University Press, 2006), p. 106.
42. Ibid., p. 107.
43. Ibid., p. 107.
44. Ibid.
45. Ibid., p. 109.

46. Ibid., p. 110.
47. Rosen, *Kant's Theory of Justice*, pp. 206–7.
48. Ibid.
49. Kant, *The Metaphysics of Morals*, p. 101. [6:326]
50. Kant, "Perpetual Peace," p. 130. [8:386]
51. Nussbaum has written many articles regarding the capabilities approach. However, I will be making my comparison from Martha Nussbaum, *Women and Human Development; The Capabilities Approach* (Cambridge: Cambridge University Press, 2000).
52. Ibid., p. 5.
53. Nussbaum justifies her argument for human dignity through Aristotle's conception of human flourishing and the idea of being "truly human." Although there are many interesting comparisons between Nussbaum and Kant's Aristotelian heritage, I cannot expend the effort here and note that they are different approaches only for clarity.
54. Ibid.
55. Onora O'Neill has also suggested that Nussbaum's capability theory could be consistent with Kantian justice and that considering justice in terms of capabilities might best express Kant's ideal of justice. However, O'Neill takes issue with prescribing these capabilities as rights, whereas Nussbaum is still open to the possibility. For more details, see Onora O'Neill, "Justice, Capabilities, and Vulnerabilities," in M. Nussbaum & J. Glover (eds), *Women, Culture and Development; A Study of Human Capabilities* (Oxford: Oxford University Press, 1995).
56. Kant, *The Metaphysics of Morals*, p. 24. [6:230]
57. Paraphrased from Nussbaum, pp. 78–80. Quotations represent her direct phrasing. It should be noted that Nussbaum's capabilities include considerable extrapolation of what are included in each. However, for my purposes a general understanding is sufficient.
58. Ibid., p. 83.
59. Ibid., p. 85.
60. Thomas Pogge, "Can the Capability Approach be Justified?," posted on *The Equality Exchange* as a draft manuscript (aran.uiv.pau.fr. 2003).
61. Cecile Fabre & David Miller, "Justice and Culture: Rawls, Sen, Nussbaum and O'Neill," in *Political Studies Review*, vol. 1 (2003), pp. 1–17.
62. John Alexander, "Capability Egalitarianism and Moral Selfhood," *Ethical Perspectives*, vol. 10 (1) (2003).
63. Kant, *The Metaphysics of Morals*, p. 24. [6:230]
64. Alexander, "Capability Egalitarianism and Moral Selfhood," p. 23.
65. Immanuel Kant, "Idea for a Universal History with a Cosmopolitan Purpose," in Hans Reiss (ed.), H. B. Nisbet (trans.), *Kant's Political Writings* (Cambridge: Cambridge University Press, 1970), pp. 51 and 45. [8:28 and 8:19]
66. Some cosmopolitan theorists, such as Thomas Pogge, have used the terminology *global economic justice* and *international distributive justice* interchangeably. It seems to me that these terms mean and function in the same way. If I am wrong, then it is due to a lack of expressed significance by various authors in relation to their use. For interchange of these terms, see Thomas Pogge, *World Poverty and Human Rights* (Cambridge: Polity Press, 2002), and Thomas Pogge, "An Institutional Approach to Humanitarian Intervention," *Public Affairs Quarterly*, vol. 6, no. 1 (1992), pp. 89–103.

67. Kant, "The Idea for a Universal History with a Cosmopolitan Purpose," p. 50. [8:27–8]

68. I discuss this topic in relation to globalization in the next chapter.

69. Kant, "Perpetual Peace," p. 106. [8:358]

70. Ibid., p. 108. [8:360]

71. As discussed in Chapter 2, Kant does outline five *laws of hospitality*, which I have suggested act as initial principles of establishing a condition of global justice. I will return to this discussion in the next chapter in relation to some contemporary concerns about globalization and global justice.

72. Immanuel Kant, Appendix, "Transcendental Logic II, Dialectic, I, Ideas in General," in J. M. D. Meiklejohn (trans.), *The Critique of Pure Reason* (New York: The Colonial Press, 1900). [4:201]

73. Ibid.

74. Thomas Pogge, "Cosmopolitanism and Sovereignty," *Ethics*, 103 (1992), pp. 49–50.

75. Simon Caney, *Justice Beyond Borders: A Global Political Theory* (Oxford: Oxford University Press, 2005), p. 103.

76. Martha Nussbaum, "Beyond the Social Contract: Capabilities and Global Justice," in G. Brock & H. Brighouse (eds), *The Political Philosophy of Cosmopolitanism* (Cambridge: Cambridge University Press, 2005).

77. Thomas Pogge, *World Poverty and Human Rights*, p. 197.

78. David Miller, *Citizenship and National Identity* (Cambridge: Polity Press, 2000), p. 162.

79. David Miller, *National Responsibility and Global Justice* (Oxford: Oxford University Press, 2007), p. 264.

80. Thomas Nagel, "The Problem of Global Justice," *Philosophy and Public Affairs*, 33 (2005), p. 115.

81. An excellent cosmopolitan response to both Miller and Nagel is given by Simon Caney, "Global Distributive Justice and the State," *Political Studies*, vol. 56, no. 3 (2008).

82. Charles Beitz, "Cosmopolitan Liberalism and the State System," in C. Brown (ed.), *Political Restructuring in Europe: Ethical Perspectives* (London: Routledge, 1994), p. 124.

83. Brian Barry, "International Society from a Cosmopolitan Perspective," in D. Maple & T. Nardin (eds), *International Society: Diverse Ethical Perspectives* (New Jersey: Princeton University Press, 1998), p. 144.

84. Ibid., p. 145.

85. Kant, *The Critique of Pure Reason*. [4:201]

86. Rawls claims that his "description of justice is an attempt to interpret Kant's conception of moral legislation." See John Rawls, "Kantian Constructivism in Moral Theory: The Dewey Lectures 1980," *Journal of Philosophy*, 77 (1980), p. 517.

87. John Rawls, *The Laws of Peoples* (Cambridge, MA: Harvard University Press, 1999), p. 51.

88. Kant, "Perpetual Peace," p. 118. [8:372]

89. It is useful to restate Kant's definition of cosmopolitanism, because it not only supports my Kantian comparison with capability theory, but also shows that Kant's definition of justice is to be globally applied. Kant defines cosmopolitanism as, "the matrix within which all the original capacities of the human race may develop . . . [by]

attaining a civil society which can administer justice universally." Kant, "The Idea for a Universal History with a Cosmopolitan Purpose," pp. 51 and 45. [8:28 and 8:19]

90. Thomas Pogge, "Priorities of Global Justice," in T. Pogge (ed.), *Global Justice* (Oxford: Blackwell, 2001).

91. Kant, *The Metaphysics of Morals*, p. 24. [6:230]

92. Brian Barry, "Statism and Nationalism. A Cosmopolitan Critique," in I. Shapiro & L. Brilmayer (eds), *Global Justice* (New Jersey: Princeton University Press, 1998), p. 36.

93. Kant, "Perpetual Peace," p. 104. [8:356]

94. Immanuel Kant, "The Contest of Faculties," in Hans Reiss (ed.), H. B. Nisbet (trans.), *Kant's Political Writings* (Cambridge: Cambridge University Press, 1970), p. 190. [7:93–4]

95. George Cavallar, *Kant and the Theory and Practice of International Right* (Cardiff: University of Wales Press, 1999), p. 150.

# CHAPTER 6

# Conclusion: Applied Theory and a Continued Cosmopolitan Enthusiasm

"However uncertain I may be and may remain as to whether we can hope for anything better for mankind, this uncertainty cannot detract from the maxim I have adopted, or from the necessity of assuming for practical purposes that human progress is possible." – Immanuel Kant

Immanuel Kant was well aware of the difficulties involved in establishing a cosmopolitan order. In response to the idea of a world federation, he knew that "such proposals have always been ridiculed by great statesmen, and even more by heads of states, as pedantic, childish and academic ideas."[1] Kant also realized that any condition of universal justice "is the most difficult to establish, and even more so to preserve, so that many maintain that it would only be possible within a [world] of *angles*, since men, with their self-seeking inclinations, would be incapable of adhering to a constitution of so sublime a nature."[2] Despite the difficulties of implementing his theory, Kant never lost faith in humankind's capacity to employ practical moral reason and to therefore eventually create a cosmopolitan order based on a mutually consistent understanding of justice and public right.[3] As the quote above illustrates, Kant believed that the maxim of universal public right is true a priori, despite the obstacles of empirical circumstance. For it is only within a condition of universal public right that humans can enjoy an environment of secured external freedom. As Kant argues, "such is the requirement of pure reason, which legislates a priori, regardless of all empirical ends."[4] It is for that reason that we should assume for all practical purposes that a cosmopolitan condition is possible.

Nevertheless, this does not mean that Kant's cosmopolitanism is necessarily a utopian abstraction beyond the realm of human experience.

As has been illustrated throughout this book, Kant's cosmopolitanism is premised on the empirical fact that humans are bounded together within a spherical globe and therefore are interlocked in already existing and potentially existing *communities of overlapping fate*,[5] which suggests that in one way or another human beings "must necessarily tolerate one another" if any external form of freedom is to be possible.[6] It is because of our bounded interconnectedness that "the earth has thus entered in varying degrees into a universal community, and it has developed to the point where a violation of right in *one* part of the world is felt *everywhere*."[7] Since human contact is unavoidable and various circumstances potentially threaten the existence of any form of public right and external freedom, practical reason dictates the establishment of a cosmopolitan legal condition of mutually consistent public right, where the freedom of each can coexist with the freedom of all the others.[8]

The purpose of this book has been to examine and develop the normative principles necessary for a Kantian cosmopolitan constitution and for the creation of a condition of cosmopolitan law. In outlining the normative requirements consistent with and necessary to a Kantian-based cosmopolitan constitution, this project has attempted to provide an exegetical reading of Kant's cosmopolitanism while also providing alternative interpretations to Kant's more problematic or ambiguous concepts. As was discussed in the Introduction, this methodology holds that exegesis and reformulation are not mutually exclusive, so that it can: (A) Outline and examine Kant's cosmopolitan vision from primary and secondary sources, while (B) reexamining and reinterpreting ambiguous aspects of Kant's cosmopolitanism in order to provide a more robust and coherent vision of a Kantian cosmopolitan position. Although many will believe this methodology to be a beneficial and profitable tool in developing a vision of Kantian cosmopolitanism, many others, most notably some strict exegetical Kantian scholars, will undoubtedly look unfavorably on my treatment of Kant. For some, the arguments presented in this book will have gone too far with an interpretation of Kant that is in drastic opposition to their own exegetical reading of Kantian philosophy. However, as was mentioned at the outset, this project was concerned with developing a tenable form of Kantian cosmopolitanism that not only was coherently consistent, but was also able to effectively respond to contemporary arguments against cosmopolitan law by relativists, pluralists, realists and communitarians. In this regard, there is an underlying theme throughout the arguments in this book concerning the useful relationship between examining Kant's cosmopolitanism in the strict contextual and textual sense, and with reformulating a variation of Kantian cosmopolitanism that is consistent with his overall normative principles.

In some ways the method of reconstruction employed throughout this book is more Kantian than critics of this approach would like to accept. This is because Kant firmly believed in a process of human progress that not only built upon the knowledge of the past, but was also a process of abstracting beyond current understanding, pressing the envelope of possible human development. As Kant suggests, progress requires an "incalculable series of generations, each passing on its enlightenment to the next," and it "requires that we should abstract at the outset from present hindrances, which do not arise inevitably out of human nature, but are rather occasioned by the neglect of genuine ideas."[9] Consequently, reexamining and expanding on existing ideas are crucial components for human development. In this light, the arguments in this book should be understood as being engaged in a normative dialogue with Kant's cosmopolitanism, building from his baseline positions, while also allowing the flexibility to reinterpret, rethink and reformulate Kant's more ambiguous cosmopolitan thoughts. This was not done in an attempt to assert the final word on Kant's cosmopolitanism, but merely to examine an alternative way that Kantian cosmopolitanism might be understood in relation to a modern world that is in desperate need of continued philosophical examination.

In providing a tenable account of Kantian cosmopolitanism this book has examined the history of cosmopolitan thought and the way in which Kant moved away from both the Stoic and natural law paradigm, instigating his own argument for a condition of cosmopolitan law. From that background, this project outlined and explored Kant's cosmopolitanism; examining the principle of cosmopolitan law, cosmopolitan right, the laws of hospitality, the normative principles behind the pacific federation, a cosmopolitan epistemology of culture and a possible normative basis for a Kantian form of global distributive justice. In doing so, I have interpreted Kant's cosmopolitan theory as a less demanding vision of ethical order than has been suggested by some contemporary cosmopolitan theorists. Contrary to many contemporary conceptions of cosmopolitanism, I have interpreted Kant's cosmopolitan thought as a form of global constitutional jurisprudence that requires minimal ethical/legal obligations versus the more rigorous demand of establishing a world state or a utopian moral order. By viewing Kant's cosmopolitan theory as a form of cosmopolitan jurisprudence, my Kantian interpretation of cosmopolitanism has better promise to satisfy communitarian, realist and pluralist concerns without surrendering cosmopolitan principles of human worth and global ethical order. Contrary to the views of some contemporary cosmopolitan theorists, this project suggests that cosmopolitan theory is difficult to take seriously when it uncompromisingly demands the removal of state interest and communal ties required by an *extreme* form of cosmopolitanism.[10] In contrast to an extreme approach, this book has attempted to provide an alternative Kantian version of cosmopolitan law that allows for various ethical perspectives on a culturally local and state level, while providing a minimal global ethical umbrella for international cooperation and universal law.

One question that could be asked of the Kantian model outlined in this book pertains to the degree to which it is actually cosmopolitan in scope. Thus, some might be tempted to object that the cosmopolitan position outlined is exclusively limited to members of the *pacific federation* and is not sufficiently global enough. It could be charged that if the federation only included a specific number of states, then it is unclear how a Kantian cosmopolitan constitution really creates a sense of world citizenship and mutual public right beyond the federation's own borders. Although this book provides a response to this question, it is useful to draw out some of the implications that a Kantian model has in relation to five contemporary issues involved with discussions of cosmopolitanism and global justice. In order to supply some link between theory and practice, the discussion below will examine five contemporary issues in cosmopolitan theory, namely, the debate surrounding the global economy and inequality, the furtherance of a global forum for transnational debate, a distinction between humanitarian assistance and distributive justice, the idea of universal human rights as a foundation for cosmopolitan right, and the question of how to move cosmopolitan theory to practice. The point of this exercise is to illustrate how a Kantian cosmopolitan position could respond to these issues and how it might in theory and practice further a cosmopolitan condition.

## I. IMPLICATIONS OF KANT'S COSMOPOLITANISM: GLOBALIZATION, GLOBAL MARKETS AND INEQUALITY

As has been touched upon in prior chapters, the term globalization generally refers to a condition of growing interdependence and connectedness between various global communities. Although the word globalization itself takes on various meanings depending on its source, most scholars generally understand that globalization is actually occurring, and that it has created both positive opportunities for continued human progress and negative effects that have hampered the life prospects of various communities.[11] In some circles globalization is seen as having expanded new markets for cultural and economic goods, as well as allowing for the cross-pollination of ideas and transnational communication. For others, globalization has become a threatening force to the idea of a cosmopolitan condition, creating institutionalized systems of global inequality, resource depletion and the overall effect of human exploitation.[12]

One significant area within contemporary debates about globalization revolves around the concept of the global economy, the effects of global capitalism, multinational corporations and particular practices of exploitation that are either directly promoted or implicitly sanctioned by various states, corporations and trade organizations. The concern is that current global economic policies promote institutionalized systems of global inequality, injustices and human rights violations. Another significant concern involves the fear that globalization has in effect threatened opportunities for expanded democratic governance by limiting the choice and power of individuals to be *decision makers*, thus reducing large segments of the global population to be merely the *decision takers* of the politically powerful and rich. One only has to look at poverty indexes and mortality statistics of the UNDP and the World Bank to see the massive disparities in terms of annual income, life expectancy and living standards between the rich and poor.[13] As Kok-Chor Tan has aptly pointed out, "differences in detail notwithstanding, the general agreement is that the current global economic structure, and the norms and principles that drive and regulate economic practices, precipitate and perpetuate gross inequality and poverty."[14]

As was alluded to in Chapter 2, Kant's cosmopolitan laws of hospitality have several implications for globalization and the fair regulation of global markets. For example, the fifth law of hospitality explicitly forbids federated members from exploiting non-federated communities through extorted or misrepresented contracts. In other words, federated members can only engage in commerce by way of fairly negotiated contract and not through trade relations which have been established through undue economic, military or political pressure. This is because federated members obligate themselves to conduct international commerce in such a way that the possibility of future peaceful relations can be maintained. According to Kant, the only way to guarantee continued relations and a mutual condition of cosmopolitan public right is by having federated members maintain a consistent normative position between the treatment of federated and non-federated communities. This means that in issues of trade, federated states must negotiate in good faith and in such a way that resulting conditions are seen as mutually beneficial. This in itself suggests that federated members must act in accordance to mutually consistent principles of global justice, thus operating within the parameters of cosmopolitan law. Although these restrictions do not provide a particularly detailed analysis of how federal trade laws would in practice operate, they do establish a normative framework from which a mutually consistent system of global trade should be institutionally organized. Therefore, if formalized through practice, these normative restrictions would go a long way to establish a system of trade regulations that would alleviate many of the concerns about the exploitative nature of global markets and help to correct existing inequalities between various trading communities.

To be sure, it would be disingenuous to suggest that by instituting these principles into economic practice the federation would single-handedly eradicate the problems of global inequality. For it is possible that states outside the scope of federal jurisdiction would continue to engage in unfair trade practices without regard for global consequences. In addition, it is also simply a fact of circumstance that some communities have been blessed with greater natural resources – a good basis for wealth creation – than others. Certain communities are at a natural advantage in regard to resource capital and strategic trading location. Nevertheless, the practice of equal trade relations by federated members would be a vital step toward a more balanced and equal condition of globalization. For what cosmopolitan law establishes is the normative belief by federated states that global economic institutions and practices should be aligned with principles of hospitable public right and that violations of these normative principles are not only unethical, but also violate the possible establishment of a condition of global justice.

## II. THE PROTECTION OF COSMOPOLITAN RIGHT AND THE GLOBAL FORUM

As in the case with global markets, the cosmopolitan federation obligates itself to the hospitable treatment of all human beings regardless of state, ethnic or communal origin. As was discussed in Chapters 2 and 3, a Kantian cosmopolitan federation is committed to the principle of cosmopolitan law. This specifically disallows the inhospitable treatment of individuals living both internally and externally to the federation. In addition, federated members are obligated to refrain from assisting and/ or conducting business with states that are despotic or who pose a direct threat to the safety of the pacific alliance. In the context of contemporary global politics, a federated state could not hold an inconsistent position between domestic public right, while systematically engaging in violations of right outside its border. One obvious example is that it would not be legitimate for a federated member to secretly prop up foreign dictators in order to suit its own political interest and/or to have unfettered access to economic resources.

Furthermore, federated members would have an obligation not to give economic assistance to any regime seeking to expand its military capacity. As was outlined in Chapter 2, federated members can only assist other states in good faith with an obligation to refrain from exploiting vulnerable communities. The implications that stem from this global commitment are considerable and would go a long way to reducing diffidence as well as feelings of inequality and exploitation that exist in the world today. Federated members could not amass large armies and would be prohibited from assisting others in creating large military forces. As was discussed in Chapters 2 and 3, the preliminary articles of the cosmopolitan constitution were designed specifically to maintain an overall sense of assured security from future military aggression. This sense of security was not only designed for federated members in their relations with one another, but was also meant to foster a global environment of perpetual peace with non-federated states.

In addition, by practicing laws of hospitality the federation helps to develop and safeguard a public forum for global dialogue and deliberation. This is because the laws of hospitality limit excessive abuses of power (both economical and military) while also protecting a cosmopolitan right for transnational communication. As was mentioned in the last section, a significant concern with globalization is the fear that systemic inequalities threaten the *opportunity* for expanded democratic governance by limiting the choice and power of individuals to be *decision makers*. Since large segments of the global population are merely *decision takers* of the politically rich and powerful, many critics of globalization argue that greater protective procedures are necessary in order to secure a global sense of democratic decision making. Accordingly, most debates within transnational democratic theory revolve around how to provide people who are affected by global decisions with an opportunity to influence those decisions. The focus for transnational democratic theory, particularly with those involved in what is called the *deliberative turn*, is that individuals have an "effective *opportunity* to participate in processes of collective judgement."[15]

Nevertheless, a central critique of deliberative democracy, along with many other transnational democratic theories, is that they rely on preexisting models of liberalism and corresponding protections already granted within liberal democracies.[16] Many critics suggest that expanding deliberative models beyond state borders is impossible because without a universal state to arbitrate against possible breakdowns in the deliberative process, then deliberation could easily be stalled into incommunicative quagmire. Deliberative democrats themselves often admit that deliberative democracy is only possible when coupled with some system of liberal rights and/or constitutional mechanisms which allow for *communicative power* within a secured public sphere.[17] According to theorists like Mark Warren, these liberal protections are necessary to guarantee a robust public sphere, the existence of a counterbalancing civil society and to adjudicate impasses in the deliberative process.[18]

However, other theorists such as John Dryzek and Anthony McGrew have argued, on the contrary, that cosmopolitanism and deliberative democratic models are not only compatible, but that "deliberative democracy should be more at home in the international system."[19] According to Dryzek, "we should think of democracy not in terms of voting or the representation of persons' interests, but rather in terms of deliberation and communication."[20] In addition, they argue that discourse already occurs on the international level and from the expansion of an active global civil society. Therefore, the inclusion or exclusion of any particular group in a political state is becoming less relevant since various associations find expression by communicating at the transnational level. As Dryzek suggests, "deliberation and communication . . . can cope with fluid boundaries, and the production of outcomes across boundaries. For we can look for democracy in the character of political interaction that generates public opinion, without worrying about whether or not it is confined to particular territorial entities."[21]

However, transnational models of deliberative democracy as defended by Dryzek seem to sidestep the criticism that certain values, mechanisms or preexisting commitments are necessary before a deliberative process is feasible. For skeptics of deliberative democracy are not arguing that communication and dialogue does not take place on a global level, but that this communication does not represent a distinct model of democracy. In other words, what deliberation seems to produce are mutually agreed resolutions at times, but it does not necessarily produce a framework for the procedures of deliberation itself in all cases. What is needed prior to any form of genuine transnational deliberative democracy is an understanding in the value of deliberation and the legitimacy of mutually negotiated resolution. According to many, including several deliberative democrats, this presupposes some conception of justice and the belief that democratic legitimacy is delivered by mutual communication and deliberation.

There are two supportive features to deliberative theory produced by the cosmopolitan model developed in this book. First, the pacific federation protects the possibility for transnational association and communication for everyone, at least within its sphere of influence. Second, the federation engages in external relations so that future negotiations and mutual relations could "eventually bring the human race nearer and nearer to a cosmopolitan constitution."[22] This commitment presupposes the idea that transnational dialogue and deliberative communication are critical components in the development of transnational governance and a cosmopolitan constitution, something that Kant firmly recognizes throughout his political writings.[23] However, unlike Dryzek's deliberative model, the Kantian model provides constitutional legal mechanisms to create an open public sphere within the federation and for the possibility of deliberative action across federated and non-federated borders, effectively bolstering a differentiated global civil society. In this regard, the cosmopolitan model defended in this book contains many aspects of deliberative theory while also providing the legal and constitutional framework which deliberative procedures could rest upon.

As was argued in Chapter 3, Kantian cosmopolitan law does not require, or in fact advocate, a liberal world state as the mechanism for generating a cosmopolitan condition. In this regard, the model of federation and the room it provides for multilateral cooperation/deliberation within the pacific federation fits well with contemporary international relation theorists who do not see the international environment as necessarily having to be either a world state or perpetually anarchic.[24] Theorists such as James Rosenau and Oran Young have argued that there is a "growing realization that the achievement of governance does not invariably require the creation of material entities of formal organizations of the sort we normally associate with the concept of government."[25] Nevertheless, both Young and Rosenau have suggested that *effective* systems of global governance would require certain rules and/or generally agreed principles of deliberation in order to "facilitate cooperation" and to "alleviate collective action problems in a world of independent actors."[26] It is in relation to this need for the establishment of common principles of public right that Kant's cosmopolitanism seeks to institute a system of cosmopolitan law. By creating a cosmopolitan constitution based on a mutually consistent concept of public right, the federation secures the possibility for an effective global forum and strives to alleviate international tensions that undermine global cooperation and/or violate freedoms granted by cosmopolitan law.

## III. HUMANITARIAN ASSISTANCE AND GLOBAL JUSTICE

Another contentious issue in contemporary global theory relates to whether global inequalities and human suffering are best addressed through humanitarian assistance or resolved through some mechanism of resource and wealth distribution. Simply presented for the purposes of comparison, there are two established positions within the western tradition of international relations theory.[27] The first position argues that states have a duty to provide humanitarian assistance (but not duties for justice) in order to alleviate human suffering which has been caused by unforeseen circumstances outside the control of those affected.[28] This includes suffering caused by misfortune, natural disaster, repressive governments, unavoidable war, drought, governmental collapse and/or the spread of disease. The second position upholds one of global distributive justice as outlined in the last chapter. This cosmopolitan position argues that humanitarian assistance alone only alleviates immediate problems associated with inequality and human suffering and therefore fails to address the institutional factors that perpetuate conditions of human suffering and global inequality.[29] In sum, there are those who favor a system of humanitarian assistance based on the particular circumstances involved in cases of human suffering[30] and those who favor a more egalitarian system of distributive global justice, which seeks to rebalance global inequalities toward some cosmopolitan conception of universal justice.[31]

A persuasive humanitarian assistance position has been presented by the international theory of John Rawls as it is outlined in *The Laws of Peoples*. According to Rawls, there exists an important distinction between humanitarian assistance and conceptions of global distributive justice. As Rawls suggests, a theory of global justice is redundant at the international level since according to his non-ideal theory liberal states already have a duty to aid nations through humanitarian assistance. As Rawls puts it, "well-ordered people have a duty to assist burdened societies. It does not follow, however, that the only way, or the best way, to carry out this duty of assistance is by following a principle of distributive justice to regulate economic and social inequalities among societies."[32] In addition, Rawls believes that unlike schemes of global distributive justice, which demand the fulfillment of egalitarian principles regardless of localized circumstances, humanitarian assistance allows for critical distinctions to be made regarding domestic self-responsibility and the prudence from which societies handle themselves. As Rawls suggests, it is unreasonable to ask well-ordered societies to transfer resources to societies regardless of the fact that they have been negligent or unwilling to implement policies necessary to improve their situation.[33] Lastly, Rawls argues that a system of global distributive justice is insensitive to various cultures and "would fail to express due tolerance for other acceptable ways of ordering society."[34] In light of the apparent contradiction with Rawls' past work, much has been written regarding the abandonment of his more egalitarian concerns as found in *A Theory of Justice*. Critics of Rawls argue that he is mistaken to abandon the *difference principle* when applying his theory of justice to the international level since the global level represents nothing more than another possible scheme of social cooperation and hence requires a corresponding system of distributive justice.[35] My concern here is not to go over the well-rehearsed material on this subject, but to relate how the Kantian model outlined in this book might respond to questions regarding the desirability of distributive justice over a system that is based solely on humanitarian assistance.

As was discussed in the last section, federated members obligate themselves to practice the laws of hospitality and to maintain a system of cosmopolitan law. It was also argued that these actions would go a long way to limit global exploitation and to help guide the regulation of fair and equal trade relations between federated and non-federated communities. Nevertheless, as was outlined in the last chapter, a system of distributive justice beyond the protection of basic external freedoms would also be necessary to approximate a cosmopolitan condition and fulfill Kant's own concern for human development as suggested by a hypothetical *kingdom of ends*. As was argued in the last chapter, there is interpretive room within Kant's discussion of social welfare and his *principle of publicity* to suggest a consistent system of distributive justice, which at the very minimum favors the establishment of institutional structures to guarantee the basic needs of individuals. Furthermore, it was argued that this system of distributive justice might be best expressed through a globally applied capability approach.

With respect to the question of whether a Kantian model would favor humanitarian assistance or a more robust system of global distributive justice, the response is that it utilizes aspects of both, but favors one more than the other. Where Kant and Rawls significantly differ is in the fact that a system of global justice is for Kant the ultimate goal, something for which the federation obligates itself to promote internally and externally. However, Kant's and Rawls' positions are similar in one respect, namely, Kant is willing to allow for pragmatism similar to Rawls' use of non-ideal theory. For example, within the Kantian model outlined, there would exist a duty for the furtherance of global justice between federated members and non-federated members. Nevertheless, humanitarian assistance could be one method to help bring about this cosmopolitan condition. Prima facie, Kant's cosmopolitan enthusiasm is similar to Rawls' own concern, in that Rawls clearly states that the long-term goal of assistance is to "bring burdened societies, like outlaw states, into the society of well ordered peoples."[36] However, whereas Rawls allows non-ideal conditions to inform the long-term arrangement of international institutions, Kantian cosmopolitanism firmly holds global justice to be an ideal on the basis of which the federation is committed to alter existing institutional schemes. This is because, for Kant, cosmopolitan justice demands a duty to reform injustices so that they gradually approach the a priori ideal of justice. In this regard, humanitarian assistance is only an immediate and pragmatic method for influencing non-federated members to move toward eventual membership and toward more robust cosmopolitan principles of distributive justice. Therefore, the Kantian position as I have argued within this book leans toward an ultimate system of global distributive justice through some preliminary systems of humanitarian assistance.

It is also important to understand that the federation as it has been developed throughout this book aims to maintain a system of public right between its members and therefore does not consider intra-federated distribution as a form of humanitarian assistance. The use of humanitarian assistance is only one of many initial tools used by federated members in order to provide aid to non-federated members. In this regard, many of Rawls' concerns regarding delivery systems, suitability of programs on the ground, to whom funding is given within a burdened society (anti-corruption measures) and its interchangeability with local systems of justice could be managed on a case-by-case basis by the federation. Nevertheless, it is important to once again stress that any humanitarian assistance by federated members would be ultimately geared towards securing the eventual possibility of establishing a cosmopolitan condition between communities which will ultimately "have influence on each other."[37] As stated above, the distinction between assistance and justice is only a pragmatic move from theory to practice in the short term. In the case of Kantian cosmopolitanism, pragmatism cannot inform the system of justice, as it seems to do for Rawls, but can only be one consideration in a move toward its ideal counterpart. In other words, humanitarian assistance is used in conjunction with the laws of hospitality and public right to create an overall condition of cosmopolitan right. A condition from which non-federated states could become participants in a larger scheme of global justice and therefore also be required to uphold the cosmopolitan commitments that such membership enjoins.

## IV. THE IDEA OF UNIVERSAL HUMAN RIGHTS AS A BASIS FOR COSMOPOLITAN RIGHT

Many cosmopolitan and human right theorists have attempted to make a connection between Kant's cosmopolitan right and the universal human rights as understood in the United Nations Charter on Human Rights (UNCHR). Sharon Anderson-Gold, for example, has argued that there is a direct connection between Kant's discussion of public right and the normative principles that underwrite the UNCHR.[38] Although she is correct to suggest that many of the negative rights listed in the UNCHR would create conditions upon which individuals could enjoy external freedom, it is not necessarily the case that Kant's theory of public right accommodates the entire list of social rights as well. As has been discussed in the previous chapter, Kant did not fully develop a robust system of social and economic justice. In this regard, any extrapolation of social rights from Kant's political theory is exactly that, an extrapolation. This is not to say that the attempt to tie universal human rights to Kant is misguided, for there are significant areas of overlap between contemporary arguments for universal human rights and the political philosophy of Kant. However, it would be deceptive to directly link Kantian cosmopolitanism with all the provisions in the UNCHR without making some critical distinctions between them.

Critics of a human rights approach have maintained that we should be somewhat skeptical of those who attach the language of human rights to Kant's cosmopolitanism, especially if these theorists insinuate that Kant conceived of universal human rights exactly as we do today. According to the duty-based approach offered by Onora O'Neill, a strict focus on assigning rights overlooks the fact that these rights must have prior duties and/or obligations by others in order to fulfill the nature of such a right.[39] In this sense, the assigning of rights comes with corresponding duties to perform the obligation presupposed by that human right. In addition, right-based theories often assume that there is a clear delineation between the right bearer and those who would have corresponding duties to fulfill the obligation. Since this is often not the case internationally, O'Neill argues that rights without such corresponding duties are "manifesto rights," since they can only produce imperfect duties toward others. As O'Neill writes, "imperfect obligations can be enforced only when they are institutionalized in ways that specify *for whom* the obligation is to be performed."[40] What is necessary, according to O'Neill, is a renewed Kantian cosmopolitan focus on the specificity of these rights in relation to corresponding duties and an institutionalization of these obligations into a global system of human responsibility.[41]

There has been much written on the relationship between universal human rights, duties to humanity and cosmopolitanism. In addition, exhaustive arguments have been made illustrating that alternative forms of cosmopolitanism, namely utilitarian and duty-based approaches, ultimately reduce into relying on some underlying normative principle of human right.[42] As Tan, Jones and Thomas Pogge have pointed out, for O'Neill the motivation for having duties to our fellow humans rests "on a Kantian duty to protect and promote individual moral agency."[43] However, as Tan and Jones further suggest, "O'Neill's duty-based approach has to rely on an account of individual moral primacy that is rather consistent with the doctrine of individual rights."[44] In other words, although O'Neill has skillfully highlighted the point that rights make the most sense when individuals have corresponding duties to respect those rights, she does not produce a "different conceptual grounding for cosmopolitan justice."[45]

Furthermore, the rights-based approach seems to provide the most viable cosmopolitan option for any future theorizing on the creation of a cosmopolitan condition. Therefore the relevant question here is not whether Kant himself would have confirmed contemporary human rights arguments as being representative of his theory of public right and moral agency, but whether universal human rights are compatible and consistent with the Kantian position of cosmopolitan law as argued in this book.

As was argued in Chapter 2, the laws of hospitality assign both rights and duties while clearly delineating who is to have these rights and who would have an obligation as a duty bearer to respect them. In the realm of cosmopolitan law, all individuals have a duty to uphold the laws of hospitality, while federated states have a further obligation to enforce the protection of cosmopolitan right. Federated states are duty bearers in the sense that the cosmopolitan constitution forbids a violation of cosmopolitan right and that this duty is confirmed by any state that contractually joins the pacific federation. In this case, O'Neill's concern about the identification of duty bearers is resolved since the cosmopolitan constitution would clearly delineate who has international and cosmopolitan rights, what those rights entail, and who has duties to uphold those rights.

Furthermore, there is no theoretical reason as to why a rights-based approach is incompatible with Kant's cosmopolitanism. As has been argued throughout the chapters of this book, Kant's entire cosmopolitan project is premised on the protection of individual moral agency and the establishment of a mutually consistent condition of global public right. Given the language of current global politics, the human rights approach seems to provide the best philosophical invention that allows for the respect of an individual's moral agency based exclusively on the fact that the person is a human being regardless of geographical location or citizenship. In this regard, a rights-based approach fits comfortably with the inherent individualist, egalitarian and universalized demands of Kant's cosmopolitanism. In relation to Kant's pragmatism and a transition from theory to practice, it would seem that "rights are on their way to becoming the accepted international currency of moral, and especially political debate."[46] Therefore, the argument that the language of human rights is a non-identifiable concept to many cultures is simply no longer the case, since almost every culture now at least understands the concept of universal human rights, regardless of the fact that they might ultimately reject them.[47]

However, some communitarians and relativists have argued that the very rejection of human rights by some communities illustrates that it is

200

a western concept that cannot account for non-western values. The argument has generally been raised that the practice of exporting a language of universal human rights is tantamount to an act of liberal imperialism. In this regard, the language of universal human rights has an attached normative agenda to replace communal values with a non-identifiable universal conception of human entitlement. Many modern-day politicians, such a Lee Kuan Yew, feel that the language of human rights destabilizes communal obligations and cultural self-determination, suggesting that there is a theoretical conflict between universal human rights and local communities. As Yew put it, "Asians have little doubt that a society with communitarian values, where interests of society take precedence over that of the individual, suits them better than a society of individuals."[48] From this communitarian perspective, critics maintain that the concept of universal human rights should be seen as meta-ethically opposed to various cultural beliefs and that some communities are better suited without the cosmopolitan principles which underpin universal human rights.

The question of cultural difference and its relationship to cosmopolitan law has already been addressed in Chapter 4. Nevertheless, it behoves a cosmopolitan position that is concerned about a transition between theory and practice to highlight the faulty logic of the two aforementioned arguments. First, it should be pointed out that the argument presented by critics like Yew is guilty of a *reductionist sociology of culture* as outlined in Chapter 4.[49] In this regard, Yew's argument is premised on the fact that cultures are clearly definable, that a clear description of that culture is possible and that subgroup variants pose no problem in describing its cultural identity. Not only is there the immediate problem that Yew alone cannot represent the entire 'Asian' population, but there is little credibility in claiming that an entire anthropological group shares the exact communitarian position. This argument not only presumes that every Asian shares a similar communitarian commitment, but that human rights are necessarily incompatible with those communal aspirations. As has been argued by numerous theorists, the presumed incompatibility between cultural commitments and universal human rights is overstated and does not necessarily represent the fact that an acceptance of human rights is impossible.[50] As John Charvet points out, many inequalities in human rights are a matter of political authority versus a fundamental article of religious or cultural faith, and therefore can be modified without abandoning an overall vision of community.[51]

The second fallacy committed by Yew's argument is that he assumes that cultures cannot undergo internal normative shifts and that they are unable to fuse external ideas with their own cultural views. As was argued in Chapter 4, there is no theoretical reason to suggest that cultures are impregnable fortresses that are impervious to a cross-cultural pollination of ideas and values. An argument of this kind is unrepresentative of human history and immediately strikes us as contrary to the cultural evidence that suggests otherwise. It would seem that cultures are relating with other communities and that they often borrow, steal and interfuse various external cultural values with their own. In this regard, the difficult and important element in the formulation of a cosmopolitan order based on human rights is the fact that cultural communities will have to acknowledge some indispensable amount of human agency and external freedom. Although difficult to imagine as happening in tyrannical communities, this immediate difficulty does not necessarily mean that the people within those communities are themselves unwilling or psychologically unable to accept human rights if they were presented with the choice. Given the possibility for multifarious cultural identities and cultural normative shifts, it is not impossible to imagine various levels of subjective obligation and identification, one of which could be universal human rights under a unified system of cosmopolitan law.

## V. APPLIED THEORY: TOWARD A COSMOPOLITAN CONDITION

There is considerable debate among cosmopolitans in relation to applied theory and how a movement from cosmopolitan theory to cosmopolitan practice might be possible. As was outlined in Chapter 3, some cosmopolitans maintain that a cosmopolitan institutional order would be best practiced through the creation of a world state. These theorists argue that robust principles of cosmopolitan democracy,[52] global justice[53] or a cosmopolitan form of mutual security[54] can only be maintained through the organization of something resembling a world state. Implicit in these arguments, however, is a reliance on a thoroughgoing condition of cosmopolitan law and the corresponding requirement for a centralized authority to create, institute and enforce that legal order. Alternatively, many cosmopolitans have argued that a meaningful cosmopolitan condition can be fostered and maintained without establishing a world state and without a reliance on classical forms of political and legal power.[55] According to these cosmopolitan theorists, what is needed are more innovative mechanisms for democratic global governance,[56] the multilateral enforcement of existing cosmopolitan laws[57] and the fostering of international legal norms that already regulate human coexistence without a "formal juridical apparatus."[58] However, it is here, between the world state model and more minimal models of "mundane" cosmopolitan norms, that the Kantian model presented within this book can be situated. This is because, unlike world state cosmopolitans, the Kantian federation that I have argued for allows states to maintain a significant amount of local legal control while also providing a condition of cosmopolitan law by means of a normative cosmopolitan constitution. In this regard, as it has been argued, the federation enacts a form of *normative positivism* through a commitment to the principles that underpin the cosmopolitan constitution. Nevertheless, unlike some world state advocates, this constitution is designed to limit power while also assigning positive duties to its members, without also establishing a world authority beyond the self-regulated principles of the constitution itself.

In this regard, the Kantian model as it has been presented rejects the world state argument as the only, and certainly the best, possible formulation of a meaningful cosmopolitan condition. This has been based on both practical and theoretical considerations. First, the Kantian model, as it has been presented, suggests that any feasible move to a cosmopolitan condition, in whatever form that may eventually take, would necessarily have to start from current circumstances. This is because, for better or worse, the current global order is made up of states and it would seem that any move from theory to practice should be able to accommodate this empirical reality. For it seems more worthwhile to consider what various iterative steps could lead to a more robust cosmopolitan condition, than immediately designing a world state from a hypothetical vacuum. Second, as has been argued by Kant, there are serious theoretical reasons why we should be concerned about a world state and we should not so easily dismiss the fact that properly constituted states can have profoundly positive impacts on our lives.[59] It is from an understanding of these concerns that a cosmopolitan constitution might provide a middle position, in that it generates global commitments to cosmopolitan law while also allowing these commitments to be the result of co-legislation between states that best approximate Kant's condition of internal justice. In other words, the Kantian model outlined throughout this book can occupy a middle and transitory position between a world that only reflects some cosmopolitan norms and the future possibility of establishing a more robust system of global governance based on cosmopolitan law.

However, it would be naïve to assume that my Kantian model does not face its own practical difficulties. As Seyla Benhabib has recently suggested, even a more moderate move from cosmopolitan principles to global practice presents cosmopolitans with a big hurdle to jump. This is because serious questions remain about "how to create quasi-legal binding obligations through voluntary commitments . . . in the absence of an overwhelming sovereign power with the ultimate right of enforcement."[60] In this regard, Benhabib is correct to suggest that this is a crucial question facing cosmopolitanism. As she further argues, "the modern state system is caught between sovereignty and hospitality, between the prerogative to choose to be a party to cosmopolitan norms and human rights treaties, and the obligation to extend recognition of these human rights to all."[61]

Nevertheless, as Benhabib and many cosmopolitans maintain, the global situation is not as bleak as we might first expect. As Jeremy Waldron has recently expressed, the world is already made up of a "dense thicket" of interlocking laws, treaties, regulations and applied norms.[62] According to Waldron, this thicket of "mundane" international law and norms represents, to some degree, an already functioning set of "cosmopolitan norms that structure our lives together."[63] As Waldron suggests, "if we really want to understand how the world is coming to be ordered by cosmopolitan norms, we have to look at the ordinary as well as the extraordinary, the tedious as well as the exciting, the commercial as well as the ideological."[64] In many ways, Waldron's thicket analogy remains true to Kant's teleology and his *lex mercatoria* as explored in Chapter 1. This is because there seems to be a belief that the continued interconnection between people, through commerce and trade, will create "peaceful relations with one another, and thus achieve mutual understanding, community of interests, even with the most distant of their fellows."[65] In this regard, Waldron wants to stress that the world is already made up of a complex system of laws and norms that help regulate human coexistence and that there is much to be enthusiastic about. In many ways this is an appropriate analogy and one that captures an important aspect of current international law. For Waldron is right to suggest that it is from international commerce, global communication and the increasing interaction of peoples that human beings have slowly, but surely, incorporated various cosmopolitan principles of cooperation, human rights, norms of hospitality and a sense of moral obligation to others.

In a complimentary fashion, this thicket of "mundane" international law underpins and supports what Jürgen Habermas has labeled the "constitutionalization of international law" and his suggestion that this interlocking system of cosmopolitan norms and law has come to constitute something like a world society.[66] As Habermas argues, "the everyday experience of growing [legal] interdependencies in an increasingly complex global society also imperceptibly alters the self-image of nation states and their citizens."[67] It is from this slow socializing effect of constitutionalization that states gain "latitude for a new sort of political influence" at the global level, which channels into "governance without government" and into legally constituted international organizations.[68] According to Habermas, we can witness the shaping of a "new structure of a constituted cosmopolitan society" by the increasing number of world organizations, regional governance bodies, emboldened civil societies and the "accelerated development of international law."[69] It is through this continuing process of constitutionalization that there is a strengthening of what he calls "The Kantian Project." Namely, the "legal position of the individual legal subject, who is gradually acquiring the status of a subject of international law and a cosmopolitan citizen."[70]

As stated before, Waldron's analogy of a dense thicket of international law, as well as Habermas' concept of increased constitutionalization, is able to capture something very real about the current global order and how these laws are helping to structure our lives together. Nevertheless, scholars are right to question this position, by suggesting that "mundane and repeated contact among different human groups is absolutely no guarantee of the spread of a cosmopolitan point of view that considers all human beings as individuals equally entitled to certain rights."[71] In addition, although Waldron and Habermas are correct to suggest that some cosmopolitan norms have developed through human interaction, it is also true that the current thicket of international law also allows for the perpetuation of massive inequality, injustices, war, genocide, exploitation and a sustained devaluation of human worth. In this regard, although there is some basis from which a cosmopolitan enthusiasm can be generated, it still lacks a coherent normative direction toward a more robust cosmopolitan condition. It is with this in mind that the Kantian cosmopolitan constitution, as presented in this book, is meant to provide the normative and legal grounding toward a more thoroughgoing cosmopolitan legal condition.

Therefore, the key to advancing cosmopolitanism is to combine the "mundane" bottom-up approach of Waldron and Habermas with the more formal constitutional approach as developed in the previous chapters. Nevertheless, this process itself generates questions of its own. For in practice, the Kantian federation would need a group of like-minded democratic states that are willing to ground cosmopolitan law into their own legal codes and then to promote these laws in their dealings with all people. As Kant recommends, this should be done not only for the protection of domestic right, but also to advance these principles to all humanity, in order to bring about a more just and cooperative cosmopolitan condition. The question then becomes why certain democratic states might be willing to obligate themselves to cosmopolitan law under a federated system and to broaden the scope of public right to include others.

As was discussed in Chapter 3, Kant predicates the foundation of a cosmopolitan federation on the *definitive article* that "the civil constitution of every state be republican."[72] Kant grounds the expansion of cosmopolitan law on domestic law because he believed that a democratic constitution is the only order that can secure and approximate the ideal of justice both internally and externally.[73] Kant believed that a domestic sense of justice between democratic peoples lends itself to viewing other democratic peoples as sharing similar values of justice and that they will seek to be more cooperative with each other. In addition, implicit in Kant's understanding of democratic law is an additional reference to democracy's intermediary quality. By intermediary, Kant suggests that democratic people not only concern themselves with the protection of domestic right, but also that they concern themselves with establishing a condition of justice with anyone who they have contact with, even non-democratic and potentially hostile peoples. This sociological element of democratic law forms the foundation for Kant's democratic peace theory, but also is held as the motivational component behind why "like-minded" democratic peoples would be more willing to create a federation that included cosmopolitan law and the laws of hospitality.

Nevertheless, Kant does not elaborate as to why democratic peoples are sociologically more accepting and thus more willing to legally protect the cosmopolitan value of those beyond their borders. In attempts to explore this prospect, Benhabib has recently suggested that democratic law is a process of *democratic iteration*, which helps to arbitrate "between universal norms and the will of democratic majorities."[74] Benhabib suggests that through a process of repeated reiteration and reconstruction, democratic law engages in progressive modification by its democratic population, resulting in what she calls "jurisgenerative politics." Benhabib further argues that through continued iteration "a democratic peoples, which considers itself bound by certain guiding norms and principles, engages in iterative acts by reappropriating and reinterpreting these, thereby showing itself not only the subject but also the author of the laws."[75] Through this process of jurisgenerative politics, democratic law sequentially reflects and then expands the boundaries of ethical universalism. This occurs because the democratic concern for justice and individual autonomy is systematically incorporated into domestic positive law and these laws in turn eventually come to guide the behavior of that political body towards non-citizens. In order to illustrate the force behind this process, Benhabib asks us to examine the continued broadening of cosmopolitan norms between democratically liberal countries and peoples beyond their borders. Although not always representative of a progressive trajectory, liberal democracies, especially within the European Union, have extended their own domestic laws to include and protect the rights of non-citizens. In addition, these same liberal democracies have sought to expand many cosmopolitan norms at the international level, as witnessed by a growing commitment to humanitarian intervention, humane migration law and to the punishment of crimes against humanity.

However, there are considerable perplexities involved with Benhabib's account of why democratic law produces progressive iterations toward a cosmopolitan ethic. Similar to Kant, Waldron and Habermas, Benhabib relies on the fact that cosmopolitan principles are intrinsically valid and she does not fully explain why democratic iteration would necessarily lead to universal ethical norms versus promoting nationalistic tendencies. In addition, as Bonnie Honig rightly suggests, many of the injustices involved with the global system are the results of the very same democracies that purport to have the greatest concern for cosmopolitan human worth.[76] In this regard, although democracies under the guidance of democratic law might be the most likely candidates to help advance a cosmopolitan condition under applied cosmopolitan law, it is not necessarily the case that this is inevitable.

In spite of the fact that the democratic theory of both Kant and Benhabib does not sufficiently explain why democracies necessarily promote cosmopolitanism, there is empirical justification to recommend that democratic states represent the most likely candidates for the expansion of cosmopolitan law. As the history of universal human rights law would help to illustrate, cosmopolitan principles are more likely to come from liberal democracies than from non-democratic or from more authoritarian regimes. Although theorists are not sure why democratic law can have an intermediary function between the domestic and the global, prima facie it would seem that democratic law does have an ability to move domestic concerns for justice to global laws of hospitality. Despite the fact that many cosmopolitans might view this process as insufficiently slow and without a clear linear progression, it would seem that any movement to a cosmopolitan order would have to begin with existing democratic political communities and from the enlargement of existing cosmopolitan norms. Nevertheless, this continued growth toward more applied cosmopolitan law is not guaranteed and will require prolonged deliberation and ethical acceptance through the formation of identification relationships, domestically and globally, between states and peoples, both legally and extra-legally. In addition, it will require liberal peoples to consistently apply domestic concerns for justice and the protection of human worth equally to those beyond their borders. Given the current political order, it would seem that the move to ground cosmopolitan theory into practice will need to come from both internal and external deliberative processes to expand domestic legal codes to include others and to then establish a condition of cosmopolitan law.[77] Through some form of Benhabib's iterative process or Kant's intermediary system, democratic peoples will need to demand that a consistent relationship between domestic justice and global justice be maintained. Although this process as of now remains a rather intuitive speculation, it is also not totally unreasonable to suggest that there are both theoretical and empirical reasons to think this is possible, and also, as Waldron might suggest, that the world is already slowly engaged in this process.

The key to this process is the establishment of robust commitments by democratic peoples and their popular sovereigns to pursue a mutually consistent condition of justice beyond their borders. This commitment must not only be held as a moral obligation, but also as a legal obligation, so as to secure cosmopolitan law as a set of legal expectations that express and facilitate the furtherance of a continued universal ethic toward others.

In many ways, Kant's cosmopolitan law seeks to provide those global norms and standards that will produce a condition of soft-positivism and compliance pull between political communities. This is bolstered by the federal constitution as it has been outlined in this book, for it is meant to objectify the normative and juridical principles that underwrite a cosmopolitan order. It secures obligation through contractual agreement and thus commands normative authority through a legally binding agreement. Furthermore, the federated order establishes a condition of soft-positivism in that it generates constitutional authority to persuade compliance and obligation by setting the terms of federated membership and by setting legitimacy standards of global practice. In addition, the constitution acts as a reference point for the creation of a continued global identity and ethic, since individuals can form an identification relationship with a set of juridical standards that have positive impacts upon their lives. For Kant, a constitution refers to the totality of laws that should be publicized so as to create a rightful condition of mutual freedom between individuals, states and associations. As Kant himself proclaimed, what is ultimately needed is "a system of laws . . . for a multitude of peoples, which, because they affect one another, need a rightful condition under a will uniting them, a constitution (constitutio), so that they may enjoy what is laid down as right."[78] Although Kant did not refer specifically to a written constitutional document, he did refer to contractarian principles of self-binding obligation that were to limit power as well as give authority to a juridical condition of mutual public right. It is for this reason that it might be reasonable to think creatively about a Kantian-based written constitution and its ability to ground self-binding commitments by political communities, individuals and states to a cosmopolitan order.

As was stated in Chapter 2, in order to facilitate a continued sense of cosmopolitan community, it is necessary to create positive ethical and legal experiences of global interaction by way of the formation of additional norms that grow through the fulfillment of existing legal and extra-legal expectations. By objectifying the minimal laws of hospitality into the written constitution of a normatively based Kantian federation, it would help to foster what Habermas describes as a condition of *constitutional patriotism* beyond borders and could help to provide a global point of reference for continued global deliberation and legal expectation.[79] This is because the continued application of juridical procedures has the ability to foster identification relationships between peoples and the normative principles that underwrite a legal constitution. Thus a sense of patriotic identification can be generated beyond local political obligations by cultivating a belief that these global legal practices have bearing and meaning on human coexistence and well-being.

# VI. CONCLUSION

In many ways it could be argued that the world is moving toward a cosmopolitan condition and that there is much to be enthusiastic about. The current world order sustains unprecedented levels of cooperation between states, communities and individuals. Peoples of the world currently find themselves embroiled in international organizations, systems of global trade, global communication, economic interdependence, cross-media infusion, complex international treaties, and other effects of globalization that bring the remoteness of communities together. Furthermore, the rise of democracy on the global level since the 1980s and the need for communities to solve global problems such and global warming and SARS has created greater opportunities, partnerships, mutual commitments, international norm building and a growing possibility for continued cosmopolitan enthusiasm.[80] In addition, there has been a steady increase in what has been labeled global civil society. According to many theorists, a robust global civil society has acted as an *insurgent* element, which challenges the current global order and forces grass-root global concerns to be addressed by international institutions.[81] Lastly, as was insinuated in the previous section, the language of universal human rights is beginning to find a global audience and more states than not have embraced the language of human rights by signing human right covenants.

Nevertheless, despite this continued globalization of interests and a durable dialogue on human rights, our global order still produces extraordinary poverty, senseless death, human right violations and dismal inequality. What is perhaps the most striking feature of these global issues is the fact that many of these problems could be eliminated if a political will to do so existed.[82] Furthermore, although the world has suffered two devastating world wars and the threat of nuclear annihilation, it would seem that humanity refuses to learn from history and that the world is largely unwilling to embrace anything closely resembling a system of mutual public right and global justice. It would seem that Kant's reliance on David Hume's *heroic medicine* has had more difficulty producing the enlightened progress he had hoped, since states are still "bludgeoning each other" like "two drunken wretches in a china-shop" without ever realizing that they will "have to pay for all the damages they have caused."[83] Focusing on the apparent realism of the global system, many theorists argue that the current level of cooperation is as good as it gets, that communal self-interest, cultural boundaries, political brinkmanship, economic models and the nature of the international system itself are all inherently anti-cosmopolitan. The best that can be hoped for, according to this anti-cosmopolitan stance, is that states will control themselves through the self-interested pursuance of a balance of power and that enough well-minded states will organize themselves in such a manner as to secure a power balance for the foreseeable future.

So given the fact that the world does not resemble a cosmopolitan ideal, what possibility is there for the existence of a cosmopolitan condition of public right? As Michel De Montaigne poignantly remarked, "one cannot change anything without judging whatever one abandons to be bad, and whatever one adopts to be good."[84] In many regards, any change towards a cosmopolitan condition will only result from a conscious decision to change current international relations and the way states and individuals beyond state borders behave. In order for this to be possible, we as human beings will have to abstract from current hindrances toward more universal and encompassing visions of global cohabitation. In some respects we will have to start thinking in terms of the categorical imperative and whether our current behavior could be or should be universalizable.

Regardless of current hindrances, there still remain certain indisputable facts about the world that scholars of contemporary political theory must continue to try and resolve. It is indisputable that humanity is enclosed within the bounded sphere of the earth and that our actions toward one another greatly affect our mutual ability to live well. Furthermore, it is indisputable that any concept of communal right is incoherent unless it is couched within a system of global rights and obligations. For it is absurd to suggest that any state, community or individual can enjoy self-determined freedom when they are under a constant threat from external forces. Furthermore, as they stand, global institutions are organized in such a way that they perpetuate massive injustices and inequalities between various peoples of the earth. If we take these injustices and inequalities as an affront to the valuation of human beings as having ends in themselves, then it is important to seek out recognizable principles that not only facilitate greater cooperation, but that also protect the human concerns of various people impacted by global cohabitation. In Kantian terms, what is needed is "a constitution allowing the greatest human freedom in accordance with the laws which ensure that the freedom of each can coexist with the freedom of all the others."[85] This condition of justice "is at all events a necessary idea which must be made the basis not only of the first outline of a political constitution but of all laws as well."[86]

211

In this regard, "all politics must bend a knee before right . . . [if we are to] arrive, however slowly, at a stage of lasting brilliance."[87]

To this end, the purpose of this book has been to provide a Kantian alternative to the global order and to outline what a tenable form of Kantian constitutional cosmopolitanism would resemble. In doing so, this book has focused on the normative principles that would underwrite a cosmopolitan condition of public right and the formation of a Kantian cosmopolitan constitution. Undoubtedly, some will argue that this project is nothing more than a theoretical exercise and that it has abstracted too far from real world circumstances that limit the prospect of a cosmopolitan condition. To this I can only side with Kant and "put trust in the theory of what the relationships between men and states *ought to be* according to the principle of right."[88] In this regard, this project is a continuation of Kant's cosmopolitan enthusiasm, for "it recommends to us earthly gods the maxim that we should proceed in our disputes in such a way that a universal federation may be inaugurated, so that we should therefore assume that it is *possible*."[89] This underlining enthusiasm stems from the premise that just because a theory has a degree of difficulty, it does not mean that it cannot be achieved, but simply that there will be complications involved in the effort to realize it. Furthermore, and most importantly, just because a theory has a degree of difficulty does not also mean that it is not something we *should strive to do*. In this regard, "it thus remains true to say that whatever reason shows to be valid in theory, is also valid in practice."[90]

## NOTES

1. Immanuel Kant, "On the Common Saying: This May be True in Theory, But it Does not Apply in Practice," in Hans Reiss (ed.), H. B. Nisbet (trans.), *Kant's Political Writings* (Cambridge: Cambridge University Press, 1970), p. 92. [8:313]

2. Immanuel Kant, "Perpetual Peace: A Philosophical Sketch," in Hans Reiss (ed.), H. B. Nisbet (trans.), *Kant's Political Writings* (Cambridge: Cambridge University Press, 1970), p. 112. [8:366]

3. I borrow the phrase cosmopolitan enthusiasm from Georg Cavallar, *Kant and the Theory and Practice of International Right* (Cardiff: University of Wales Press, 1999).

4. Kant, "On the Common Saying: This May be True in Theory, But it Does not Apply in Practice," p. 73. [8:290]

5. I borrow this phase from David Held, "From Executive to Cosmopolitan Multilateralism," in Mathias Koenig-Archibugi & David Held (eds), *Taming Globalization: Frontiers of Governance* (Cambridge: Polity Press, 2003), pp. 160–86.

6. Kant, "Perpetual Peace," p. 106. [8:358]

7. Ibid., pp. 107–8. [8:360]

8. Immanuel Kant, *The Metaphysics of Morals*, Mary Gregor (trans.) (Cambridge: Cambridge University Press, 1996), pp. 40–1. [6:246–53]

9. Immanuel Kant, "Idea for a Universal History with a Cosmopolitan Purpose," in Hans Reiss (ed.), H. B. Nisbet (trans.), *Kant's Political Writings* (Cambridge: Cambridge University Press, 1970) p. 43 [8:19] and "Appendix: Transcendental Logic II, Dialectics, I, Ideas in General," *The Critique of Pure Reason*, J. M. D. Meiklejohn (trans.) (New York: Colonial Press, 1900). [4:201]

10. I refer here to Scheffler's distinction regarding *moderate* and *extreme* cosmopolitanism, namely that an extreme cosmopolitan position requires that all moral commitments, even localized sentiments for the family, must be justified in relation to a particular cosmopolitan ideal or principle without exception. Alternatively, a moderate form of cosmopolitanism allows for the acceptance that some special obligations can be held independently and in mutual compatibility with cosmopolitanism. For his more detailed delineation, see Samuel Scheffler, *Boundaries and Allegiances* (Oxford: Oxford University Press, 2001), pp. 115–19.

11. Garrett Wallace Brown, "Globalization is What We Make of It: Contemporary Globalization Theory and the Future Construction of Global Interconnection," *Political Studies Review*, vol. 6, no. 1 (2007), pp. 42–53.

12. For a broad overview of the various positions on globalization, see David Held & Anthony McGrew, *Globalization/Anti-Globalization* (Cambridge: Polity Press, 2002).

13. An excellent overview of these statistics can be found in Thomas Pogge, *World Poverty and Human Rights* (Cambridge: Polity Press, 2002).

14. Kok-Chor Tan, *Justice Without Borders: Cosmopolitanism, Nationalism and Patriotism* (Cambridge: Cambridge University Press, 2004).

15. Mark Warren, "Deliberative Democracy," in A. Carter and G. Stokes (eds) *Democratic Theory Today* (Cambridge: Polity Press, 2002), p. 174. Italics are mine.

16. Deborah Cook, "The Talking Cure in Habermas's Republic," in *New Left Review*, 12 (Nov. 2001), pp. 135–51.

17. Jürgen Habermas, *Between Facts and Norms*, W. Rehg (trans.) (Cambridge: Polity Press, 1996).

18. Warren, p. 174.

19. John Dryzek, *Deliberative Democracy and Beyond* (Oxford: Oxford University Press, 2000). Anthony McGrew, "Transnational Democracy," in A. Carter & G. Stokes (eds) *Democratic Theory Today* (Cambridge: Polity Press, 2002). Quote from Dryzek, p. 115.

20. Dryzek, *Deliberative Democracy and Beyond*, p. 129.

21. Ibid.

22. Kant, "Perpetual Peace," p. 106. [8:358]

23. Ibid., pp. 102–15. [8:354–60] Arguments of this sort are scattered throughout Kant's political writings. The most significant and compelling are located in "The Idea for a Universal History with a Cosmopolitan Purpose," especially pp. 50–3 [8:27–31]; "An Answer to the Question: 'What is Enlightenment?'," pp. 54–60 [8:35–42]; "The Contest of Faculties," especially pp. 180–1 [7:83–4] & 186–90 [7.90–4]; "On the Common Saying: This May be True in Theory, But it Does not Apply in Practice," especially pp. 84–92 [8:304–13]. These essays are all found in Hans Reiss, *Kant's Political Writings*. Similar arguments can also be found throughout Kant's *The Metaphysics of Morals*, especially Part II.

24. Jürgen Habermas, *The Divided West*, Ciaran Cronin (ed. & trans.) (Cambridge: Polity Press, 2006).

25. Oran Young, *International Governance: Protecting the Environment in a Stateless Society* (Ithaca: Cornell University Press, 1994), p. 14. For a similar conclusion, see James Rosenau, "Governance, Order and Change in World Politics," in J. Rosenau and E. Czempiel (eds), *Governance without Government: Order and Change in World Politics* (Cambridge: Cambridge University Press, 1992), pp. 1–29.

26. Young, p. 15.

27. There are certainly more than two traditions in international relations theory. These positions can range from a more Malthusian position to more extreme forms of cosmopolitanism. Nevertheless, for my purposes here I am concerned only with the two arguments outlined above. This is because both share similar values concerning the alleviation of human suffering and an additional normative concern for the basic needs of individuals. These positions share a similarity with the philosophy of Kant and therefore are the positions from which a comparison will be most lucrative.

28. Thomas Nagel, "The Problems of Global Justice," *Philosophy and Public Affairs*, 33 (2005).

29. Thomas Pogge, "Moral Universalism and Global Economic Justice," *Politics, Philosophy and Economics*, vol. 1, no. 1 (2002). For a similar argument, see Patrick Hayden, *Cosmopolitan Global Politics* (Aldershot: Ashgate, 2005).

30. David Miller, *National Responsibility and Global Justice* (Oxford: Oxford University Press, 2007).

31. Simon Caney, *Justice Beyond Borders* (Oxford: Oxford University Press, 2005).

32. John Rawls, *The Laws of Peoples* (Cambridge, MA: Harvard University Press, 1999), p. 106.

33. Ibid., pp. 117–19.

34. Ibid., p. 59.

35. Although I tend to agree with most of these criticisms I simply cannot dedicate significant space to this subject. The tip of the iceberg includes, Thomas Pogge, "Rawls and Global Justice," *Canadian Journal of Philosophy*, 18 (2) (1988), pp. 227–56. Simon Caney, *Justice Beyond Borders* (Oxford: Oxford University Press, 2005), especially Chapter 4. Kok-Chor Tan, *Justice Without Borders* (Cambridge: Cambridge University Press, 2004), especially Chapters 3 & 4. Patrick Hayden, *John Rawls Towards a Just World Order* (Cardiff: University of Wales Press, 2002). Allan Buchanan, "Rawls's Law of Peoples," *Ethics*, 110 (2000), pp. 697–721.

36. Rawls, p. 59.

37. Kant, *The Metaphysics of Morals*, p. 121. [6:352]

38. Sharon Anderson-Gold, *Cosmopolitanism and Human Rights* (Cardiff: University of Wales Press, 2001).

39. Onora O'Neill, *Constructions of Reason: Exploration of Kant's Practical Philosophy* (New York: St. Martin's Press, 1989).

40. Ibid., p. 191.

41. Ibid., p. 199.

42. Charles Jones, *Global Justice: Defending Cosmopolitanism* (Oxford: Oxford University Press, 1999), Chapter 4. Also see Tan, Chapter. 3.

43. Tan, p. 52. For a similar argument, see Thomas Pogge, "O'Neill on Rights and Duties," *Grazer Philosophische Studien*, 43 (1992), pp. 233–47.

44. Tan, pg 52. Jones, p. 107.
45. Tan, p. 53.
46. L. Sumner, *The Moral Foundations of Rights* (New Jersey: Princeton University Press, 1987), p. vii.
47. Jack Donnelly, *Universal Human Rights in Theory and Practice* (Ithaca: Cornell University Press, 1989).
48. Taken from Nathan Gardels, "Interview with Lee Kuan Yew," *New Perspectives Quarterly*, 9, I (Winter 1992).
49. A *reductionist sociology of culture* and the three corresponding features are attributed to Seyla Benhabib, *The Claims of Culture: Equality and Diversity in the Global Era* (Princeton: Princeton University Press, 2002).
50. John Charvet, "The Possibility of a Cosmopolitan Order Based on the Idea of Universal Human Rights," *Millennium* (3), vol. 27 (1998), pp. 523–41.
51. Ibid., p. 536.
52. Raffaele Marchetti, *Global Democracy: For and Against* (Oxford: Routledge, 2008).
53. Luis Cabrera, *Political Theory of Global Justice: A Cosmopolitan Case for the World State* (New York: Routledge, 2004).
54. Daniel H. Deudney, *Bounding Power: Republican Security Theory from the Polis to the Global Village* (New Jersey: Princeton University Press, 2007).
55. Jürgen Habermas, *The Divided West*. Patrick Hayden, *Cosmopolitan Global Politics* (Aldershot: Ashgate, 2005).
56. David Held, "Reframing Global Governance: Apocalypse Soon or Reform!," in D. Held & A. McGrew (eds), *Globalization Theory* (Cambridge: Polity Press, 2007). Daniele Archibugi, *The Global Commonwealth: Toward Cosmopolitan Democracy* (New Jersey: Princeton University Press, 2008).
57. Hayden, *Cosmopolitan Global Politics*.
58. Jeremy Waldron, "Cosmopolitan Norms," in P. Post (ed.), *Another Cosmopolitanism* (Oxford: Oxford University Press, 2006), p. 83.
59. Jeremy Waldron, "Kant's Theory of the State," in P. Kleingeld (ed.), *Toward Perpetual Peace and Other Writings on Politics, Peace and History* (New Haven: Yale University Press, 2006).
60. Seyla Benhabib, "The Philosophical Foundations of Cosmopolitan Norms," in R. Post (ed.), *Another Cosmopolitanism* (Oxford: Oxford University Press, 2006), p. 23.
61. Ibid., p. 31.
62. Waldron, "Cosmopolitan Norms," p. 49.
63. Ibid.
64. Ibid., p. 97.
65. Kant, "Perpetual Peace," p. 111. [8:364]
66. Jürgen Habermas, *Between Naturalism and Religion*, Ciaran Cronin (trans.) (Cambridge: Polity Press, 2008), p. 316.
67. Jürgen Habermas, *The Divided West*, p. 177.
68. Ibid., p. 176–177.
69. Habermas, *Between Naturalism and Religion*, pp. 322–42.
70. Ibid., p. 335.
71. Seyla Benhabib, "Hospitality, Sovereignty, and Democratic Iterations," in R. Post (ed.), *Another Cosmopolitanism* (Oxford: Oxford University Press, 2006), p. 153.
72. Kant, "Perpetual Peace," p. 99. [8:349]

73. Kant, *The Metaphysics of Morals*, pgs. 89-95. [6:311-318]
74. Seyla Benhabib, "Democratic Iterations: The Local, the National and the Global," in R. Post (ed.), *Another Cosmopolitanism* (Oxford: Oxford University Press, 2006), p. 49.
75. Ibid.
76. Bonnie Honig, "Another Cosmopolitanism?: Law and Politics in the New Europe," in R. Post (ed.), *Another Cosmopolitanism* (Oxford: Oxford University Press, 2006).
77. I acknowledge that democratic change can come from both internal processes and from external processes. These external processes often take the form of an insurgent global civil society or through pressures exerted by existing cosmopolitan norms that are seen as standards from which other nations might urge compliance. However, given the political organization of states, these external processes do not legislate from outside the political community, but simply influence internal political rethinking. In this regard, any real adoption of cosmopolitan legal principles by a political community can only come from its internal legislative process and its self-determined belief to morally and legally obligate itself to others. This might naturally occur through increased global interaction as Waldron seems to suggest, or it can also happen, in conjunction with natural interaction and extra-legal norm building, through the self-motivated extension of legal codes to include others, thus creating a baseline cosmopolitan condition.
78. Kant, *The Metaphysics of Morals*, p. 89. [6:311]
79. Jürgen Habermas, *Between Facts and Norms*, p. 499.
80. David Held, "Democracy and the New International Order," in D. Archibugi & D. Held (eds), *Cosmopolitan Democracy* (Cambridge: Polity Press, 1995).
81. Mary Kaldor, *Global Civil Society: An Answer to War* (Cambridge: Polity Press, 2003).
82. For a more detailed argument outlining the manageable cost of eliminating poverty and its feasibility, see Thomas Pogge, *World Poverty and Human Rights*.
83. Immanuel Kant, "The Contest of Faculties," in Hans Reiss (ed.), H. B. Nisbet (ed. & trans.), *Kant's Political Writings* (Cambridge: Cambridge University Press, 1970), p. 190. [7:93–4]
84. Michel De Montaigne, "On Common; and Never Easily Changing a Traditional Law," in M. A. Screech (trans.), *The Complete Essays* (London: Penguin Classics, 1993), p. 136.
85. Kant, *Critique of Pure Reason*. [4:201]
86. Ibid.
87. Kant, "Perpetual Peace," p. 125. [8:380]
88. Kant, "Theory and Practice," p. 92. [8:313]
89. Ibid.
90. Ibid.

# Bibliography

Alexander, John, "Capability Egalitarianism and Moral Selfhood," *Ethical Perspectives*, vol. 10 (1) (2003).

Alexander, Larry, *Constitutionalism: Philosophical Foundations* (Cambridge: Cambridge University Press, 1998).

Allan, R., *The Oxford Latin Dictionary: Collectors Edition* (Norwalk: The Easton Press, 1993).

Allison, Henry E., *Kant's Theory of Freedom* (Cambridge: Cambridge University Press, 1990).

Ameriks, Karl, *Kant and the Fate of Autonomy* (Cambridge: Cambridge University Press, 2000).

Ameriks, Karl, *Kant's Theory of Mind* (Oxford: Oxford University Press, 2000).

Anderson-Gold, Sharon, *Cosmopolitanism and Human Rights* (Cardiff: University of Wales Press, 2001).

Andrews, William, *Constitutions and Constitutionalism* (Princeton: Van Nostrand Co., 1968).

Apel, Karl-Otto, *Understanding and Explanation: A Transcendental-Pragmatic Perspective* (Cambridge, MA: MIT Press, 1984).

Apel, Karl-Otto, "Kant's Toward Perpetual Peace as Historical Prognosis from the Point of View of Moral Duty," in J. Bohman & M. Lutz-Bachmann, *Perpetual Peace: Essays on Kant's Cosmopolitan Ideal* (Cambridge, MA: MIT Press, 1997).

Appiah, Kwame Anthony, *Cosmopolitanism: Ethics in a World of Strangers* (New York: Norton, 2006).

Archibugi, Daniele, "Models of International Organization in Perpetual Peace Projects," *Review of International Studies*, 18 (1992), pp. 295–317.

Archibugi, D. & Held, D. (eds), *Cosmopolitan Democracy: An Agenda for a New World Order* (Cambridge: Polity Press, 1995).

Archibugi, Daniele, "Immanuel Kant, Cosmopolitan Law and Peace," *European Journal of International Relations*, vol. 1 (4), 1995.

Archibugi, D. & Koening-Archibugi, M., "Globalization, Democracy and Cosmopolis: A Bibliographical Essay," in D. Archibugi (ed.), *Debating Cosmopolitics* (London: Verso, 2003), pp. 273–91.

Archibugi, Daniele, *The Global Commonwealth of Citizens: Toward Cosmopolitan Democracy* (New Jersey: Princeton University Press, 2008).

Aune, Bruce, *Kant's Theory of Morals* (New Jersey: Princeton University Press, 1979).

Aurelius, Marcus, *The Meditations* (New York: Hackett, 1983).

Avineri, S. & de-Shalit, A. (eds), *Communitarianism and Individualism* (Oxford: Oxford University Press, 1992).

Axinn, Sidney, "Kant on World Government," in G. Funke & T. Seebohm (eds), *Proceedings of the Sixth International Kantian Congress*, vol. 2 (Washington, DC: University Press of America, 1989).

Barry, Brian, "International Society from a Cosmopolitan Perspective," in D. Maple & T. Nardin (eds), *International Society: Diverse Ethical Perspectives* (New Jersey: Princeton University Press, 1998).

Barry, Brian, "Statism and Nationalism: A Cosmopolitan Critique," in I. Shapiro & L. Brilmayer (eds), *Global Justice* (New Jersey: Princeton University Press, 1998).

Barry, Brian, *Culture and Equality* (Cambridge, MA: Harvard University Press, 2001).

Baucock, R. & Rundell, J. (eds), *Blurred Boundaries: Migration, Ethnicity, Citizenship* (Aldershot: Ashgate, 1998).

Bauer, J. & Bell, D. (eds), *The East Asian Challenge for Human Rights* (Cambridge: Cambridge University Press, 1999).

Beiner, Ronald, "Nationalism, Internationalism, and the Nairn-Hobsbawn Debate," *Archives for European Sociology*, XL, 1 (1999), pp. 171–84.

Beitz, Charles, *Political Theory and International Relations* (New Jersey: Princeton University Press, 1979).

Beitz, Charles, "International Liberalism and Distributive Justice: A Survey of Recent Thought," *World Politics* 51, 1992.

Beitz, Charles, "Cosmopolitan Liberalism and the State System," in C. Brown (ed.), *Political Restructuring in Europe: Ethical Perspectives* (London: Routledge, 1994).

Benhabib, Seyla, *The Claims of Culture: Equality and Diversity in the Global Era* (Princeton: Princeton University Press, 2002).

Benhabib, Seyla, *The Rights of Others: Aliens, Residents and Citizens* (Cambridge: Cambridge University Press, 2004).

Benhabib, Seyla, "The Philosophical Foundations of Cosmopolitan Norms," in R. Post (ed.), *Another Cosmopolitanism* (Oxford: Oxford University Press, 2006).

Benhabib, Seyla, "Democratic Iterations: The Local, the National, and the Global," in R. Post (ed.), *Another Cosmopolitanism* (Oxford: Oxford University Press, 2006).

Benhabib, Seyla, "Hospitality, Sovereignty, and Democratic Iterations," in R. Post (ed.), *Another Cosmopolitanism* (Oxford: Oxford University Press, 2006).

Bernard, F. M. (ed.), *Herder on Social and Political Culture* (Cambridge: Cambridge University Press, 1969).

Bohman, James, "The Public Spheres of the World Citizen," in J. Bohman & M. Lutz-Bachmann (eds), *Perpetual Peace: Essays on Kant's Cosmopolitan Ideal* (Cambridge: The MIT Press, 1997).

Bohman, J. & Lutz-Bachmann, M. (eds), *Perpetual Peace: Essays on Kant's Cosmopolitan Ideal* (Cambridge, MA: MIT Press, 1997).

Breckenridge, Carol (ed.), *Cosmopolitanism* (Durham: Duke University Press, 2002).

Brennan, Timothy, *At Home in the World: Cosmopolitanism Now* (Cambridge: Cambridge University Press, 1997).

Brown, Chris (ed.), *Political Restructuring in Europe: Ethical Perspectives* (London: Routledge, 1994).

Brown, Garrett Wallace, "Globalization is What we Make of It: Contemporary Globalization Theory and the Future Construction of Global Interconnection," *Political Studies Review*, vol. 6, no. 1 (2007), pp. 42–53.

Brown, Garrett Wallace, "Moving from Cosmopolitan Legal Theory to Legal Practice: Models of Cosmopolitan Law," *Legal Studies*, vol. 28, no. 3 (2008).

Bryant, John, "Nowhere a Stranger: Melville and Cosmopolitanism," *Nineteenth-Century Fiction*, vol. 39, no. 3 (1984).

Buchanan, Allan, "Rawls's Law of Peoples," *Ethics*, 110 (2000), pp. 697–721.

Buchanan, Allan, *Justice, Legitimacy and Self-Determination: Moral Foundations for International Law* (Oxford: Oxford University Press, 2004).

Bull, Hedley, *The Anarchical Society* (London: Macmillan, 1977).

Cabrera, Luis, *Political Theory of Global Justice: A Cosmopolitan Case for the World State* (New York: Routledge, 2004).

Caney, Simon, "Cosmopolitan Justice and Equalizing Opportunities," in T. Pogge (ed.), *Global Justice* (Oxford: Blackwell, 2001).

Caney, Simon, *Justice Beyond Borders: A Global Political Theory* (Oxford: Oxford University Press, 2005).

Caney, Simon, "Global Distributive Justice and the State," *Political Studies*, vol. 56, no. 3 (2008).

Carter, A. & Stokes, G. (eds), *Democratic Theory Today* (Cambridge: Polity Press, 2002).

Cavallar, Georg, *Kant and the Theory and Practice of International Right* (Cardiff: University of Wales Press, 1999).

Cavallar, Georg, *The Rights of Strangers* (Aldershot: Ashgate, 2002).

Caygill, Howard, *A Kant Dictionary* (Oxford: Blackwell, 1995).

Charvet, John, "The Possibility of a Cosmopolitan Order Based on the Idea of Universal Human Rights," *Millennium* (3), vol. 27 (1998).

Cicero, Marcus, *De Officiis*, M. T. Griffin & E. M. Atkins (eds) (Cambridge: Cambridge University Press, 1991).

Clarks, I., Neumann, I. & (eds), *Classical Theories of International Relations* (Basingstoke: Macmillan Press, 1996).

Cohen, G. A., *Self-Ownership, Freedom and Equality* (Oxford: Oxford University Press, 1995).

Cook, Deborah, "The Talking Cure in Habermas's Republic," in *New Left Review*, 12 (Nov. 2001), pp. 135–51.

Cook, John W., *Morality and Cultural Differences* (Oxford: Oxford University Press, 1999).

Covell, Charles, *Kant and the Law of Peace: A Study in the Philosophy of International Law and International Relations* (New York: Palgrave, 1998).

Czempiel, E. & Rosenau, J. (eds), *Governance Without Government: Order and Change in World Politics* (Cambridge: Cambridge University Press, 1992).

Delanty, Gerard, *Citizenship in a Global Age* (Buckingham: Open University Press, 2000).

Derrida, Jacques, "Foreign Question," R. Bowlby (trans.), *Of Hospitality* (Stanford: Stanford University Press, 2000).

Derrida, Jacques, "On Cosmopolitanism," in *On Cosmopolitanism and Forgiveness*, M. Dooley & M. Hughes (trans.) (London: Routledge, 2002).

Deudney, Daniel H., *Bounding Power: Republican Security Theory from the Polis to the Global Village* (New Jersey: Princeton University Press, 2007).

Donaldson, Thomas, "Kant's Global Rationalism," in T. Nardin & D. Maple (eds), *Traditions of International Ethics* (Cambridge: Cambridge University Press, 1992).

Donnelly, Jack, *International Human Rights* (Boulder, CO: University of Colorado Press, 1989).

Donnelly, Jack, *Universal Human Rights in Theory and Practice* (Ithaca: Cornell University Press, 1998).

Dower, Nigel, *An Introduction to Global Citizenship* (Edinburgh: Edinburgh University Press, 2003).

Doyle, Michael, "Kant, Liberal Legacies, and Foreign Affairs," *Philosophy and Public Affairs*, 12 (3) (1983), pp. 204–35.

Doyle, Michael, "Kant, Liberal Legacies, and Foreign Affairs," *Philosophy and Public Affairs*, 12 (4) (1983), pp. 323–53.

Doyle, Michael, "Kant and Liberal Internationalism," in P. Kleingeld (ed.), *Toward Perpetual Peace and Other Writings on Politics, Peace and History* (New Haven: Yale University Press, 2006).

Dryzek, John, *Deliberative Democracy and Beyond* (Oxford: Oxford University Press, 2000).

Dunn, T. & Wheeler, N. (eds), *Human Rights in Global Politics* (Cambridge: Cambridge University Press, 1999).

Durkheim, Emile, *Ethics and the Sociology of Morals*, T. Hall (trans.) (Buffalo: Prometheus Books, 1993).

Evens, T. (ed.), *Human Rights Fifty Years On: A Reappraisal* (Manchester: Manchester University Press, 1998).

Fabre, Cecile, *Social Rights Under the Constitution: Government and the Decent Life* (Oxford: Oxford University Press, 2000).

Fabre, Cecile & Miller, David, "Justice and Culture: Rawls, Sen, Nussbaum and O'Neill," *Political Studies Review*, vol. 1 (2003), pp. 1–17.

Falk, Richard, *On Humane Governance: Towards a New Global Politics* (Cambridge: Polity Press, 1995).

Fidler, David, "Desperately Clinging to Grotian and Kantian Sheep: Rousseau's Attempt to Escape the State of War," in I. Clarks & I. Neumann (eds), *Classical Theories of International Relations* (Basingstoke: Macmillan Press, 1996).

Flikschuh, Katrin, *Kant and Modern Political Philosophy* (Cambridge: Cambridge University Press, 2000).

Franceschet, Antonio, *Kant and Liberal Internationalism: Sovereignty, Justice and Global Reform* (New York: Palgrave, 2002).

Franck, Thomas, M., *The Power of Legitimacy Among Nations* (Oxford: Oxford University Press, 1990).

Frost, Mervyn, *Towards a Normative Theory of International Relations* (Cambridge: Cambridge University Press, 1986).

Gardels, Nathan, "Interview with Lee Kuan Yew," *New Perspectives Quarterly* 9, I (Winter 1992).

Geertz, Charles, *The Interpretation of Cultures* (New York: Basic Books, 1973).

Gellner, Ernest, *Nations and Nationalism* (Oxford: Blackwell, 1983).

Giddens, Anthony, *The Consequences of Modernity* (Stanford: Stanford University Press, 1990).

Glossop, Ronald, J., *World Federation?: A Critical Analysis of Federal World Government* (North Carolina: McFarland & Company, 1993).

Gray, Thomas, "Constitutionalism: An Analytic Framework," in J. Pennock & J. Chapman (eds), *Constitutionalism* (New York: New York University Press, 1979).

Gregor, Mary, *The Laws of Freedom: A Study of Applying the Categorical Imperative in the Metaphysics of Morals* (Oxford: Blackwell, 1963).

Gregor, Mary, "Kant's Approach to Constitutionalism," in A. Rosenbaum (ed.), *Constitutionalism: The Philosophical Dimension* (New York: Greenwood Press, 1988).

Grillo, R., *Pluralism and the Politics of Difference: State, Culture and Ethnicity in Comparative Perspective* (Oxford: Clarendon Press, 1998).

Guyer, Paul, *Kant on Freedom, Law and Happiness* (Cambridge: Cambridge University Press, 2000).

Habermas, Jürgen, *Between Facts and Norms*, W. Rehg (trans.) (Cambridge: Polity Press, 1996).

Habermas, Jürgen, *The PostNational Constellation*, M. Persky (trans.) (Cambridge, MA: MIT Press, 2001).

Habermas, Jürgen, *The Divided West*, Ciaran Cronin (ed. & trans.) (Cambridge: Polity Press, 2006).

Habermas, Jürgen, *Between Naturalism and Religion*, Ciaran Cronin (trans.) (Cambridge: Polity Press, 2008).

Harris, Hugh, "The Greek Origins of the Idea of Cosmopolitanism," *The International Journal of Ethics*, vol. 38, no. 1 (1927), pp. 1–10.

Harrison, Ewan, "Waltz, Kant and Systematic Approaches to International Relations," *Review of International Studies*, 28 (2002), pp. 143–62.

Hatch, Elvin, *Theories of Man and Culture* (New York: Columbia University Press, 1973).

Hayden, Patrick, *John Rawls Towards a Just World Order* (Cardiff: University of Wales Press, 2002).

Hayden, Patrick, *Cosmopolitan Global Politics* (Aldershot: Ashgate, 2005).

Hayek, F. A., *Law, Legislation and Liberty* (London: Routledge, 1973).

Heater, Derek, *World Citizenship and Government: Cosmopolitan Ideas in the History of Western Political Thought* (New York: St. Martin's Press, 1996).

Heater, Derek, *World Citizenship* (London: Continuum, 2002).

Hegel, G. W. F., *The Philosophy of Right*, S. W. Dyde (trans.) (New York: Prometheus Books, 1996).

Hegel, G. W. F., *The Phenomenology of Spirit*, A. Miller (trans.) (Oxford: Oxford University Press, 1977).

Held, David, *Democracy and the Global Order: From the Modern State to Cosmopolitan Democracy* (Cambridge: Polity Press, 1995).

Held, David, "Democracy and the New International Order," in D. Archibugi & D. Held (eds) *Cosmopolitan Democracy* (Cambridge: Polity Press, 1995).

Held, David (ed.), *Political Theory Today* (Cambridge: Polity Press, 1995).

Held, D., McGrew, A., Goldblatt, D. & Perraton, J., *Global Transformations* (Cambridge: Polity Press, 1999).

Held, D., & McGrew, A., *Globalization/Anti-Globalization* (Cambridge: Polity Press, 2002).

Held, David, "Cosmopolitanism: Globalization Tamed?," *Review of International Studies*, 29 (2003), pp. 465–80.

Held, David, "From Executive to Cosmopolitan Multilateralism," in Mathias. Koenig-Archibugi & David. Held (eds), *Taming Globalization: Frontiers of Governance* (Cambridge: Polity Press, 2003), pp. 160–186.

Held, David, "Reframing Global Governance: Apocalypse Soon or Reform!," in D. Held & A. McGrew (eds), *Globalization Theory* (Cambridge: Polity Press, 2007).

Herskovits, Melville, *Cultural Relativism: Perspectives in Cultural Pluralism*, F. Herskovits (ed.) (New York: Random House, 1972).

Hinsley, F. H., *Power and the Pursuit of Peace* (Cambridge: Cambridge University Press, 1963).

Hoffe, Otfried, *Kant's Cosmopolitan Theory of Law and Peace* (Cambridge: Cambridge University Press, 2006).

Holsti, Kalevi J., *Peace and War: Armed Conflicts and International Order 1648–1989* (Cambridge: Cambridge University Press, 1992).

Honig, Bonnie, "Another Cosmopolitanism?: Law and Politics in the New Europe," in R. Post (ed.), *Another Cosmopolitanism* (Oxford: Oxford University Press, 2006).

Huntington, Samuel, *The Clash of Civilizations and the Remaking of the World Order* (New York: Simon and Schuster, 1996).

Hurrell, Andrew, "Kant and the Kantian Paradigm in International Relations," *Review of International Studies*, 16 (3) (1990), pp. 183–205.

Jackson, Robert, *The Global Covenant* (Oxford: Oxford University Press, 2000).

Jones, Charles, *Global Justice: Defending Cosmopolitanism* (Oxford: Oxford University Press, 1999).

Kaldor, Mary, *Global Civil Society: An Answer to War* (Cambridge: Polity Press, 2003).

Kant, Immanuel (1784), "Idea for a Universal History with a Cosmopolitan Purpose," in Hans Reiss (ed.), H. B. Nisbet (trans.), *Kant's Political Writings* (Cambridge: Cambridge University Press, 1970).

Kant, Immanuel (1784), "An Answer to the Question 'What is Enlightenment?'", in Hans Reiss (ed.), H. B. Nisbet (trans.), *Kant's Political Writings* (Cambridge: Cambridge University Press, 1970).

Kant, Immanuel (1785), *Grounding for the Metaphysics of Morals*, J. Ellington (trans.) (Cambridge, MA: Hackett Publishing Company, 1981).

Kant, Immanuel (1787), *The Critique of Pure Reason*, J. M. D. Meiklejohn (trans.) (New York: The Colonial Press, 1900).

Kant, Immanuel (1790), *Critique of Judgement*, J. Meredith (trans.) (Oxford: Oxford University Press, 1973).

Kant, Immanuel (1793), "On the Common Saying: This May be True in Theory, But it Does not Apply in Practice," in Hans Reiss (ed.), H. B. Nisbet (trans.), *Kant's Political Writings* (Cambridge: Cambridge University Press, 1970).

Kant, Immanuel (1795), "Perpetual Peace: A Philosophical Sketch," in Hans Reiss (ed.), H. B. Nisbet (trans.), *Kant's Political Writings* (Cambridge: Cambridge University Press, 1970).

Kant, Immanuel (1797), *The Metaphysics of Morals*, M. Gregor (ed. & trans.) (Cambridge: Cambridge University Press, 1996).

Kant, Immanuel (1798), *Anthropology from a Pragmatic Point of View*, V. Dowdell (trans.), H. Rudnick (ed.) (Carbondale: Southern Illinois University Press, 1978).

Kant, Immanuel (1798), "The Contest of Faculties," in Hans Reiss (ed.), H. B. Nisbet (trans.), *Kant's Political Writings* (Cambridge: Cambridge University Press, 1970).

Kaufman, Alexander, *Welfare in the Kantian State* (Oxford: Clarendon Press, 1999).

Kelly, Paul (ed.), *Multiculturalism Reconsidered* (Cambridge: Polity Press, 2002).

Koenig-Archibugi, M. & Held, D. (eds), *Taming Globalization: Frontiers of Governance* (Cambridge: Polity Press, 2003).

223

Korner, Steven, *Kant* (Harmondsworth: Penguin, 1955).

Korsgaard, Christine, M., "Aristotle and Kant on the Source of Value," *Ethics*, 96 (April 1986), pp. 486–505.

Korsgaard, Christine, M., *Creating the Kingdom of Ends* (Cambridge: Cambridge University Press, 1996).

Kroeber, Alfred, *Anthropology* (New York: Harcourt Brace, 1948).

Kukathas, Chandran, *The Liberal Archipelago: A Theory of Diversity and Freedom* (Oxford: Oxford University Press, 2003).

Kymlicka, Will, *The Rights of Minority Cultures* (Oxford: Oxford University Press, 1995).

Kymlicka, Will, *Politics in the Vernacular: Nationalism, Multiculturalism and Citizenship* (Oxford: Oxford University Press, 2001).

Laberge, Pierre, "Kant on Justice and the Law of Nations," in D. Maple & T. Nardin (eds), *International Society: Diverse Ethical Perspectives* (New Jersey: Princeton University Press, 1998).

Laertius, Diogenes, *The Lives of Eminent Philosophers*, vol. II, R. Hicks (trans.) (Cambridge, MA: Loeb Classical Library, 1925).

Linklater, Andrew, *Men and Citizens in the Theory of International Relations*, 2nd edn (Basingstoke: Macmillan, 1990).

Lévi-Strauss, Claude, *Elementary Structures of Kinship* (Boston: Beacon Press, 1967).

Lu, Catherine, "The One and Many Faces of Cosmopolitanism," *Journal of Political Philosophy*, vol. 8 (2), June 2000.

Lutz-Bachmann, Matthias, "Kant's Ideal of Peace and the Philosophical Conceptions of a World Republic," in J. Bohman & M. Lutz-Bachmann (eds), *Perpetual Peace: Essays on Kant's Cosmopolitan Ideal* (Cambridge, MA: MIT Press, 1997), pp. 59–77.

Lyotard, Jean-François, *The Postmodern Condition: A Report of Human Knowledge*, G. Bennington (trans.) (Minneapolis: University of Minneapolis Press, 1984).

Maple, D. & Nardin, T. (eds), *International Society: Diverse Ethical Perspectives* (New Jersey: Princeton University Press, 1998).

Maple, D. & Nardin, T. (eds), *Traditions of International Ethics* (Cambridge: Cambridge University Press, 1992).

Marchetti, Raffaele, *Global Democracy: For and Against: Ethical Theory, Institutional Design and Social Struggles* (Oxford: Routledge, 2008).

McGrew, Anthony, "Human Rights in a Global Age: Coming to Terms with Globalization," in T. Evens (ed.), *Human Rights Fifty Years On: A Reappraisal* (Manchester: Manchester University Press, 1998), pp. 188–210.

McGrew, Anthony, "Transnational Democracy," in A. Carter & G. Stokes (eds), *Democratic Theory Today* (Cambridge: Polity Press, 2002).

McKim, Robert & McMahan, Jeff (eds), *The Morality of Nationalism* (Oxford: Oxford University Press, 1997).

McIlwain, Charles, *Constitutionalism: Ancient and Modern* (Ithaca: Cornell University Press, 1947).

Melvill, Henry, "Partaking in Other Men's Sins," *The Golden Lectures* (London: Chapter House, 1855), p. 454.

Miller, David, *On Nationality* (Oxford: Oxford University Press, 1995).

Miller, David, "The Limits of Cosmopolitan Justice," in D. Maple & T. Nardin (eds), *International Society* (New Jersey: Princeton University Press, 1998).

Miller, David, *Citizenship and National Identity* (Cambridge: Polity Press, 2000).

Miller, David, *National Responsibility and Global Justice* (Oxford: Oxford University Press, 2007).

Monaghan, John & Just, Peter, *Social and Cultural Anthropology* (Oxford: Oxford University Press, 2000).

Montaigne, Michel De, "On Common; and Never Easily Changing a Traditional Law," in M. A. Screech (trans.), *The Complete Essays* (London: Penguin Classics, 1993).

Mulholland, Leslie, *Kant's System of Rights* (New York: Colombia University Press, 1990).

Munzel, Felicitas, *Kant's Concept of Moral Character: The Critical Link of Morality, Anthropology, and Reflective Judgement* (Chicago: University of Chicago Press, 1999).

Muthu, Sankar, *Enlightenment Against Empire* (Princeton: Princeton University Press, 2003).

Nagel, Thomas, "The Problem of Global Justice," *Philosophy and Public Affairs*, 33 (2005), pp. 113–47.

Nell, Onora, *Acting on Principle: An Essay on Kantian Ethics* (New York: Columbia University Press, 1975).

Neumann, Franz, *The Rule of Law: Political Theory and the Legal System in Modern Society* (Dover: Berg Publishing, 1986).

Nozick, Robert, *Anarchy, State, and Utopia* (New York: Basic Books, 1974).

Nussbaum, Martha, *Cultivating Humanity* (Cambridge, MA: Harvard University Press, 1997).

Nussbaum, Martha, "Kant and Cosmopolitanism," in J. Bohman & M. Lutz-Bachmann (eds), *Perpetual Peace: Essays on Kant's Cosmopolitan Ideal* (Cambridge, MA: MIT Press, 1997).

Nussbaum, Martha, "Patriotism and Cosmopolitanism," *The Boston Review*, 19 (5) (1995).

Nussbaum, M. & Glover, J. (eds), *Women, Culture and Development: A Study of Human Capabilities* (Oxford: Oxford University Press, 1995).

Nussbaum, Martha (ed.), *For Love of Country: Debating the Limits of Patriotism* (Boston: Beacon Press, 1996).

Nussbaum, Martha, *Women and Human Development: The Capabilities Approach* (Cambridge: Cambridge University Press, 2000).

Nussbaum, Martha, "Beyond the Social Contract: Capabilities and Global

Justice," in G. Brock & H. Brighouse (eds), *The Political Philosophy of Cosmopolitanism* (Cambridge: Cambridge University Press, 2005).

Oneal, John & Russett, Bruce, "The Kantian Peace: The Pacific Benefits of Democracy, Interdependence, and International Organizations, 1885–1992," *World Politics*, 52 (1999).

O'Neill, Onora, *Faces of Hunger: An Essay on Poverty, Justice and Development* (London: Allen & Unwin, 1986).

O'Neill, Onora, *Constructions of Reason: Exploration of Kant's Practical Philosophy* (New York: St. Martin's Press, 1989).

O'Neill, Onora, "Justice, Capabilities, and Vulnerabilities," in M. Nussbaum & J. Glover (eds), *Women, Culture and Development: A Study of Human Capabilities* (Oxford: Oxford University Press, 1995).

O'Neill, Onora, "Transnational Justice," in D. Held (ed.), *Political Theory Today* (Cambridge: Polity Press, 1995).

Orend, Brian, *War and International Justice: A Kantian Perspective* (Waterloo: Wilfrid Laurier University Press, 2001).

Pakulski, Jan, "East European Revolutions and Legitimacy Crisis," in J. Frentzel-Zagorska (ed.), *From One Party State to Democracy* (Amsterdam: Rodopi, 1993), pp. 67–87.

Parekh, Bhiku, "Non-Ethnocentric Universalism," in T. Dunn & N. Wheeler (eds), *Human Rights in Global Politics* (Cambridge: Cambridge University Press, 1999).

Parekh, Bhiku, *Rethinking Multiculturalism* (Basingstoke: Palgrave, 2000).

Pennock, J. Roland & Chapman, John W. (eds), *Constitutionalism* (New York: New York University Press, 1979).

Plutarch, "On the Fortune of Alexander," in A. Long & D. Sedley (eds), *The Hellenistic Philosophers*, vol. I (Cambridge: Cambridge University Press, 1987).

Pogge, Thomas, "Kant's Theory of Justice," *Kant-Studien*, 79 (1988).

Pogge, Thomas, "Rawls and Global Justice," *Canadian Journal of Philosophy*, 18 (2) (1988), pp. 227–56.

Pogge, Thomas, "Cosmopolitanism and Sovereignty," *Ethics*, 103 (1992).

Pogge, Thomas, "An Institutional Approach to Humanitarian Intervention," *Public Affairs Quarterly*, vol. 6 no. 1 (1992), pp. 89–103.

Pogge, Thomas, "O'Neill on Rights and Duties," *Grazer Philosophische Studien*, 43 (1992), pp.233–47.

Pogge, Thomas (ed.), *Global Justice* (Oxford: Blackwell, 2001).

Pogge, Thomas, "Priorities of Global Justice," in T. Pogge (ed.), *Global Justice* (Oxford: Blackwell, 2001).

Pogge, Thomas, *World Poverty and Human Rights* (Cambridge: Polity Press, 2002).

Pogge, Thomas, "Moral Universalism and Global Economic Justice," *Politics, Philosophy and Economics*, vol. 1, no. 1 (2002).

Pogge, Thomas, "Can the Capability Approach be Justified?", *The Equality Exchange* (aran.uiv.pau.fr, 2003).

Pogge, Thomas, "A Cosmopolitan Perspective on the Global Economic Order," in G. Brock & H. Brighouse (eds), *The Political Philosophy of Cosmopolitanism* (Cambridge: Cambridge University Press, 2005).

Popper, Karl, *The Poverty of Historicism* (London: Routledge, 1957).

Post, Robert (ed.), *Another Cosmopolitanism* (Oxford: Oxford University Press, 2006).

Rawls, John, *A Theory of Justice* (Cambridge, MA: Harvard University Press, 1971).

Rawls, John, "Kantian Constructivism in Moral Theory: The Dewey Lectures 1980," *Journal of Philosophy*, 77 (1980).

Rawls, John, *The Laws of Peoples* (Cambridge, MA: Harvard University Press, 1999).

Reich, Klaus, "Kant and Greek Ethics," *Mind*, 48 (1939), pp. 338–54.

Reiss, Hans (ed.), *Kant's Political Writings* (Cambridge: Cambridge University Press, 1970).

Roosevelt, Grace, *Reading Rousseau in the Nuclear Age* (Philadelphia: Temple University Press, 1990).

Rosen, Allen, *Kant's Theory of Justice* (Ithaca: Cornell University Press, 1993).

Rosenau, James, "Governance, Order and Change in World Politics," in J. Rosenau & E. Czempiel (eds), *Governance without Government: Order and Change in World Politics* (Cambridge: Cambridge University Press, 1992), pp. 1–29.

Rosenbaum, A. (ed.), *Constitutionalism: The Philosophical Dimension* (New York: Greenwood Press, 1988).

Rummel, R. J., "Democracies ARE Less Warlike Than Other Regimes," *European Journal of International Relations*, vol. 1 (4) (1999), pp. 429–56.

Russett, Bruce, *Grasping the Democratic Peace* (Princeton: Princeton University Press, 1993).

Sandel, Michael, *Liberalism and the Limits of Justice* (Cambridge: Cambridge University Press, 1982).

Scheffler, Samuel, *Boundaries and Allegiances* (Oxford: Oxford University Press, 2001).

Seneca, *De Otio*, A. Long & D. Sedley (eds) (Cambridge: Cambridge University Press, 1987).

Shapiro, Ian & Brilmayer, Lea (eds), *Global Justice* (New Jersey: Princeton University Press, 1998).

Shue, Henry, *Basic Rights* (New Jersey: Princeton University Press, 1996).

Singer, Peter, "Famine, Affluence, and Morality," *Philosophy and Public Affairs* (1) (1971–2), pp. 229–43.

Smith, Anthony, *The Ethnic Origins of Nations* (Oxford: Blackwell, 1986).

Sumner, L., *The Moral Foundations of Rights* (New Jersey: Princeton University Press, 1987).

Tamir, Yael, *Liberal Nationalism* (Princeton: Princeton University Press, 1993).

Tan, Kok-Chor, *Justice Without Borders: Cosmopolitanism, Nationalism and Patriotism* (Cambridge: Cambridge University Press, 2004).

Taylor, Charles, "Atomism," in S. Avineri & A. de-Shalit (eds), *Communitarianism and Individualism* (Oxford: Oxford University Press, 1992), pp. 29–50.

Taylor, Charles, *Philosophical Arguments* (Cambridge, MA: Harvard University Press, 1995).

Taylor, Charles, "Conditions of an Unforced Consensus on Human Rights," in J. Bauer & D. Bell (eds), *The East Asian Challenge for Human Rights* (Cambridge: Cambridge University Press, 1999).

Taylor, Charles T., *Toward World Sovereignty* (Lanham, MD: University Press of America, 2002).

Teson, Fernando, *A Philosophy of International Law* (Boulder, CO: Westview Press, 1998).

Teson, Fernando, "Kantian International Liberalism," in D. Maple & T. Nardin (eds), *International Society: Diverse Ethical Perspectives* (Princeton: Princeton University Press, 1998).

Thomas, Scott, *The Global Resurgence of Religion and the Transformation of International Relations* (New York: Palgrave, 2005).

Tully, James, *Strange Multiplicity* (Cambridge: Cambridge University Press, 1995).

Tully, James, "The Kantian Idea of Europe: Critical and Cosmopolitan Perspectives," in A. Pagden (ed.), *The Idea of Europe* (Cambridge: Cambridge University Press, 2002).

Turner, Terence, "Anthropology and Multiculturalism: What is Anthropology and What Multiculturalists should be Mindful of?," *Cultural Anthropology*, vol. 8, no. 4 (1993), pp. 411–29.

Waldron, Jeremy, "Minority Cultures and the Cosmopolitan Alternative," *University of Michigan Journal of Law Reform*, 25 (1992), pp. 751–93.

Waldron, Jeremy, "Minority Cultures and the Cosmopolitan Alternative," in Will Kymlicka (ed.), *The Rights of Minority Cultures* (Oxford: Oxford University Press, 1995).

Waldron, Jeremy, "Kant's Legal Positivism," *Harvard Law Review*, vol. 109 (1996).

Waldron, Jeremy, "What is Cosmopolitan?," *Journal of Political Philosophy* vol. 8, no. 2 (2000), pp. 227–43.

Waldron, Jeremy, "Kant's Theory of the State," in P. Kleingeld (ed.), *Toward Perpetual Peace and Other Writings on Politics, Peace and History* (New Haven: Yale University Press, 2006).

Waldron, Jeremy, "Cosmopolitan Norms," in R. Post (ed.), *Another Cosmopolitanism* (Oxford: Oxford University Press, 2006).

Waltzer, Michael, "Pluralism: A Political Perspective," in Will Kymlicka (ed.), *The Rights of Minority Cultures* (Oxford: Oxford University Press, 1995).

Ward, Keith, *The Development of Kant's View of Ethics* (Oxford: Blackwell, 1972).

Warren, Mark, "Deliberative Democracy" in A. Carter & G. Stokes (eds), *Democratic Theory Today* (Cambridge: Polity Press, 2002).

Weber, Martin, "Keeping it Real? Kant and Systematic Approaches to IR – A Response to Harrison," *Review of International Studies*, 29 (2003), pp. 145–50.

Westin, Charles, "Temporal and Spatial Aspects of Multiculturality," in R. Baucock & J. Rundell (eds), *Blurred Boundaries: Migration, Ehinicity, Citizenship* (Aldershot: Ashgate, 1998).

Wheare, K. C., *Modern Constitutions* (Oxford: Oxford University Press, 1951).

Wight, Martin, "An Anatomy of International Thought," *Review of International Studies*, 13 (1987).

Wight, Martin, *International Theory: The Three Traditions*, G. Wight & A. Roberts (eds) (Leicester: Leicester University Press, 1991).

Williams, Howard, *Kant's Political Philosophy* (New York: St. Martin's Press, 1983).

Wolff, Christian, *The Laws of Nations Treated According to a Scientific Method*, H. Drake (trans.) (Oxford: Clarendon Press, 1934).

Wood, Allen W., "Kant's Compatibilism," in A. Wood (ed.), *Self and Nature in the Philosophy of Kant* (Ithaca: Cornell University Press, 1984).

Wood, Allen (ed.), *Self and Nature in the Philosophy of Kant* (Ithaca: Cornell University Press, 1984).

Wood, Allen W., "Kant's Philosophy of History," in P. Kleingeld (ed.) *Toward Perpetual Peace and Other Writings on Politics, Peace and History* (New Haven: Yale University Press, 2006).

Young, Iris Marion, *Justice and the Politics of Difference* (Princeton: Princeton University Press, 1990).

Young, Oran, *International Governance: Protecting the Environment in a Stateless Society* (Ithaca: Cornell University Press, 1994).

# Index

Akhnaton, 4
Anderson-Gold, Sharon, 49, 59, 198
Apel, Karl-Otto, 38–41
Aristotle, 8, 96
aspect capacity, 157–9, 167–8
Aune, Bruce, 161
Aurelius, Marcus, 5–9, 31, 32, 50
autonomy, 34, 38, 41, 150, 151–3, 154–5,
    155–9, 162–3, 166, 169, 170–1, 173, 174,
    178, 180n; see also effective autonomy;
    freedom of will

Bacon, Francis, 7
balance of power, 90, 211; see also modus
    vivendi
Barry, Brian, 10–11, 109, 140, 176
Beiner, Ronald, 127
Beitz, Charles, 10–11, 109, 176
Benhabib, Seyla, 56, 65, 128, 130, 204, 206–7,
    208
Bohman, James, 48
Bull, Hedley, 16, 107, 110

Cabrera, Luis, 13
Caney, Simon, 174
capability approach, 150, 159, 166, 167–71,
    175
categorical imperative, 1, 34–5, 94, 99, 153,
    155, 158, 161, 168
    as cosmopolitan regulatory principle, 34–7,
        94, 171, 211
Cavallar, Georg, 56, 60, 65, 96–7, 180
Charvet, John, 201
Chrysippus, 5
Church of England, 1
Cicero, Marcus, 5–9
civic cosmopolitanism, 13, 205–6
civil justice, 153–6, 161–2, 167

civil society, 35–7, 153–6, 161–2, 163–6,
    192–5, 210
commerce, 39, 47, 62–3, 100, 101, 104, 172–3,
    204
communitarianism, 15–17, 127, 128, 129, 133,
    136, 140, 177, 187, 188, 200–2
constitutional patriotism, 71–2, 209
constitutionalism, 69–73, 98–9, 113–15, 149,
    159, 165–6, 167, 169, 171
cosmopolitanism
    basic definition, 9–10
    classic tradition, 5–9
    contemporary models, 9–15
cosmopolitan citizenship 5–9, 10, 47, 65, 103–6,
    112, 189, 205
cosmopolitan constitutionalism
    as constitutionalization, 60, 63, 66–7, 98,
        105, 113–15, 142–3, 172, 177–8, 204–10
    idea of formal constitution, 66–78, 100,
        105–6, 113–15, 150, 167–8, 175, 178, 187,
        189, 192, 194–5, 203, 205–10, 211
    Kant's constitutionalism, 31, 36–7, 44, 66,
        71, 98, 106, 159, 165–6, 174–5, 177,
        209
    the need for a cosmopolitan constitution, 17,
        36, 39, 43–4, 60, 66–7, 71, 78–9, 98–9,
        106, 141, 142, 159, 172, 173, 175, 177,
        178, 205–10, 211
    see also public right
cosmopolitan democracy, 115–16, 190–1,
    191–5, 202, 203, 206
cosmopolitan federation see pacific federation;
    world federation
cosmopolitan jurisprudence, 44–7, 66, 73–8, 91,
    94–5, 98, 103–6, 140–1, 142, 174–5, 177,
    188, 202–10
cosmopolitan justice see cosmopolitan right;
    global justice; public right; universal justice

cosmopolitan law, 17, 37, 44–50, 58–9, 66, 72,
  87, 91, 95, 103–6, 112–15, 123–4, 128,
  129, 139–40, 140–1, 142–4, 164, 187, 188,
  191–5, 196, 200, 202–10
  and globalization, 4, 60, 104, 124, 144, 175,
  191, 204
  and Stoicism, 5–9
  as distinct from natural law tradition, 7,
  89–94
  see also cosmopolitan right
cosmopolitan matrix, 31–7, 47–50, 51, 60, 172
  as developing human capacities, 31–3, 41–3,
  51, 60, 169, 171, 175–8, 177, 196–7
  see also cosmopolitan law
cosmopolitan right, 17, 37, 44–7, 55–6, 58–66,
  69, 75–8, 88, 95, 103–6, 171, 173, 188,
  189, 191–5, 198, 208; see also law of
  hospitality
cosmopolitan teleology, 6, 39–44; see also Kant's
  teleology; teleology
Covell, Charles, 47, 60, 103–4
Crate of Thebes, 5
criminal justice, 153
critical philosophy, 23–4, 33–7
cultural cosmopolitanism, 13, 125, 131–3, 135,
  137, 138–9, 143–4, 189, 201–2
cultural pluralism, 15–17, 123–5, 126–31,
  140–3, 143, 144, 170, 176, 177, 187, 188,
  196
cultural relativism, 125, 126–31, 134–40, 143,
  170, 171, 187, 188, 200–2
Cynics, 5

definitive articles for perpetual peace, 75–8,
  95–106, 107, 112, 206
Delanty, Gerald, 12
deliberative democracy, 191–5, 209
democratic law, 115–16, 206–9, 216n
democratic peace theory, 93, 119n, 206
dependency thesis, 134–7
Derrida, Jacques, 55–6, 59, 60, 64–5, 78
Diderot, Denis, 7
Diogenes of Sinope, 4–5, 10
distributive justice, 117, 150–1, 153–9, 159,
  160, 161, 162–6, 167, 168, 169, 173–8,
  188, 189–91, 195–8; see also global justice
diversity thesis, 134, 137–40
Doctrine of Right, 94, 98, 161, 165
domestic law, 45–6, 76, 93, 95–9, 164, 206; see
  also Kant's tripartite of law; pacific
  federation
Donaldson, Thomas, 103
Dryzek, John, 193–4
duties of right, 161; see also public right
duties of virtue, 161, 165

effective autonomy, 150, 151, 156–9, 160, 166,
  167–71, 173, 175, 177, 178–9, 181n

enculturative conditioning, 134, 136
English School, 112
European balance of power see balance of power
European Union, 207
exegesis and interpretation, 20–3, 187–8
experiments in living, 142
external freedom, 37, 44, 90, 108, 116, 151–3,
  154–9, 160, 161, 163, 165, 166, 167, 169,
  170, 171, 179, 180n, 186–7, 198, 202, 211;
  see also justice; public right
extreme cosmopolitanism, 11, 26n, 189, 213n;
  see also strong cosmopolitanism

federation of states, 14, 100; see also pacific
  federation
Flikschuh, Katrin, 43–4
foedus pacificum see pacific federation
Franceschet, Antonio, 98–9
Franck, Thomas, 102–3
free will, 34, 151, 155, 170, 180n; see also
  autonomy; freedom of will
freedom of will, 34, 41, 151–3, 164; see also
  autonomy

general united will see united general will
global civil society, 31, 38, 193–5, 210
globalization, 2–4, 39–40, 104, 187, 189–91,
  192, 204, 210
  as dialectic, 3, 40, 52n, 210
global justice, 13, 37, 93, 150, 159, 171–8,
  183n, 189, 191, 195–8, 202, 210; see also
  cosmopolitan right; public right
Gregor, Mary, 44, 58, 73, 94
Grotius, Hugo, 6, 7, 90

Habermas, Jürgen, 13, 71–2, 78, 113–15, 149,
  205–6, 207, 209
Hegel, G. W. F., 56
Hegelian critiques of Kant, 88, 98, 107
Held, David, 116
Hinsley, F. H., 59
Hobbes, Thomas, 7, 90, 91, 93, 96, 111, 160,
  172
Hoffe, Otfried, 22, 163, 165–6
Honig, Bonnie, 207
hospitality see law of hospitality
humanitarian assistance, 189, 195–8
Hume, David, 33, 151, 179, 210
Hurrell, Andrew, 112

institutional cosmopolitanism, 10, 109, 176,
  179
internal freedom, 151–3, 154–9, 162, 169, 181n
international law, 45–7, 95, 99–103, 112,
  113–15, 116, 164, 204–10
  in Kant's tripartite of law, 45, 75–7, 89, 95,
  99, 111
  see also international right

international right, 45–7, 76, 88–9, 93, 99–103, 107, 111–12

Jones, Charles, 56, 199
jurisgenerative politics *see* democratic law
jus gentium, 7, 88, 91–3; *see also* natural law theory
justice, 149–50, 150–9, 162–7, 179, 180n
  commutative, 153–5
  protective, 153–5
  *see also* cosmopolitan right; distributive justice; domestic right; international right; public right

Kant, Immanuel
  and globalization, 1–5, 39–40, 104, 186–7
  anthropology, 131–3
  as anti-colonialist / anti-imperialist, 8, 64–66, 105, 111, 124
  critical philosophy, 23–4, 33–7, 132–3, 186
  defined as a legal cosmopolitan, 14–15, 31–2, 44–7, 184n
  enlightenment and the history of ideas, 22, 48, 60, 124, 140, 141–2, 178–80, 186, 188, 211–12
  idea of morality, 33–7
  natural law theory, 7, 93–4, 188; *see also* natural law theory
  naturalistic teleology, 31, 37–44, 142; *see also* teleology
  tripartite of law, 45, 67, 75–7, 95, 111, 184n, 206
Kantian ethics, 33–7
kingdom of ends, 35–7, 51, 52n, 151, 155, 156, 158–9, 160, 163, 167, 169, 171, 174, 175, 178–9, 197
kosmopolites, 4, 5
Kukathas, Chandran, 139

las Casas, Bartolomé de, 7
law of hospitality, 46–8, 55–6, 58–66, 75–7, 103–6, 172, 188, 190–1, 192, 196, 198, 200, 204, 206, 208
  and asylum seekers, 59, 64–6
  besuchsrecht and gastrecht, 64–6, 104–5
  *see also* cosmopolitan right
law of nations, 7; *see also* natural law theory
law of nature
  and the categorical imperative, 34–5
  Stoic natural law, 6–7
  *see also* natural law theory
Law of Peoples, 112–13, 177–8, 196–8
law of publicity *see* principle of publicity
legal cosmopolitanism, 12
  Kant as a legal cosmopolitan, 14–15, 31–2
  Kant's cosmopolitan law, 44–7; *see also* cosmopolitan law; cosmopolitan right

legal naturalism, 72–3
legal nihilism, 27n
legal positivism, 14, 72–3, 102
  hard positivism versus soft positivism, 102
legal realism, 14
lex mercatoria *see* commerce
Linklater, Andrew, 35, 112
Locke, John, 6, 7
Lutz-Bachmann, Matthias, 108

McGrew, Anthony, 193
Melvill, Henry, 1
metaphysics, 33–7, 170, 180n
  and cosmopolitanism, 41–4, 132–3, 170–1, 177, 211
Mill, John Stuart, 142
Miller, David, 176
moderate cosmopolitanism, 11, 26n, 213n; *see also* weak cosmopolitanism
modus vivendi, 28n, 111–12
Montaigne, Michel de, 123–5, 126, 143, 151, 211
moral cosmopolitanism, 10, 109, 176, 179
multiculturalism *see* cultural pluralism

Nagel, Thomas, 176
nationalism, 128, 176; *see also* cultural pluralism
natural law theory
  as distinct from cosmopolitan law, 7, 89–94, 188
  natural law tradition, 6, 89–94
natural slave, 8
negative freedom, 151, 153–6, 161, 174, 178
Newtonian science, 33
normative positivism, 15, 73
noumenal beings, 34; *see also* autonomy
Nussbaum, Martha, 8, 150, 159, 166–71

O'Neill, Onora, 56, 59, 199–200

pacific federation, 48, 67–70, 72, 87–8, 93, 99–103, 110–17, 188, 189, 197–8, 211
  as made up of republican states, 93–4, 95–9, 206–10; *see also* popular sovereignty
  as opposed to world state / republic, 68, 75–6, 88, 91–4, 95, 100–3, 106–10, 113–15, 194–5, 203–10
  constitutional foundations for, 73–8, 93–4, 99–103, 110–17, 189, 190–1, 191–5, 196, 197, 200, 203, 206, 208–10
Paine, Thomas, 7
particularism 136; *see also* communitarianism
perpetual peace, 90–4, 106, 142, 192
  as guaranteed by nature, 37–40
  definitive articles for grounding of, 75–8
  preliminary articles for grounding of, 73–5, 192
  *see also* pacific federation

phenomenal beings, 34; see also autonomy; free will
Pogge, Thomas, 10, 170, 175, 199
political cosmopolitanism, 12, 50
Popper, Karl, 40–1
popular sovereignty, 95–9, 173, 208; see also republicanism
positive freedom, 151, 153–6, 174, 178
practical reason, 87, 123, 143, 169, 186–7, 212
preliminary articles for perpetual peace, 73–5, 192
principle of humanity, 164, 182n
principle of publicity, 44, 162, 163–5, 166, 173, 175, 177, 182n, 197
private right, 153–4; see also public right
providence, 38–40; see also teleology
public reason, 48–9, 62, 164, 166, 174, 178, 192–5
public right, 35, 43, 44–7, 57–8, 60, 67, 71, 88, 93, 94–5, 108, 110–11, 116, 152–3, 153–9, 160, 161, 163–6, 168, 174, 177, 180n, 186, 187, 189, 191, 195, 197, 198, 200, 206, 209, 210, 211, 212; see also universal justice
    cosmopolitan public right, 103–6, 191, 192, 195, 197, 198; see also cosmopolitan law; cosmopolitan right
    domestic public right, 95–9, 160–7, 192, 206; see also domestic law; republicanism; state sovereignty
    international public right, 95–103; see also international law; international right
Pufendorf, Samuel, 90

Rawls, John, 112, 149, 177–8, 196–8
reductionist sociology of culture, 128–9, 130, 131–2, 133, 134, 201
reflective judgement, 40
relativism, 15–17
republicanism, 93, 95–9, 173
    relationship with liberal democracy, 96–9; see also popular sovereignty
Rosen, Allen, 163–6
Rosenau, James, 194–5
Rousseau, Jean-Jacques, 92–4, 96

Saint-Pierre, Abbé de, 92–4
Seneca, 5, 8
social welfare and Kant, 159–67, 173; see also distributive justice
state of nature, 94–5, 160, 172; see also state of war
state of war, 90, 94; see also state of nature
state sovereignty, 90, 96, 99–103, 110–12, 117, 118n; see also republicanism
Stoic cosmopolitanism, 5–9, 188

strong cosmopolitanism, 11; see also extreme cosmopolitanism

Tan, Kok-Chor, 190, 199
teleology, 31–2
    and producing peace, 39–44
    Kant's cosmopolitan teleology, 37–44
Tennyson, Alfred, 87–8
Teson, Fernando, 111
transcendental deduction, 34, 41
Treaty of Westpahilia, 90–1, 93, 99–100, 110
Tully, James, 127
Turner, Terence, 129

united general will, 96–7, 152–3, 156, 162, 163, 164, 165, 173
United Nations Charter on Human Rights, 198–9
United Nations Declaration of Human Rights, 59
United Nations Development Program, 190
universal human rights, 190, 198–202, 204, 208, 210
    in relation to cosmopolitan right, 49, 104, 105–6, 107, 189, 198–202
universal justice, 31, 35–7, 44–7, 58–9, 95, 116
    and teleology, 38
    see also cosmopolitan right; global justice; public right
US Constitution, 68

Vattel, Emeric de, 90–1
Vitoria, Francisco de, 7
Voltaire, 7

Waldron, Jeremy, 15, 73, 99, 135, 138, 139, 144, 204, 205–6, 207, 208
Waltzer, Michael, 129
Warren, Mark, 193
weak cosmopolitanism, 11; see also moderate cosmopolitanism
Westin, Charles, 138
Wight, Martin, 56, 110, 127
Wolff, Christian, 91–3
World Bank, 190
world citizen see cosmopolitan citizenship
world federation, 87–8, 106–10, 202–3; see also pacific federation
world republic / state, 88, 106–10, 188, 202–3; see also pacific federation
Wood, Allen, 41

Yew, Lee Kuan, 201–2
Young, Oran, 194–5

Zeno of Citium, 5